Teaching of Mathematics

Teaching of Mathematics

Mujibul Hasan Siddiqui

A P H PUBLISHING CORPORATION
4435-36/7, ANSARI ROAD, DARYA GANJ
NEW DELHI-110 002

Published by
S.B. Nangia
A.P.H. Publishing Corporation
4435–36/7, Ansari Road, Darya Ganj,
New Delhi-110002
Phone: 011–23274050
e-mail: aphbooks@gmail.com

2027

Typeset by
Ideal Publishing Solutions
C-90, J.D. Cambridge School,
West Vinod Nagar, Delhi-110092

Printed at
RD DIGITAL PRINTERS
Ansari road Daryaganj Delhi-110002

Contents

Preface

The effective teacher of mathematics should have competency in the mathematics being taught as well as its prerequisites. If the teacher is not competent and confident with the subject matter, difficulties will be encountered creating positive mathematical experiences best suited for the development of the learner. You must have the desire to learn mathematics. You must have the desire to learn how to educate the students. You must have the desire to learn how to supply the optimum mathematics environment for each student. An effective teacher continues to investigate now mathematical knowledge and effective teaching strategies. As you do, your thirst and excitement will easily be seen by your students. If you do not know an answer to a question asked of you by a student, hopefully your thirst for knowledge will drive you to pursue the situation until you do possess that information. At the same time, you can stimulate your student to make similar pursuits, as you travel the road to new knowledge together, each at your respective level and pace.

The effective teacher of mathematics must be devoted to the profession. A teacher must create a stimulating atmosphere conducive to learning. Whether in mathematics or in some other area, the teacher must possess the desire, passion, and patience to facilitate the learning of others. An effective teacher of mathematics wants to help erase the fear and anxiety that mathematics represents to so many students. A true teacher is always willing to learn new methods and strategies for introducing concepts to students.

This book is an excellent resource for those who are investigating the teaching of mathematics at the elementary and middle school levels. Above all, the emphasis on student-centered problem solving is consistent with current trends and practices. This book is unique in that it challenges assumptions and traditional practices.

Editor

1

Learning Theory, Curriculum, and Assessment in Mathematics

Introduction

- Specific mathematics education examples of concepts covered in general education courses
- Communicating with individuals teaching the same course, the next course in the sequence, the previous course in the sequence, and those in "feeder schools"
- Equity issues in the mathematics curriculum
- Error patterns
- Diagnostic teaching
- Evaluation of cooperative groups
- Assessment techniques
- Mathematics competitions available to secondary students
- Pressures on the secondary mathematics curriculum

Ed Begle said, "We have learned a lot about teaching better mathematics but not much about teaching mathematics better". When perusing the history of teaching mathematics, it appears as if we constantly look for a magic method or strategy that will serve all students. There is no enchanted formula that fits every learner. We need to realize that a variety of methods are necessary to meet the mathematical learning needs of all students. Our task, as teachers of mathematics, is to determine which method will be most beneficial to the mathematical learning of each student and when these strategies will be most effective. If a teacher uses a strategy with no positive result from the learner, at what point is that method abandoned in favor of another? The decision is most often influenced by our own background, training, experiences, bias, and current curriculum.

It is assumed you have had exposure to learning theories, curriculum, and assessment in foundational education classes. These are some of the topics to be discussed in this chapter. The intent here is not to provide an extensive discussion about these topics but, rather, to briefly touch on many aspects of them. It is assumed you will investigate selected issues in greater depth as you see the need. The order in which the topics are presented is not to be construed as an indication of the value or importance of each topic.

Constructivism

Adherents of constructivism support the notion that children learn effectively through interactions with experiences in their natural environment. Steffe and Killion stated that, from a constructivist perspective, "mathematics teaching consists primarily of the mathematical interactions between a teacher and children". This indirect approach to instruction effectively allows the student to learn in the context of meaningful activities Learning is an endless, lifelong process that results from interactions with a multitude of situations. The constructivist approach does not solely focus on the action of the teacher or the learner, but on the interactions between the two. The teacher should make a conscious effort to see personal actions as well as the student's from the student's point of view.

Constructivism has multiple roots in the psychology and philosophy of this century. There is no single concrete definition of constructivism. Piaget is thought to be one of the first learning theorists to advocate a constructivist teaching approach, even though he did not identify himself as such. He believed in the importance of human interaction and physical manipulation in the gaining of knowledge. The emphasis of the constructivist classroom begins with the student! The constructivist educator demonstrates a respect for the student. The classroom should be a place that fosters and nurtures learning and development of knowledge.

The constructivist classroom creates an environment that encourages learning. The teacher should create surroundings where students can make sense of mathematics as it relates to the real world. Students are to be treated with respect and responsibility. The fear of failing must be erased in order to foster the idea that students can learn from their mistakes. If we are to expect our students to comprehend and deal with complex problems, we need to establish an atmosphere rich with exposures. Students should become aware of their own thinking process, strategies, and critical thinking abilities. Each student should become aware of the ability to invent and explore new ideas and concepts. The effective teacher of mathematics must be willing to capitalize on these natural thinking abilities.

Constructivism focuses on student-centered instruction, which is not new in education. The student plays a major role in the decision-making process as to what, when, and how learning is to occur. This is a bold approach, but students have great insight into themselves that teachers cannot always see! We need to show respect to each student by providing the opportunity to shape individual learning.

Other learning theorists stress that information students assimilate can be taught more effectively and efficiently by providing a structured approach. Providing a clear sequence of steps will allow the learner to incorporate a greater amount of knowledge, is the behaviorists' claim.

Behaviorism

The work of Edward Thorndike's connectionism paved the way for the behaviorist movement. *Connectionism* describes the link between stimuli and responses that can be initiated and fortified through reinforcements or repeated use of the stimuli. Thorndike's work led to B. F. Skinner's belief that only a small portion of learned behaviors were due to classical conditioning. Skinner proposed that operant conditioning played a significant role in learned behaviors.

Operant conditioning is learning in which behavior is altered by events that precede and follow the behavior. Reinforcement is an example of operant conditioning. Positive reinforcement is used to strengthen a behavior by presenting a desired stimulus after an action. Rewarding a student for effort is an example of positive reinforcement. If a student will not stop distracting a neighboring student, the teacher can change the student's seat assignment. This is an example of negative reinforcement. The teacher is strengthening the behavior by removing the adverse stimulus.

Thorndike's investigations, which looked at learning in terms of selected associations to related actions, strongly influenced the development of behaviorism. Behaviorism was introduced into American psychology by John B. Watson. Skinner, who followed Watson and became the major advocate of behaviorism, believed that a person's behavior is a function of environmental actions and results.

Behaviorism centers around a direct approach. This has been the dominant strategy for teaching mathematics in the United States for many years. Behaviorism centers around a direct approach and has been the dominant strategy for teaching mathematics in the United States for many years. The behaviorist approach essentially treats mathematics as a collection of skills. Learn all the skills and learn mathematics.

Robert Gagne used the idea that a sequence of tasks could be established for a desired learning outcome. If the student practiced each required task as it was learned and developed, that student would then be able to move on to the next step in the continuum. When discussing addition of fractions, can a continuum for addition of fractions be established? Can a similar list be built for each concept in mathematics? Do you have adequate time and background to build a list for each concept you teach? Are you willing to trust someone else to build the list for you? (Essentially, this is what textbooks often do.) What happens if you do not agree with the established list? It appears that the emphasis has shifted from how students learn mathematics to what mathematics should be learned. Is this what we are after?

Within a department, suppose not everyone accepts the behaviorist approach to teaching. What is the impact on text selection? If departmental examinations are used, how are the different concepts tested? What impact will this have on students who move from a behaviorist-based class to a non-behaviorist-based class? What is the impact on students learning a procedure without conceptually grasping the reason for it?

The discussion about the learning theories becomes focused on whether it is wisest to provide an efficient learning environment that results primarily in the acquisition of academic knowledge, or an approach that provides a more in-depth, indirect process encompassing the whole learner. If a basic concept is not fully comprehended, should the student move on? If the student is taught how to mechanically do a problem but does not understand the process or application, is the knowledge useful to the learner? There is a need to consider the amount of time students are actively taught or supervised. In a direct instruction classroom, the teacher presents information and develops concepts through lecture and demonstration. As students question, respond to teacher queries, react to assignments, and do practice exercises, elaborations are given that are designed to clarify and strengthen understanding. Reteaching and emphasis shifts are inserted by the teacher as needed. The teacher carries the curriculum to the students.

Behaviorism and constructivism generate a question about which is the best way to teach mathematics: give the students the information, or encourage them to use the various curriculum materials and teacher support to actively discover the information in context through learning activities?

Again, what is the best way, direct or indirect instruction?

Assuming the student understands each skill as it is presented and is capable of performing the defined tasks before moving on to the next, more complicated, concept, the need to preserve the current knowledge is present. How often should addition of fractions be reviewed and practiced? How many of each type problem is necessary? Where do boredom and restlessness with the repetition begin? What do we do when we are confident that some students have mastered the task and others have not? When do we go on to a new concept that builds on the ability to add fractions? Is it mandatory that *all* students master the skill before you, as a teacher, proceed? None of these questions is easy to answer, but this last one is especially perplexing.

Mastery learning permits the teacher to go on as long as a student's learning pace is not hurried just to keep up with the rest of the class. This is based on the realization that we all learn at different rates. Mastery learning implies that each student will master a subordinate skill before proceeding to the next skill level. When using mastery learning with direct instruction, the teacher begins a unit of study by using techniques involving lecture, demonstrations, and review, along with drill and practice. At an appropriate interval (often about 3-5 days) the teacher deviates from the normal routine to administer some form of evaluation to assess student understanding. This evaluation is strictly for diagnostic purposes and not for assigning grades. Students meeting the standards set on the evaluation instrument will be given alternative assignments that might be considered enrichment activities. If half the class has mastered the task, what do we do with them while the other half is still working on it? Suppose only one student remains who has not mastered the task. Do we go on or do we persist until that one remaining student exhibits the necessary competence at performing the task? Do "silly" arithmetic mistakes count against mastery? Should the class move on to new material leaving that one student behind to master the concept? Will the one student continue to fall behind?

If only we could dissect each student's brain and somehow tell what has been learned, the processes that are most likely to succeed, and the propensities for learning. If that could be done, perhaps a better connection between theory and practice could be established. Then learning theories could be more solid and identifiable. Alas, we cannot dissect a student's brain so we are reduced to studying tendencies and creating theories. How many times have you heard, Where is a difference between theory and practice"? Many theories will "sound good" or "make sense" on paper. Often theories are created out of observation, knowledge of student learning, thought, and discussion. The background is often built in a specific, sometimes controlled, setting or with a limited number of cases. The real world of the classroom often does not resemble the theory environment. Putting theory into practice is not that simple. Implementation of a learning theory also assumes the practitioner (teacher) is well versed in the related ideas. That assumption is often unrealistic from the standpoint of a teacher who was exposed to the theory or strategy in a class or in-service session but is swamped with all the details related to classroom production.

We think back to our own learning environments, searching for clues about how we learned different skills and concepts. The assumption is that if we are "normal" and if we can figure out how we learned to perform a given task, we might gain some insight into what can be done to help students learn as they advance through the world of mathematics. Considering time and memory, the likelihood of our remembering minute details from our learning is not great. Besides, most of us who are involved in the teaching and learning of mathematics are not "typical" representatives of students found in secondary mathematics classes. Students and how they perceive or learn mathematics change from year to year. We are talking about learning theories. Is it good, accepted, acceptable, or desirable to lockstep a class? Given that class sizes are close to 40 students in some areas, is it reasonable to think in terms of applying any of these theories? Would it be acceptable to create three groups within a class? Will all the students get the basics of the class? Will average and higher ability groups be able to go beyond the basics with additional applications, extensions, and applications? This group of questions is purposely left unanswered. These are things you need to begin pondering as you enter the teaching profession.

Change

We no longer live in the industrial age. We live in the technological age. Times have changed. Yet, much of the curriculum seems to have stayed in the industrial age. Over the years, many calls for change have been heard. One of the most famous, or infamous, is "modern math." More recently, various works have called for change. They inc'ude:

The Underachieving Curriculum: *Assessing Indian School Mathematics from an International Perspective Curriculum and Evaluation Standards for School Mathematics*

Everybody Counts: *A Report to the Nation on the Future of Mathematics Education*

Mathematics Education: *Wellspring of U.S. Industrial Strength*

Reshaping School Mathematics: *A Philosophy and Framework for Curriculum Professional Standards for Teaching Mathematics*

The State of Mathematics Achievement: *NAPE's 1990 Assessment of the Nation and the Trial Assessment of the States and the Trial Assessment of the States*

These publications discuss the current status of school mathematics programs. They describe what has happened in mathematics classrooms of the past, what is happening now, and what should happen in the classrooms of the future. You might find some of these requests for change radical. Again, this becomes something for you to ponder. You need to arrive at an educated, informed, well-thought-out decision.

In the not too distant past, "modern math" was a change element. Many thought "modern math" was created because of the space race and the launching of Sputnik in 1957. In reality, the "modern math" movement had begun several years earlier. Educators and mathematicians realized that the mathematics being taught in the high schools in the early 1950s was not providing an effective background for individuals who would become future users of mathematics. They also were aware that the plug and chug, drill and practice approach was not creating the preparation for effective citizenry of that day. These "modern math" creators and developers were looking to the future. They realized the system of teaching and learning mathematics of that time was not effective at building for the future. The system was broken and needed to be fixed.

There is debate as to whether or not "modern math" was effective. In the early 1960s, when "modern math" was beginning to be used in some schools, new texts were produced. "Algebra II" books were revised to be "Modern Algebra II" texts. Comparison of the "Algebra II" book with the "Modern Algebra II" book by the same publisher revealed some startling insights. The "Modern Algebra II" text might have had a few pages dealing with sets, subsets, set operations (union and intersection), and the field axioms (properties). Let us assume this information was covered in the first five pages of the new text. Page six of the new text was the same as page one of the old; new seven was the same as old two; new eight was old three; and so on.

Rarely, if ever, were sets and field axioms directly referred to in the "Modern Algebra II" book. Frequently teachers skipped the first five pages of the "Modern Algebra II" text and taught the same old course. Many teachers of the early 1960s had not covered the set topics or field axioms per se in their college work. They received little, if any, instruction dealing with the changes called for in the "modern math" movement. Yet, teachers were expected to insert the new ideas into their curriculum. It did not work. Curriculum proceeded as usual, and "modern math" rarely made it into the classrooms. Many people (experts, teachers, and citizens) and written commentaries presented "modern math" as a dismal failure.

Certainly there were exceptions to this. Individuals who developed and tested the School Mathematics Study Group (SMSG) materials delivered solid secondary mathematics courses. Each of these programs, and many like them, were well-founded and offered a strong mathematics program that would have moved our curriculum beyond the drill and practice stage. For a variety of reasons, those programs never made it into the mainstream curriculum. We now have publications, like those referred to earlier, calling for change in the way secondary mathematics is taught and learned. This time it is not called "modern math," but many are aware that the system we use is not fulfilling the needs of society and the scientific world now, let alone that of the future. The motivation for these changes comes from a variety of representatives from industry. They list mathematical expectations from the perspective of an employer and say employers want people who:

- Are capable of setting problems up, not just following formulas.
- Know how to interpret the numbers or answers they get.
- Are aware of a variety of approaches for solving problems.
- Understand the mathematical features of a problem and can work in groups to reach solutions.
- Recognize commonalities of mathematics in different problems.
- Can deal with problems that are not in the format often presented in the learning environment.
- Value mathematics as a useful learning and work tool.

This list of workplace desires is different from the student abilities produced in many secondary mathematics programs. It is time to change.

The Standards

Some members of the mathematics community realized in the mid-1980s that "business as usual" would not be effective for future mathematics teaching and learning. NCTM took the lead and published *Curriculum and Evaluation Standards for School Mathematics.* The guidelines presented in the Standards are formative ideas indicating mathematics learning that is desirable in school settings. The Standards focus on five general goals, which adopt the position that all students should:

- Learn to value mathematics.
- Develop confidence in their ability to use mathematics.
- Become problem solvers, not answer finders.
- Learn to communicate mathematically. Know how to reason mathematically.

Problem solving, reasoning, communication, and mathematical connections are common strands through all levels, but there are other standards for various grade ranges. The additional standards for Grades K-4 are:

- Estimation
- Number sense and numeration
- Concepts of whole number operations
- Whole-number computation
- Geometry and spatial sense
- Measurement
- Statistics and probability
- Fractions and decimals
- Patterns and relationships

For Grades 5-8:

- Number and number relationships
- Number systems and number theory

- Computation and estimation
- Patterns and functions
- Algebra
- Statistics
- Probability
- Geometry
- Measurement

For Grades 9-12:

- Algebra
- Functions
- Geometry from a synthetic perspective
- Geometry from an algebraic perspective
- Trigonometry
- Statistics
- Probability
- Discrete mathematics
- Conceptual underpinnings of calculus
- Mathematical structure

The final section of the Standards focuses on evaluation. The basic premise is that evaluation is not a separate act within the classroom but, rather, a part of teaching. There is a need for viewing more than an answer and whether it is right or wrong. A variety of assessment techniques needs to be present in different formats.

Addenda Series

As the Curriculum and Evaluation Standards for School Mathematics was being developed, it became apparent that supporting publications would be needed to aid in interpreting and implementing the curriculum and evaluation standards and the underlying instructional themes.

The Addenda to the Standards were to clarify the recommendations contained in some of the standards and to give examples of how they could realistically be implemented in the school curriculum. The Addenda Series provides plenty of examples involving problem solving, reasoning, communicating, connections, technology, and assessment. They have been designed to reflect the "realities of today's classrooms and to make them 'teacher friendly'".

The Standards show mathematics as more than a body of knowledge. Mathematics is something we must *do*. Each student is expected to become an active, reflective participant as learning progresses. Students should recognize connections between topics, see applications of the material being learned, and appreciate the subject. In the process, the learning environment must change from teacher-centered to teacher-motivated. No longer can the teacher be the "sage on the stage." Rather, the effective teacher of mathematics is expected to function as a catalyst and facilitator of learning. This attitude is reflected in the Standards by the request for increased attention to:

> *actively involving students in constructing and applying mathematical ideas; using problem solving as a means as well as a goal of instruction; promoting student interaction through the use of effective questioning techniques; using a variety of instructional formats – small cooperative groups, individual explorations, whole-class instruction, and projects; using calculators and computers as tools for learning and doing mathematics.*

The Addenda Series contains several features throughout the volume. "Try This" encourages students to do problems, exercises, and explorations related to the content. "Teaching Matters" contains suggestions and ideas that could prove helpful in introducing a topic, using technology, or understanding areas where students might generate misconceptions with the topic. Assessment is an integral part of the topics presented in the Addenda Series. "Sustainable change must occur first in the hearts, minds, and classrooms of teachers and then in their departments and school districts". We cannot ask our students to change unless we first change how we teach mathematics.

Professional Standards

The *Professional Standards for Teaching Mathematics* also deal with how we should change the way we teach mathematics. The

Professional Standards focus on teacher knowledge, beliefs, and strategies that will deliver the Standards into the classroom. The Professional Standards also include a discussion of methods of teacher support and evaluation necessary to promote reform. It is important to note that the Professional Standards, like the Standards, are broad frameworks designed to guide school mathematics reform.

> *To reach the goal of developing mathematical power for all students requires the creation of a curriculum and an environment, in which teaching and learning are to occur, that are very different from much of current practice. The image of mathematics teaching needed includes elementary and secondary teachers who are more proficient in –*

- selecting mathematical tasks to engage students' interests and intellect;
- providing opportunities to deepen their understanding of the mathematics being studied and its applications;
- orchestrating classroom discourse in ways that promote the investigation and growth of mathematical ideas;
- using, and helping students use, technology and other tools to pursue mathematical investigations;
- seeking, and helping students seek, connections to previous and developing knowledge;
- guiding individual, small-group, and whole class work.

Change does not come easy. Barriers include student and teacher beliefs regarding how mathematics is taught as well as learned blockages in mathematics education. To a large extent, these impressions are developed by prior experiences in mathematics. Here is a familiar scenario:

- Attendance is taken.
- Homework is reviewed with the teacher doing some problems.
- Examples of "today's" problem types are worked or students are told to read the book and see how to do the problems.
- Seat work is assigned related to the assignment of the day.

This is how many students, and teachers, think mathematics is learned – the teacher models how to do the problem and the students mimic what they see. One thing organizations like the NCTM, Mathematical Sciences Education Board (MSEB), and Mathematical Association of America (MAA) have repeatedly asked for is that post-secondary teachers of mathematics model different behavior in their classrooms. If these educators take the lead, individuals studying to become teachers of mathematics will see a more modern teaching behavior modeled. The sad fact is, as you know, few post-secondary teachers of mathematics exhibit the desired behavior—most of the classes are lectures revolving around "here is how you do this kind of problem."

Student and teacher impressions are not the only obstacles to changing mathematics education. Administrators, parents, and society have strong ideas about how to educate our children as well. The Professional Standards were built on two basic assumptions: "Teachers are key figures in changing the ways in which mathematics is taught and learned in schools. Such changes require that teachers have long term support and adequate resources". Because the Professional Standards ask for such a significant difference in how mathematics is taught and learned, they also implicitly expect ongoing professional development by each teacher of mathematics. It is unreasonable to expect a teacher to take one class, attend one workshop, or read and discuss a few articles and then be an effective agent of new ideas about teaching and learning mathematics. Can one class, workshop, or a few articles be powerful enough to negate the conditioning from prior learned examples of how mathematics is taught, show how it should be done, and provide the strength to continue to do it for the rest of that individual's professional career? Teachers need to see classes taught that model the desired new behavior, and they need continued exposure to new strategies and methods of instruction. Only then can they be expected to consistently deliver effective mathematics classes to their students.

The kind of instruction needed to implement the NCTM Standards requires a high degree of individual responsibility and professionalism on the part of each teacher. To give guidance to the development of such professionalism in mathematics teaching, the Professional Standards for Teaching Mathematics consists of five components:

1. Standards for teaching mathematics
2. Standards for the evaluation of the teaching of mathematics
3. Standards for the professional development of teachers of mathematics
4. Standards for the support and development of mathematics teachers and teaching
5. Next steps

The section on "Standards for Teaching Mathematics" develops a vision of what a teacher must know and be able to do if the curriculum goals outlined in the Standards are to be delivered. The assumption is that there are several important decisions teachers make in determining the learning environment:

- Select goals and mathematical tasks designed to assist students in achieving desirable mathematical growth.
- Establish a classroom environment that clarifies for both the students and the teacher what is being learned.
- Create a classroom atmosphere that is supportive of the teaching and learning of mathematics.
- Continually analyze student learning and the classroom environment in order to make ongoing instructional decisions.

These assumed teacher decisions help focus on the curriculum that is to be delivered and how to do so in the most effective manner. Sample vignettes are included that illustrate many of the Standards. These sample scenarios provide a setting that assists in judging the effectiveness of the lesson. The section on "Evaluation of the Teaching of Mathematics" presents the NCTM vision for how mathematics teaching should be evaluated. It is assumed that evaluation is present to assist in improving teaching. The section gives guidance to teachers who want to improve their professionalism and presentation skills. Vignettes are used to show a variety of assessment activities. Although they present a wide variety of examples, it is not an exhaustive supply. The "Standards on Professional Development" indicate the NCTM vision of the "well-prepared" teacher of mathematics. The vision begins with the first post-secondary mathematics course taken and continues throughout the individual teacher's professional career. "These standards focus on what a teacher needs to know about mathematics, mathematics education, and pedagogy to be able to carry out the vision of teaching discussed in the first component of the document". The following aspects of both the pre-service and in-service phases of the professional development of teachers are addressed:

- Modeling good mathematics teaching
- Knowing mathematics and school mathematics
- Knowing students as learners of mathematics
- Knowing mathematical pedagogy
- Developing as a teacher of mathematics
- Teachers' roles in professional development

These standards provide guidance to colleges, schools, and anyone involved in the development of teachers of mathematics. They stress the need for communication between individuals at all levels so that each is aware of the needs and actions of the other. Then the mathematical community, as a whole, can grow toward the desired goals. This last statement becomes an integral part of the basic assumption that teaching mathematics is a professional endeavor at all levels. Each teacher is a member of a learning community. The *"Standards for Support and Development"* outline the responsibilities of decision makers. Decisions of individuals from government, business, industry, schools, colleges, and professional organizations can either enable or hamper teachers of mathematics as we move toward the vision of teaching described in the Professional Standards. These decisions influence the environment in which the teaching and learning of mathematics is to take place. The final section in the Professional Standards deals with issues on developing mathematical power for all students. The entirety of the Professional Standards is not intended to be a checklist. Instead they are directions for moving toward a stronger, more meaningful mathematics education for *all* students at *all* levels: pre-K through postgraduate. The Professional Standards:

furnish guidance to all who are interested in improving teaching, including teachers, universities, state departments of education and provincial ministries of education, local school districts, private schools, teacher organizations, the National Board on

Professional Teaching Standards, and others who license or certify teachers or who evaluate teaching or teacher education programs.

Assessment Standards

The *Assessment Standards for School Mathematics* are based on research, experiences of the writing team, and "developments related to national efforts to reform the teaching and learning of mathematics. In particular, a recent report from MSEB, *Measuring What Counts*, provided an initial scholarly base for the development of these Assessment Standards":

At present, a new approach to assessment is evolving in many schools and classrooms. Instead of assuming that the purpose of assessment is to rank students on a particular trait, the new approach assumes that high public expectations can be set that every student can strive for and achieve, that different performances can and will meet agreed-on expectations, and that teachers can be fair and consistent judges of diverse student performances. Setting high expectations and striving to achieve them are quite different from comparing students with one another and indicating where each student ranks. A constant theme of this document is that decisions regarding students' achievement should be made on the basis of a convergence of information from a variety of balanced and equitable sources.

The six standards presented in the document state that assessment should:

1. **Reflect the mathematics that all students need to know and be able to do:** This refers to providing examples from the real world of students as viewed by students, not adults.
2. **Enhance mathematics learning:** Due to some form of assessment, a student becomes aware of an inability to readily find the sum of rational expressions and realizes the deficiency is related to finding least common denominators. The student's choice should be to correct the deficiency in order to enhance the ability to deal with the problem at hand and build appropriate background for future work.
3. **Promote equity:** Stereotyping is a well documented problem.

Everyone has the ability to succeed in mathematical settings. An effective assessment program should depict individuals of all races, creeds, and gender in environments showing true equity.

4. **Be an open process:** A teacher's assessment tool to measure statistical abilities should be open to colleagues for scrutiny. The more people viewing the assessment tool and process, the stronger the program becomes. This will enhance the program's ability to respond to the needs of each student.
5. **Promote valid inferences about mathematics learning:** The greater the number of assessments used to determine a student's understanding of a concept, the greater the likelihood that you have made a valid decision. These decisions come from your knowledge of students and how they learn as well as your professional judgment.
6. **Be a coherent process:** Not only should the student understand the assessment, but the [illegible] should reflect the overall program that is most [illegible] the lifelong learning goals of that individual.

We need to value the [illegible] of all students. Assessment should not be a tool used [illegible] mathematical learning. Assessment should be used to [illegible] growth toward higher mathematical expectations. [illegible] the best from each student is akin to washing [illegible] respective individual. The Assessment Standards [illegible] expand on the evaluation section of the Standards [illegible]

- student assessment be [illegible] integral to, instruction;
- multiple sources of assessment [illegible];
- assessment methods be appropriate for [illegible] purposes;
- all aspects of mathematical knowledge and its connections be assessed;
- instruction and curriculum be considered equally in judging the quality of a program.

The Assessment Standards reiterate the call for systematic changes toward:

- A richer variety of mathematical topics and away from just arithmetic.
- Investigation of problems and away from memorizing and repeating.
- Teacher questioning and listening and away from teacher telling.
- Assessment that gathers evidence from several sources and away from a single test.
- Using concepts and procedures in problem solving and away from mastering isolated pieces of information.

The Assessment Standards are designed to be a guideline as is the case with the other NCTM Standards publications, not a cookbook to be followed. Assessment is defined as:

> *the process of gathering evidence about a student's knowledge of, ability to use, and disposition toward, mathematics and of making inferences from that evidence for a variety of purposes. Furthermore, by evaluation we mean the process of determining the worth of, or assigning a value to, something on the basis of careful examination and judgment.*

Assessment is viewed in The Assessment Standards as a process that describes what mathematics students know and what they can do with what they know. This outlook goes beyond the typical student interpretation reflected by the question, "Will this be on the test?" The assessment process consists of four phases: planning the assessment, gathering evidence, interpreting the evidence, and using the results. Each part can be characterized through the following questions. Planning the assessment:

- What purpose does it serve?
- What framework is used to give focus and balance to the activities?
- What methods are used for gathering and interpreting evidence?
- What criteria are used for judging performance on activities?
- What formats are used for summarizing judgments and reporting results?

Gathering evidence:

- How are activities and tasks created or selected?
- How are procedures selected for engaging students in the activities?
- How are methods for creating and preserving evidence of the performances to be judged?

Interpreting the evidence:

- How is the quality of the evidence determined?
- How is an understanding of the performances to be inferred from the evidence?
- What specific criteria are applied to judge the performances?
- Have the criteria been applied appropriately?
- How will the judgments be summarized as results?

Using the results:

- How will the results be reported?
- How should inferences from the results be made?
- What action will be taken based on the inferences?
- How can it be ensured that these results will be incorporated in subsequent instruction and assessment?

Professionalism

NCTM, MSEB, MAA, and many state and local groups deal specifically with teaching and learning mathematics. None of these organizations mandate how to operate your classroom. All of them provide a plethora of suggestions for you to select from. The formats of the information include publications, workshops, conferences, summer institutes, and evaluations of textbooks, software, manipulatives, classroom aids, and so on. You are studying to become a professional educator and the information is available to you. As such, you should accept certain responsibilities. One of those is to be a member of your professional organizations.

Professional conferences dealing with the teaching of mathematics provide a multitude of opportunities. These meetings allow you the opportunity to hear and meet textbook authors, college faculty, colleagues, and suppliers of support products. Classroom scenarios from colleagues who have been successful in presenting information to their students are described in sessions and workshops. Others describe the latest research findings and developments dealing with the teaching of mathematics. Publishers maintain exhibits that show the latest texts, teaching aids, games, software, computers, and calculators. Not only can you look at these items but, in many instances, you have the opportunity to talk with a professional about how to use them in a classroom. Granted, the representative might be selling, but the example is still available to you. The final analysis is that, as a professional, you are obligated to maintain awareness in your chosen area of specialization. Otherwise, you continue in the same old rut as the sage on the stage, wondering why students are not absorbing what you tell them.

Many organizations provide publications ranging from one-page newsletters to books, with almost anything imaginable between those two ends. NCTM publishes newsletters, journals (one is included as a part of the student membership), research journals, and yearbooks on a regular basis. The newsletter (*Bulletin for Leaders*) contains information about recent curricular or commercial developments, federal legislative action that could impact the teaching of mathematics, activity ideas for students, discussions about developments within NCTM, and so on. Journals, written for elementary (*Teaching Children Mathematics*—formerly called *Arithmetic Teacher*), middle-school (*Mathematics Teaching in the Middle School*, and high-school (*Mathematics Teacher* teaching, contain articles by classroom teachers, textbook authors, professors, students, and professional authors. Often the presentation will be a description of some successful lesson from the classroom. The *Journal for Research in Mathematics Education* is a collection of studies dealing with how to teach mathematics more effectively. The yearbooks cover a variety of topics, and usually the titles adequately describe the content of the book: *The Teaching of Secondary School Mathematics; Professional Development for Teachers of Mathematics; Assessment in the Mathematics Classroom; Calculators in Mathematics Education; Computers in Mathematics Education; Applications in School Mathematics; The Secondary School Mathematics Curriculum*; and so forth. NCTM members receive a 20% discount on all of their non-journal publications. Other national, state, and local organizations provide a variety of alternative publications.

Professionalism carries responsibilities with it. It is your obligation to keep the community and parents aware of recent developments in the field. They need to be educated and reminded about how things are different from when they learned mathematics in school. Otherwise, pressures to continue teaching mathematics as it has always been done will be so great that change will be difficult to accomplish. The broader and stronger your mathematics background and the more you know about how to teach it, the easier it will be for you to establish community trust. It is imperative that you become a self-motivated, lifelong professional who is involved in the field of teaching and learning mathematics. As a professional, you will need to evaluate and alter the needs of your students as they embark on the rest of their lifelong mathematical journey as consumers and learners.

Equity

If we believe that all children can learn meaningful mathematics and science, there are significant educational structures and contextual conditions that must be changed to reflect a system that is equitable for all students. When equity is a fundamental principle of the reform movement, it serves as a template for designing and implementing programs, practices, and policies. The perspectives on equity vary, but the following statements provide guidance for thinking about this concept:

Equity has a variety of connotations, depending on who is using it. It is used to mean equal access of all children to instruction, inclusion of all in the classroom, capacity building, diversity, or the offering of special services. Some, however, fear equity in any form.

Equity is providing all that is needed to help students overcome the consequence of barriers, regardless of where we find them.

Equity as diversity or multiculturalism is not the addition of materials or ideas from under represented cultures; rather, it involves the integrated use of context and approaches of all cultural perspectives.

Equity means equal distribution of resources, particularly money, which implies that one school or district receives the same amount as another, usually in the same district or state.

The preceding statements illustrate how diverse the discussion on equity can be. However, some common language emerges: inclusion, access, fairness, enabling, diversity, multiculturalism, capacity building, special services, and learning.

Equity issues in education have been a focal point in the study of students learning mathematics. The NCTM Standards deal with the affective domain. A common theme focuses on students' self-confidence in their personal ability to learn and do mathematics. Society often presents views of mathematics that are not always conducive to good mathematics learning or instruction. Many times good performance in mathematics is viewed as the exception rather than the rule. Frequently, boys were expected to perform better than girls in mathematical settings. For years there was an unstated position that "nice girls" did not do mathematics. Thankfully that attitude has changed. There is still peer pressure in some segments of school society that place negative value on good performance in mathematics. Such perceptions can destroy the ambitions of some students. As a teacher of mathematics it is your responsibility to "sell" the subject to all students. Race and gender should not be deterrents. Perhaps they should be viewed as challenges. As an effective representative of your product, what do you do to create an appealing atmosphere? How do you convince *all* students in your classes they can succeed? Can you demonstrate applications of the concepts being learned? When a student says "When will I ever use this junk?" (perhaps not in those words, but the message will be that clear), what will you say? Students have become hardened to the learning of mathematics. Many of them are convinced there is no earthly value to the subject. We give them examples supposedly from everyday life. For some strange reason, the answers to our problems are almost always integers. Somehow the students are aware that, in the real world, the answers are not always integers. We give them real-world problems to work with, but often these situations are not from their world, and rarely are they aimed at girls. We must provide equity for all students, who must be encouraged in all mathematical settings.

Student perception is that we frequently make them learn mathematics as a means of torturing them and making their lives more miserable. Perhaps there is some truth to that last statement. Suppose we want to know the zeros of $f(x) = x^2 + 3^x - 7$. The quadratic formula can be used to compute the values, but it could be easier to use a graphing calculator or software to plot the curve shown in Fig. 1.1. Then, either zoom as seen in Fig. 1.2 on the location where the curve crosses the x-axis, or use a table function as shown in Fig. 1.3 to approach the value.

As another example, we spend long periods of time explaining how to divide one fraction by another. Somehow it is difficult to see where a problem like that appeals to either girls or boys. Yes, that is a skill they need to have for future work, but we cannot continually cite upcoming topics as the mason for learning something. Selling mathematics to students is not always easy. Selling mathematics to *all* students is difficult. Selling new or different mathematics or procedures to parents is often more difficult than student sales. It needs to be done because parental support can prove invaluable as you seek to provide a better mathematics education for *all* students.

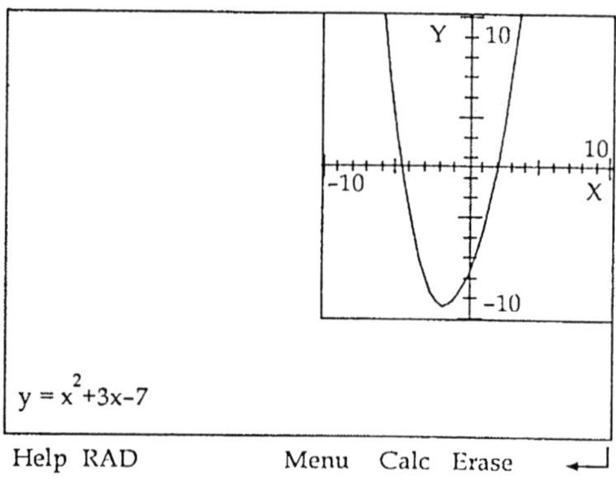

Fig. 1.1. Created with IBM's Algebra Series

More students are taking more mathematics, as reflected in the 1994 American College Test (ACT) and Scholastic Aptitude Test (SAT) scores. In particular, more girls are becoming mathematically involved. Both test results show that since 1987 the number of girls taking advanced mathematics classes in high school has increased.

ACT information indicates a 12% increase in the number of girls taking Algebra II. SAT information shows that 34% of the girls who took the test had taken pre-calculus; 19% had taken calculus; and 41% had taken physics. This information is good news. It is your responsibility to maintain this momentum of change, and increase it. Math is an equal opportunity subject.

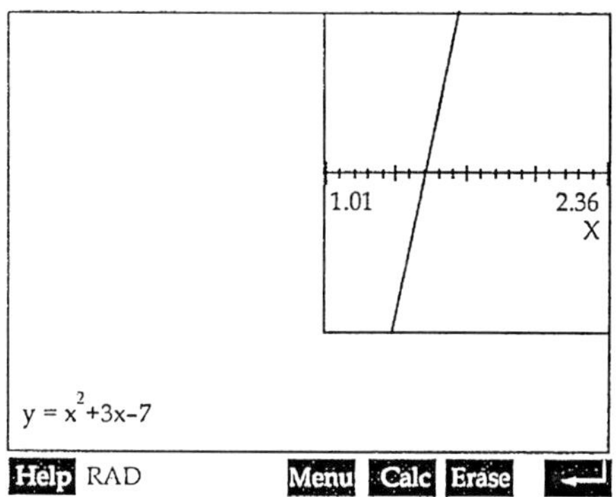

Fig. 1.2. Created with IBM's Algebra Series

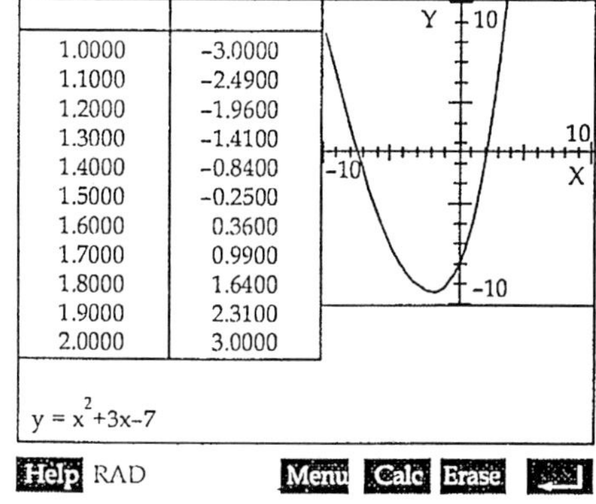

Fig. 1.3. Created with IBM's Algebra Series

Curriculum

The definitions of curriculum vary. Students often describe it in terms of some of the computations they learn in a given class. Students believe that the teacher has the power to teach whatever is appealing whenever desired. The students feel that the teacher is the ultimate controller of curricular power. They generally are not aware of the forces outside the classroom that drive the curriculum. Teachers would define curriculum as what they teach to the students. Administrators view curriculum as a body of course offerings and all other planned school events. Members of the community view the school curriculum as a group of courses designed to produce what they want. A philosopher says the curriculum is the group of courses designed to expose the student to the necessary items that will develop an individual. Perhaps the best definition comes from the idea that curriculum is what happens in your classroom with your students. A multitude of forces affect the mathematics curriculum. Your task becomes one of determining which forces get emphasis and how much.

Test-Driven Curriculum

Some educators advocate a national test for different disciplines. If there were a national test, the likelihood is that many teachers would be forced to teach to the test. Teacher success may be judged on the success of students on standardized tests. This puts a teacher in an awkward position. If this scenario occurs, the test begins defining the curriculum. Suppose the idea of a national test comes to fruition. Suppose that the results of the test are to be used as a factor in determining placement in the mathematics course to be taken the following year. For simplicity's sake, assume that all schools in the nation operate on the same calendar year. In order to gather the tests, assess them, and get the information back to the schools in time to build student schedules for the following school year, the test would probably need to be given somewhere around the first of March. Certainly a test of this magnitude would mandate some review, so assume the review starts in mid-February. For all practical purposes, the instruction for Algebra I has to be completed by mid-February. This supposition raises some interesting questions:

- Can the essentials of Algebra I be covered in this time frame?
- Will some topics be deemphasized?
- Is it reasonable to teach to the test?
- What weight is given to the national test score in placement?

- If a student passes the course with an A but fails to achieve the minimal score on the national test, what course is taken next year?.
- What do you do for the rest of the Algebra I year?.

But, you say, there is no national test. At this point, that may be true. Does your state have a state Algebra I test? Is it coming? Did the high school you attended have such a test, just for the school?

Text-Driven Curriculum

Many educators say there is no nationally defined curriculum. In one sense that is true. On the other hand, most textbooks are similar. The similarities are rather easy to understand. States have established learning outcomes that define a course. The lists of state objectives are given to publishers who, in turn, produce texts that cover the specified material. All the lists are similar, but if differences do occur, publisher decisions are made based on potential sales. The state offering the largest sales potential would appear to have the greatest influence. State textbook adoption lists are a significant factor here, too. Publishers cannot produce a book for each set of objectives. Instead, one text is produced. The expectation is that the material in this text will meet or exceed the objectives of each state and district. Generally, this is a safe assumption. If material is in the book that is not on the district or state list of objectives, the teacher can opt to omit it. If the text does not contain material the state or district wants included, supplemental information can be supplied by the respective teachers. Basically, the text covers most, if not all, of the topics required. Because each publisher works from the same list of objectives, the texts become similar. The order of presentation may vary; colors are different; explanations are distinctive; problem sets change; and areas of emphasis or importance are not the same. The publishers use different frills to sell their books. Still, much of the content is the same. This has to be, if the list of objectives is to be met. Some texts are clearly different. Saxon, for example, approaches topics in an order and emphasis different from that of most other publishers. Saxon's approach has caused a variety of discussions and opinions to be generated within the mathematics education community. Such developments can be healthy for overall community growth. In a typical Saxon mathematics text, the specific content objectives are usually the same as those of other publishers. One difference between Saxon and other publishers relates to how content is explained. Another difference is in the approach to practice of the learned objectives. These books generally have the student continually review previously learned material. For example, if the current section introduced addition of integers, the problem set for that section would contain problems on:

- Percent
- Proportions
- Addition, subtraction, multiplication, and division of fractions
- Area of geometric shapes
- Circumference and perimeter of geometric shapes
- Algebraic identities
- Addition of integers
- Only 3 out of 25 problems on this problem set would be on addition of integers
- The student would be given more practice in the upcoming problem sets.

Teacher-Driven Curriculum

A class consists of students, a teacher, boards, an overhead projector, books, and technology. That is the same almost everywhere you go. The boards are different colors; the books vary, depending on the publisher, but they are quite similar. The availability of technology ranges from some students having calculators (the use of which may or may not be permitted) to having powerful computers equipped with the latest and greatest in software offerings. The available technology is one thing that could be quite different. There is one more thing that is the same. In almost every classroom, the expertise and knowledge reside with the teacher. In many instances, the class becomes an exercise in giving the teacher the desired answers. Curricular decisions are influenced by what the teacher knows about mathematical content, how learners think about mathematical concepts, and instructional materials used to teach mathematics.

The irony is that many students like an atmosphere where knowledge and expertise reside with the teacher. They know the rules. They are basically told what to do and how to do it, which is easier than having to think. It is less complicated for the teacher, too. Rather than having a varied set of answers, one stereotypical response is gathered. Grading—er, ah, assessment—is clear and simple. Either the student got the idea as presented, or not. Right or wrong. No shades of grey. No need for the teacher to reflect on responses that vary from the norm. Everyone is on the same wavelength. However, approaches like this are not conducive to student flexibility. Student development is fostered by encouraging self-learning. The student must be encouraged to develop personal intellect. The student is not in the classroom for the sole purpose of repeating the words of the instructor. We want to develop critical thinking skills, not robotic responses. If learners have latitudes in how they can approach a problem, the generated responses stimulate additional thought and insight on the part of everyone.

It is imperative that the current model used in many classrooms be abandoned if we are to have mathematical growth for all students. Teachers seem compelled to ask questions the students can answer. In the process, teachers ascertain that knowledge has been acquired. However, the knowledge indicators are dependent on what questions are answered by the students. However, those questions are asked by the teacher. The teacher dictates what the student is learning. Teachers define specific behaviors as being important. What latitudes are afforded to the student? Where is the problem solving? Where are the open-ended opportunities for student growth? What are the applications seen by the students?

How much better it would be if all classrooms provided for and encouraged flexible thinking, creative approaches, a variety of ideas, an atmosphere of curiosity, and a compilation of prior knowledge to be applied to some new challenging situation: What a wonderful world that would be! Students must be taught and encouraged to think! Teachers are no longer the centers of attention. Rather, they are motivators, simulators, instigators, co-investigators, participants, and cheerleaders. They have to work much harder. Because teaching is already a demanding, time-consuming profession, perhaps it is unreasonable to ask for such changes in the classroom. Maybe the teacher should continue to be the "sage on the stage." Eventually the good students will learn that the world of mathematics can be exciting and invigorating. After all, you did, didn't you?

Curriculum as Usual

The preceding sections have dealt with test-, text-, and teacher-centered curriculums. Is it reasonable to continue in these manners? Leaders from NCTM, MSEB, MAA, and state and local groups almost universally answer that question "No!" We essentially have a basic skills curriculum. "Over the long term, basic skills only give you the right to compete against the Third World for Third World wages"

External Pressures on the Curriculum

What drives curriculum: standardized tests, learning theories, textbooks, tradition? Certainly all these influence what is covered in the classroom, but there are other forces as well. Societal needs play a role in what is taught. The current value placed on advanced education, coupled with the belief that an educated populace needs adequate mathematical background, sways society's judgment about what is to be covered in the mathematics curriculum.

At times, specific community needs have an impact on what is delivered as a part of the mathematical curriculum. The Greater Cleveland Project of the 1960s was formulated to meet the industrial needs in the Cleveland, Ohio, area. Industries reported that high-school graduates were unable to perform the desired mathematical tasks related to area employment. The curriculum was adjusted to include information that would resolve the dilemma. The project was successful in the Cleveland area, but it would not have been overly useful in Vail, Colorado. Why?

The discussion about the Greater Cleveland Project points out a curriculum influencing factor. We, as educators, seem to consistently strive for the one way we can use to teach all students the mathematics they need. Each time some new idea surfaces, groups of believers endorse it, seemingly saying we have finally found the thing that will solve all of our teaching problems. The idea works well with some concepts but fails miserably with others. It is then discarded and the search for the way continues. When will we learn that there is not one way to teach and learn mathematics for all students?

Effective teaching and learning of mathematics demands a variety of instructional methods to meet the needs of individual students in the curriculum. Educators cannot permit pressures from parents, administrators, specific segments of society, or influential individuals to dictate how mathematics is taught. As a professional educator, it will be your responsibility to call on all possible resources: your secondary learning experiences, college mathematics education classes, college education classes, college mathematics classes, internship experiences, mathematical applications from your life, information gathered from reading professional journals and conference attendance, and so on. Compiling your experiences with conscious thought about what you are asking your students to learn will help you define the curriculum in your classroom. So many things available to you are merely guides. You are the qualified professional. You know the students in your class. You would be the most likely person to decide what their mathematical exposures under your tutelage ought to be. Outside pressures may influence your thoughts, but they should not exclusively dictate what happens with your classes.

Some commentaries include curriculum areas in addition to school mathematics. Even those seem to mention mathematics as a focal point. Albert Shanker, president, American Federation of Teachers, responded to the 1995 report, "What Secondary Students Know: Gateway Exam Taken by Average-Achieving Students in France, Germany, and Scotland." The report said American students lag academically behind their European counterparts largely because they lack any real incentive to achieve, and because schools have no benchmarks against which to measure student progress. Shanker's response argued that the findings amplify the need to create national curriculum standards that would provide American students and teachers with clear guidelines for what should be covered in the curriculum. The argument is that students achieve high academic standards when teachers and pupils have clear goals set for them. Should we assume from this statement that teachers are not capable of establishing goals for themselves and their students?

The Virginia State School Board unanimously adopted standards for mathematics, science, English, and social studies. Many parent and teacher groups objected to the initial drafts of the standards. One source of argument was specific questions that the critics contended would stifle creative thinking by emphasizing rote memorization. Some of the questions were removed, but not all of them. The basic idea is that these standards will gauge student achievement from kindergarten through 12th grade.

Internal Pressures on The Curriculum

Parents, demands of society, tests, texts, and tradition are some of the external pressures on the mathematics curriculum. There are also internal pressures. Certainly the textbook can be an internal pressure. Usually a given text is purchased for a given class. Most parents assume a student should bring a book home to study from. If you elect not to use the purchased book, you will have to answer to the department, parents, and administration. Someone thought the text was a wise purchase for the class. In that context, the book becomes an internal pressure. Similar arguments can be made for the other elements mentioned in the first sentence of this paragraph.

There are other internal pressures. As attempts are made to integrate mathematics with other disciplines, influences will be exerted to achieve objectives from other subject areas. Some are easy to see. Can you imagine a physics class where students were unable to deal with variables? In this light, algebra becomes a prerequisite for physics. That influences when students take algebra—a pressure of sorts. Some students take Algebra II and trigonometry the same year they take physics. Can you teach concepts of sound waves without some exposure to the sine wave? This is a pressure on the timing of mathematical concepts being taught within a course. If you team teach with an ancient history teacher on a unit dealing with Egypt, students might be best served if they have had some exposure to finding surface area or volume of a square-based, right pyramid. Perhaps the general science teacher is doing a unit on the metric system and you have collaborated in the planning. If you teach the same students, it might work for you to teach part of the topic from a mathematical viewpoint and the science teacher to use a different perspective for the rest of the material. This is another example of internal pressure on what is taught when—influencing the curriculum you deliver to your students.

Examinations like the ACT and SAT are an even greater pressure on the secondary mathematics curriculum areas. Algebra and geometry topics are incorporated into these tests. Given this, shouldn't the secondary mathematics curriculum include algebra and geometry concepts that would enhance student performance? Examinations such as these are major factors in determining college admission.

Tangential Pressures on The Curriculum

External and internal pressures to deliver a certain curriculum are relatively easy to identify. Some pressures are not as obvious and yet they are felt. Tradition can be a significant factor here. Things are done a certain way because it has always been that way. This is a form of pressure. Suppose you are not too excited about teaching the First-Outer-Inner-Last (F.O.I.L.) method for finding the product of two binomials. Assume that no one at the school has ever done anything other than F.O.I.L. Prior classes have scored well on the tests. Suppose the attitude is that there is no need to confuse students with extraneous information. This acronym and process is easy for the students to memorize and for the teachers to teach. Memorization does not demonstrate true conceptual understanding, Suppose you resist the temptation to use F.O.I.L. Not changing becomes a pressure not—a direct pressure necessarily, but still one you are fully aware of. In your realization of the situation, you know better than to try to change things. That is a tangential pressure on the curriculum.

Tradition is not the only potential source of tangential pressures. Administrators, texts, tests, parents, other subject areas, and business can also apply pressures in a tangential manner. The problem is, some of these are not recognizable. Suppose some influential member of the community, who is also a faculty member in the local university's mathematics department, says something to the school superintendent, who says something to your principal, who says something to your department chair, who says something to you about how mathematics should be taught. That is pressure; but it has passed through several filters on its way to you. Is the message you got the same as the one that was sent? Do you dare approach the source for clarification? Do you dare disagree with the suggestion of such a well-placed individual? Granted this has been made up, but it is not as far-fetched as some might want to believe. This is one way tangential pressures grow.

Extracurricular Mathematics

You should be familiar with the emphasis placed on sports in secondary schools. Athletes are touted as school leaders and role models. Trophies, scholarships, and accolades abound for them. Everyone in the school and community knows the star athletes. This is a wonderful experience for students (assuming it is kept within control). Recently a splendid addition has been made to the list of school activities that generate pride, honor, and respect for leading students. Mathematics contests have become a serious business. Participants spend long hours practicing. They take road trips to contests. Students are in the stands cheering for contestants. Pride is evident in the participants, coaches, school officials, parents, and communities. Students who do not make the traveling team participate in club-level activities to build their mathematical knowledge and interest. What a wonderful opportunity for students! There are a variety of potential sources of mathematics competitions. Sponsorship for these events comes from a variety of sources. The American Mathematics Competitions are jointly sponsored by the Mathematical Association of America, Society of Actuaries, Mu Alpha Theta, National Council of Teachers of Mathematics, Casualty Actuarial Society, American Statistical Association, American Mathematical Association of Two- Year Colleges, American Mathematical Society, and American Society of Pension Actuaries. They support the following activities:

- American Junior High School Mathematics Examination
- American High School Mathematics Examination
- American Invitational Mathematics Examination
- United States of America Mathematical Olympiad
- Other competitions are available through:
- Mathcounts
- Mu Alpha Theta
- Society of Engineers

This is not an all-inclusive list of competitions, but it will provide you with a starting point.

Using Information from the Curriculum

Students regularly ask when the things they are learning will be used. The question can be translated to, "Show me a place where this occurs in my world, now." Often that is difficult to do. There are sources like *When Are We Ever Gonna Have to Use This?* that list professions and the mathematics courses needed for them. Some students will identify with such a list because they have begun career decision making. Many others will not identify with it because they may not have selected a career yet. These students want to see applications of the concept in their current lives.

It is your obligation as a professional to search for applications of the material you are covering in class. You need to be able to show students where the material being taught occurs in their world, now. This is a difficult task in many instances, but it is necessary. By answering with real-world examples as often as you can, you gain the flexibility to say at times, "This is mathematics gymnastics that you will need later." Certainly any connection with other classes they are taking would be beneficial. At other points in this text we give specific examples of connections with science, English, and social studies courses.

Vertical Communications

Items in the curriculum are influenced by a variety of people. There is a need for communication among individuals teaching the same course, those teaching the next course in the sequence, those teaching the previous course in the sequence, and even those in "feeder schools" for your school. A multitude of people can have an influence on the material taught. Formative background for the idea of variable can be approached in the early grades through using A, ?, or even B. The teacher needs to let the children know that the C, ?, or D is taking the place of the desired answer. Once the appropriate response is determined, the B, ?, or will be replaced. The subliminal gains from such a reminder by the lower grade teacher can ease some of the difficulties many students experience when encountering variables later. They are aware that the symbol A, ?, B, or even "x" is temporary in many situations. They should know it is waiting to be replaced by some value.

There is a need for vertical communication to make others aware of the mathematical background needs for your classes. Teachers from the lower grades have dealt with variables when they were taking mathematics classes in the preK-12 school environment and when they were in some college classes. In their curriculum, variables may not frequently be mentioned or stressed, so, even though they know the information, it becomes lost in the many other demands. Teachers who precede you in the curriculum want to help their students succeed just like you will. It is imperative that you let them know what will make things easier for students in your classes. It is also important that you convey to these other teachers that these ideas are only suggestions that can assist student learning in the classes you teach. Remember, these teachers are professionals with educational knowledge as well. Few teachers like to have someone else mandate how to teach a class.

Some of the pressures that are placed on teachers have been briefly discussed in other sections. The following is taken from *Counting on You* and provides a different insight and, to some extent, a summary of the environment teachers face:

> *The fact that teachers in the United States do not have the high-level of professional status and respect afforded their counterparts in other countries has been a significant factor in our nation's inability to respond to the educational changes it faces. As each cycle of would-be reform comes around, we exhort teachers to do better, lament their poor preparation in college, search for additional ways to hold them accountable, and generally treat them as objects in need of repair.*

In the current cycle of reform, U.S. teachers of mathematics—more strongly and more effectively than any other group in the nation—have risen to the challenge presented by the President and the governors. Through their standards they have set the agenda for reform. Few teachers in today's schools have the authority or resources necessary to carry out this agenda. But as schools evolve from a model with teachers as hired hands to one in which teachers function as professional educators, they should welcome the challenge to implement national standards for mathematics education.

Cooperative Learning

Cooperative learning is more than putting students into groups and giving them a task. You need to give careful thought to the tasks assigned to the groups, how the groups are formed, and the roles of members of each group. This can be shown through scored discussions. Four students form a group. In front of the class they are required to solve a problem. Prior to getting in front of the group, they have no knowledge of the question they are to be asked. The teacher uses a checklist to evaluate the students' performance solving the problem. The emphasis is placed on the processes, strategies, and cooperativeness of the participants. For example, a student gets points for drawing a group member into the conversation. The check sheet is shown in Fig. 1.4. The participants sit facing each other in front of the room. L1 refers to the student on the left side of the class, closest to the board. L2 indicates the other student on the left. Students are given 5 to 7 minutes in which to cooperatively formulate a solution to the given question. They are evaluated on their ability to work as a group, as they progress toward a solution. The teacher uses the checklist to evaluate the listed areas. Three points would be awarded to a student who develops a possible strategy for solving the problem. Three points are also awarded to a student who can successfully explain a possible solution. A question that could be asked of the group is, Which costs more per pound?

- M&Ms
- Certs
- T-bone steak
- Honda Civic

A strategy might be to determine an approximate cost of each item. Another student might ask, "What does that have to do with anything?" That student would gain three points for asking a clarifying question. Another student would respond, "If you knew how much an 8-ounce bag of M&Ms costs, you could find out how much they cost per pound." This student gets three points for successfully communicating a strategy. A silent group member might be asked how the cost per pound could be determined, and three points would be generated because a non-participant has been drawn into the discussion. As the exchange continues, students can be penalized for interrupting others or monopolizing time. Although the audience cannot receive positive points, they can earn negative points for their future discussion if they disrupt the class during this scored discussion. The scored discussion is a method of leading students to the ability to work together as a group. One hurdle to group work in mathematics is the traditional view that mathematics learning is an individual activity. The prior mathematical experiences students possess may create anxieties that hinder the ability to function in a cooperative mathematics group. Some people resist use of cooperative groups in mathematics because of their belief that only a few talented individuals are capable of learning mathematics. This is a clear contradiction of the approach that *all* students can learn meaningful mathematics

Scored Discussion

1. Determining a possible strategy (3)		1. Inattention or Distracting (-2)	
L1____	R1____	L1____	R1____
L2____	R2____	L2____	R2____
2. Successfully communicating a strategy (3)		2. Interrupting (-2)	
L1____	R1____	L1____	R1____
L2____	R2____	L2____	R2____
3. Correctly applying a property (2) application (-1)		3. Making an incorrect	
L1____	R1____	L1____	R1____
L2____	R2____	L2____	R2____
4. Recognizing misused or math errors (2)		4. Monopolizing (-3)	
L1____	R1____	L1____	R1____
L2____	R2____	L2____	R2____
5. Drawing another into discussion (2) attack (-3)		5. Making a personal	
L1____	R1____	L1____	R1____
L2____	R2____	L2____	R2____

6. Asking a clarifying question (3)

L1_____ R1_____

L2_____ R2_____

Fig. 1.4

Research results indicate that cooperative grouping generates positive results in areas of:

- Academic achievement
- Self-esteem or self-confidence in learning
- Inter-group relations, including crossrace and cross-cultural friendships
- Social acceptance of mainstreamed children
- Ability to use social skills

Additional findings about cooperative grouping in mathematics include the idea that each group member should have some accountability. There is lack of agreement about how to form groups. Some say groups should be homogeneous, while others say groups should be created to show a mix of race, ability, and gender. There seems to be agreement that forming groups comprised of all fast or slow students is not a good idea. Agreement about whether or not social skills should be modeled and taught as a part of the cooperative groups does not exist. Questions exist relating to how much interdependence is necessary within a cooperative group and whether or not there is a continuum of interdependencies. A constructivist would say the classroom becomes an arena for the learning of the entire individual, social and academic.

Diagnostic Teaching

Students send messages to teachers that give clues about their levels of understanding in any class. Are those messages received by the teacher? Sometimes the signals have full impact and at other times they have none. If a teacher asks a class to perform some readiness task and none of the students can do it, the message should be clear—some background work is necessary before proceeding. Messages are usually more subtle and require careful examination and concentration. It is common for a student to attempt to conceal a lack of knowledge to avoid more work, embarrassment, or just admitting something is not clear.

You need to be aware of the "SOS" signals students send. These distress signals might be an obscure "look" of befuddlement. It might be done that way because the student "would never be caught" asking, staying after class for clarification, or showing interest. The message is sent, though. It is a cry for help. You need to receive the signal. At other times, the signal may be much easier to interpret. In the number trick "1089" a student selects a three-digit number without repeating any digits. The selected value is reversed and the smaller of the two three-digit numbers is subtracted from the larger. In the answer, the tens digit will always be 9. Asking for individuals who do not have a 9 in the tens digit of the answer provides some fast diagnostic information. If the hands of most of the class are raised, you need to examine your instructions. Typically there is only a small number of students with raised hands. You can safely assume one of two things: the students did not understand/follow your instructions, or they have difficulty subtracting when regrouping is involved. There are other possible reasons for the error, but these are the dominant ones. You are now aware of the need to spend some extra time with selected individuals. You have diagnosed a difficulty and can now prescribe a remedy.

Diagnostic teaching is a lot like being a medical doctor. Individuals go to a doctor with symptoms of some illness. The doctor examines the person and compiles all symptoms. Based on the available information, education, and prior experiences, a diagnosis is made, corrective measures are prescribed, and the patient is told to call back in a given amount of time if the situation does not improve. The patient wants to get better and has volunteered information and asked for help. Teachers do not have that luxury. Students frequently try to conceal symptoms and rarely volunteer information. Still, teachers are expected to make these individuals better students of mathematics who are able to perform desired tasks based on their overall mathematical health. Ultimately, the teacher is expected to diagnose and prescribe for each student as needed.

Diagnostic teaching is not a simple task. Like the doctor, you must draw on a wide variety of training, experience, and understanding of the individual involved. You are expected to be aware of the basic psychological construct of all students. It is assumed you know the current social pressures they deal with. As you examine a mathematical illness, you must have a continuum of skills and conceptual developments that precede the problem area. If one, some, or all of those items are missing from the student's background, you are expected to be able to prescribe a series of remedies for the student that will correct all the deficiencies. Like the doctor, it is assumed your judgment is infallible and that you can resolve the situation quickly and effectively. Diagnostic errors and incorrect treatment in the medical arena can have dramatic consequences. Ineffective diagnosis and prescription in education can be equally tragic, because it can lead to the mathematical demise of a student. Diagnostic teaching is a serious endeavor and should be approached as such.

Error Patterns

Sometimes students use an incorrect method or algorithm for solving a problem. Error patterns can be generated from lack of understanding. There could be other reasons. Here the emphasis is on diagnosing what error has been made and how to correct it. Some errors are easy to determine.

If the subtraction problem 823 - 169 yields a response of 746, you are fairly safe in assuming the student subtracted the smaller digit from the larger in each place. Subtracting the smaller digit from the larger is a common error pattern. The motivation for such a move is often attributed to the student's being told at some time that a "big number cannot be subtracted from a little one." The genesis of this statement comes from the desire to have students realize the need for regrouping in the subtraction process.

Other error patterns are not as easy to determine. The next set of problems was submitted by a high school student. There was no scratch work. You see everything the student showed.

8431	9243	7152	8230
-2576	-1678	-2649	-4128
3965	5675	3513	3112

Here we are concerned with how to determine the error and a possible reason so corrective measures to prevent the same situation can be taken. This is not always easy because the root of the problem might begin several grades prior to yours. Before reading on, you should have attempted to determine the error being made in the four subtraction problems given.

What was that student doing with these problems? How do we fix this? It appears as if subtraction facts are under control. Assuming that, the flaw must lie within the application of the algorithm. Regrouping is performed when necessary so that is not the problem. The trouble is associated with the regrouping. Where is the regrouping performed? The student is going to the leftmost digit to regroup, skipping any places between the location of the desired regrouping and that digit. In the first problem, the necessary "11" is created and the "8" is decreased to "7". The tens-place subtraction decreases that leftmost "7" to a "6" and the hundreds makes the "6" a "5". Now, the problem becomes 5 thousand minus 3 thousand and it is done. That error is not easy to determine.

Although we cannot be certain, some guesses can be made as to the cause of this error. In this particular case, the class had most recently reviewed subtraction problems of the type 4000 - 1235, which required initial regrouping from the thousands digit of the sum. It is assumed that the student was combining the two procedures and did some "creative mathematics." Discussions with the student did not reveal a clear picture of the cause.

The preceding discussion should give insight into how this particular error pattern was disclosed and remedied. Development of the skills necessary to perform such diagnosis and prescription is rooted in your understanding of the mathematics involved, time, and experience. Achieving the ability to determine error patterns is not an easy task, but it can reap large benefits for your students.

Another error pattern that is difficult to determine was generated by a middle school student. What is the error involved?

36	45	92	68
× 47	× 68	× 63	× 98
492	640	276	964
204	420	602	1172
2532	4840	6296	12684

If you have not tried to define the error, now is the time! Otherwise you will read the solution, which will help you with this error type but will do little to build your diagnostic skills. It takes practice. Notice that, in the third problem from the left, the product of 92 and 3 is correct. This gives a partial clue. It appears as if the student has command of the multiplication facts but that the algorithm is confused. The error involves commuting steps but it has a dramatic impact. The student is adding the regrouping and then multiplying, as opposed to multiplying first and then adding the regrouped value. As your error pattern diagnostic skills increase, the problem areas are easier to detect. It does take conscious thought and practice. Each of the two error pattern types described in the text had four examples. Multiple examples are necessary to enable you to define patterns. You can easily convince yourself of the validity of that statement by attempting the following exercises, looking only at the first example in each problem set.

Another error pattern that is difficult to determine was generated by a middleschool student. What is the error involved?

Assessment

We in the mathematics community are fortunate to have the leadership provided by organizations like NCTM, Mathematics Association of America (MAA), American Mathematical Association of Two- Year Colleges (AMATYC), and MSEB. Their research and support have provided a solid background and set of guidelines we can use in the classroom. The Assessment Standards provide a beginning point from which to work. The discussion in this section provides general comments about assessment. The Assessment Standards should be a part of your professional library. You should be familiar with the recommendations providèd in the publication and work to install that direction in your curriculum. Assessment is more than paper-pencil testing. You look at the work students do and determine their strengths and weaknesses. You examine your planning, presentation, and discussion methods to decide how they impact the learning styles of your students. You look at the curriculum on a day-to-day basis and from the vantage point of the big picture, considering a class as its own entity and also as it integrates into the sequence of courses available for students. You evaluate texts to determine which is most advantageous for your students, school objectives, and school curriculum. You assess your mathematics program in order to determine:

- The success of the overall program
- Whether students are learning
- How well the established mathematical goals are met
- If students are capable of applying the mathematical knowledge in other areas of the curriculum and life
- When students are enticed to study more mathematics
- The worthiness and usefulness of the content
- If the program is teachable and learnable

As a teacher of mathematics, one of your basic goals is to help all students learn and enjoy mathematics to the fullest possible extent. Teachers assess achievement of students in the classroom because they must:

- Determine the progress of each student
- Ascertain the status of each student
- Know the extent to which content and skills are mastered

Knowing the extent to which content and skills are mastered involves diagnosing strengths and weaknesses for each student. This is necessary in order to:

- Accurately place students in the curriculum continuum
- Assign grades
- Help you learn how to teach more effectively
- Gather specific rather than global information on individuals
- Analyze how an answer is determined
- Structure your teaching style

Tests can be diagnostic instruments. If the information gathered is to be useful in your diagnosis, sufficient data must be taken. How many questions should be asked to assure adequate information about a concept? If one question is asked, you have little certainty about whether or not a student has mastered the material. Asking two questions dealing with the concept is better, but how sure can you be? If a student gets one of the two right, what do you know?

You could give another test, assess other work the student has done, or talk with the student about the issue, but those each take time. Multiply the time required by the number of times you possibly will need to do something like this times the number of students you will be dealing with and you begin to see some constraints.

Maybe asking three questions would do it. If a student gets all three right or all three wrong, you would be fairly certain about the ability level pertaining to this concept. Perhaps five is a better number of questions to ask on a given concept. Your confidence level would be much greater if a student got all five correct. The problem is, the test becomes extremely long very quickly with five questions per concept.

Test length is particularly significant if concepts are closely and finely defined. Solving X + 7 = 12 involves a different set of skills from solving 3X + 7 = 12. Realistically, even X - 7 = 12 is different from X + 7 = 12 in light of the fact that students, particularly weaker ones, frequently see these as entirely different, unrelated problem types. If you treat these as different problem types, and if you ask five questions per concept on a diagnostic test, the test will be very long. How much time can realistically be allocated to diagnostic testing?

Consider the following question that could be used to build part of a diagnostic test. Each response is generated by an error pattern. Some of the ways the problem could be done incorrectly are shown. There are others, but these will suffice for this discussion.

Solve for X

3X + 5 = 17

-5 = -5

- constant from both sides

3X = 12 simplify

X = 3 ÷ by coefficient

Another "solution"

3X+ 5 = 17

3X = 17 + 5 + constant to both sides

3X = 22 simplify

X = 7× ÷ by coefficient

Another "solution"

3X+ 5 = 17

3X = 17 - 5 - constant from both sides

3X = 12 simplify

X = 36 × by coefficient

Another "solution"

3X + 5 = 17 - constant from left side

3X = 17 simplify

X = 52/3 ÷ by coefficient

Another "solution"

3X + 5 = 17 - constant from left side

3X = 17 simplify

X = 51 × by coefficient

Good testing practices dictate that in multiple-choice tests, the same letter should not always represent the correct answer. For simplicity's sake, we will use A for the correct response in each question; B for adding the constant to both sides; C for subtracting the constant from both sides but then multiplying by the coefficient; D for subtracting the constant from the left side only and then dividing both sides by the coefficient; and E for subtracting the constant from the left side of the equation and multiplying the right by the coefficient. This will simplify the discussion for the example being built. There are five questions for the concept.

Fig. 1.5 shows additional poor testing practices ($2T + 5 = 13$ having only one decimal answer, responses not arranged in ascending or descending order, inconsistent format by using mixed numbers, improper fractions, decimals). As was noted earlier, the emphasis in this case is on diagnostic matters, and other issues are ignored for the sake of this discussion. A student selecting answer A on all five questions in the test would adequately demonstrate mastery (assuming honesty). A student selecting A in four out of five of the questions would probably be considered as having mastered the concept. As the number of correct responses decreases, the confidence level in the students ability to do that problem type also decreases.

Suppose a student selects B as the correct response for each of the problems in Fig. 1.5 . Not only do you know the student missed them, but you also have a good idea about what was done to get those answers. This makes prescription easy and, in most cases, effective. A personal comment or note on the paper stating the error and what should have been done might correct the situation. This discussion would be the same for options C, D, or E. Only when a student responds randomly would there be a need for additional time invested to analyze the error pattern. In such a situation, an immediate question would be whether or not the student is interested in learning. If the answer is negative, there is an entirely different set of circumstances that need to be resolved before tackling the errors encountered in solving the equations. This is exemplified by the statement about leading a horse to water but not being able to force it to drink.

Question	*Correct*	*+ con*	*- con/X*	*-left/÷*	*- left/X*
3M + 5 = 17	a) M = 4	b) M = 71/3	c) M = 36	d) M = 52/3	e) M = 51
2N + 4 = 18	a) N = 7	b) N = 11	c) N = 28	d) N = 9	e) N = 36
4P + 6 = 32	a) P = 6.5	b) P = 9.5	c) P = 104	d) P = 8	e) P = 128
7R + 3 = 12	a) R = 9/7	b) R = 15/7	c) R = 63	d) R = 12/7	e) R = 84
2T + 5 = 13	a) T = 4	b) T = 9	c) T = 16	d) T = 6.5	d) T = 26

Fig. 1.5

One concept has been tested. 3X - 5 = 17 is different because other skills are involved. This could lead to a very long test. Test length can be resolved by giving many short tests. The time required to create such questions is not an insignificant factor. Suppose you decide to ask five questions like the ones in Fig. 1.5 for each concept covered and that you teach the same course each year. A file of questions can be developed over a few years. In the first year you create five questions. The second year you create three more and use two of the initial five. In the third year, create two more and select three from the pool of eight developed earlier. At this point the amount of time required to create questions is drastically reduced, and you still have all in Fig. 1.5 ; B for adding the constant to both sides (+ constant in Fig. 1.5); C for subtracting the constant from both sides but then multiplying by the coefficient (- constant/X in Fig. 1.5); D for subtracting the constant from the left side only and then dividing both sides by the coefficient (- left/X in Fig. 1.5); and E for subtracting the constant from the left side of the equation and multiplying the right by the coefficient (- left/X in Fig. 1.5). This will simplify the discussion for the example being built. There are five questions for the concept.

Fig. 1.5 shows additional poor testing practices ($2T + 5 = 13$ having only one decimal answer, responses not arranged in ascending or descending order, inconsistent format by using mixed numbers, improper fractions, decimals). As was noted earlier, the emphasis in this case is on diagnostic matters, and other issues are ignored for the sake of this discussion. A student selecting answer A on all five questions in the test would adequately demonstrate mastery (assuming honesty). A student selecting A in four out of five of the questions would probably be considered as having mastered the concept. As the number of correct responses decreases, the confidence level in the students ability to do that problem type also decreases.

Suppose a student selects B as the correct response for each of the problems in Fig. 1.5 . Not only do you know the student missed them, but you also have a good idea about what was done to get those answers. This makes prescription easy and, in most cases, effective. A personal comment or note on the paper stating the error and what should have been done might correct the situation. This discussion would be the same for options C, D, or E. Only when a student responds randomly would there be a need for additional time invested to analyze the error pattern. In such a situation, an immediate question would be whether or not the student is interested in learning. If the answer is negative, there is an entirely different set of circumstances that need to be resolved before tackling the errors encountered in solving the equations. This is exemplified by the statement about leading a horse to water but not being able to force it to drink.

Observation can be a valuable assessment tool. You can watch as you move around the room during group work. As they respond to your questions, notice facial expressions and body language. Be aware of the emotional climate in the room. When a particular student asks a question, is it sincere or an attempt to get some means of praise from you? Is the student a flexible thinker who is willing to try different approaches to the same question? Is the student asking merely as an attempt to lead you away from the objective at hand?

Observations sometimes lead to the need for additional information, perhaps coming from interviews with individual students. One advantage of the interview is the removal of writing skills. Students do exist who can talk through a proof when they cannot write it. Be careful that they do not look to you for visual clues as they go through it. This approach is in line with suggestions that students be able to communicate mathematically. Interviewing requires time and rapport with the student. You are attempting to determine what the student knows. Some students will attempt to tell you what they think you want to hear. You need to be able to discern the difference. Time is a major factor in this approach, but the idea should not be discarded as an option for some students, without careful consideration.

One answer to time as an assessment tool comes from a checklist. You are aware of what a student should know about a concept. A list of items related to that concept can prove useful. As you observe or reflect on what a student has done, you should be able to quickly establish a picture of what needs to be done to strengthen that student's understandings. A checklist can be an invaluable readiness tool. One specific checklist can be used to lay the foundation for attitudinal surveys. Does the student appear to like mathematics? Does the student work well with others? The scored discussion covered earlier is an example of how a checklist could be used as an assessment tool.

Other assessment tools include items you should be familiar with from education courses: criterion-referenced tests, norm referenced tests, and standardized tests. Various versions of these tests are often supplied with the text or by the school system. Students are accustomed to this kind of test and, for the most part, comfortable with them. One significant drawback to these tests is that they often function at the knowledge level. It is imperative that we start asking students non-knowledge-level questions as a pad of their assessment program if we truly want the student to learn in a constructivist environment. Only then will we begin to have insight into each students true ability and understanding.

Another method of gathering information is the portfolio. A portfolio should contain examples of the best works of a student, as determined by the student. You can provide guidelines that suggest inclusion of an exemplary test paper, a proof, some homework problems, and so on. The portfolio should go beyond that type of information, though. Perhaps segments from a journal that indicate attitudes and feelings about the study of mathematics are appropriate. Certainly, examples of applications of topics covered would be acceptable. Demonstrations of the ability to use and interpret results generated through graphing calculators, spreadsheets, symbol-manipulating/function-plotting software, and dynamic geometry software would be appropriate. This is not an exhaustive list of elements that could be included in a student's portfolio, but it is a start. You need to consider the concept and build components into it that are appropriate for you and your students.

Some assessment is relatively easy to do. You say or do something in class and a student reacts. You know, based on the response, the impact of your action. Content goals are established for a class, and it can be determined whether or not they are met. Other assessment is not so easy. Behavior is a constant consideration. Most behavior is clearly either acceptable or unacceptable. There are actions between the two extremes, and determining when something moves from acceptable to unacceptable is not always easy.

Not all assessment ideas are successful or accepted. This compounds the issue immensely. What methods should be adopted. Which ones are trends that will vanish? Will some of the new ideas have a lasting impact on the school mathematics curriculum? The curriculum and its associated tentacles are not easily altered.

Fourteen schools across the country that were considered pioneers in the use of performance assessment in evaluating their students' progress were studied for 3 years. The conclusion was that performance assessments are having little effect on what gets taught in the classroom. One part of the discussion was that multiple choice and short-answer questions readily gauge what students know. On the other hand, performance assessments are aimed at evaluating what students can do with what they know. Researchers found that content taught in the classrooms had changed little. Teachers complained because the new assessment methods allowed them less time to cover all the material they had taught in the past. Students were writing more, but the writing was not necessarily better. The researchers concluded that the schools where changes in teaching and learning had taken a firmer hold were those in which teachers had been involved with the new assessment systems from the start.

The state of Kentucky instituted a student assessment program that was classified as a "ground breaking battery of tests." A panel of testing experts concluded that the battery, which assesses student achievement in mathematics, reading, science, social studies, and writing, has produced misleading results. They contend the test is not reliable in determining which schools should receive cash awards and which should be penalized (is this an external pressure?). The five-member panel of experts asked, "Are the intended uses of the tests appropriate?" Accusations are that the gain scores have been exaggerated. Panel members concluded that scoring of portfolios is too subjective and inconsistent, efforts to equate assessments from one year to the next are problematic, and student gains on the tests do not match changes in performance on other standardized tests. The forms of the test reviewed contained no multiple-choice questions. It is suggested that multiple-choice questions be added and counted as a part of the score and that the portfolio scores be removed from consideration. Assessment is a continuing integral aspect of teaching mathematics. It helps you determine if the students are learning what you think they should. It helps the student know if the ideas garnered are those the teacher deems valuable. Assessment involves appraisal as well as measurement. No one form is appropriate for all aspects of assessment. You need to be aware of the multitude of avenues available to you and select those that will prove most beneficial to you in assisting your students to learn and appreciate as much mathematics as possible for each one of them.

Conclusion

You have traveled from beginning foundations through the latest thinking of the mathematics education community as you looked at learning theory, curriculum, and assessment. The associated topics and ideas are intertwined to such a degree that it is difficult to discuss one without the other. You need to blend these discussions with those from your other classes into a position that is comfortable for you. You cannot include an item in your construct because we, or some authorities, say so. It should be there because it fits with your philosophy and beliefs about the teaching of mathematics. The only feasible way you can create your own view of teaching mathematics is to be familiar with all the facets of the arena. It takes time and energy to learn all the aspects, but the benefits you and your students will reap will be worth the effort.

2

Social Interaction and Learning Mathematics

In this chapter, teaching and learning mathematics are viewed as linked in the local processes of classroom interaction. The special interest is in how mathematical meanings are negotiated and become taken to be shared in the classroom discourse. In the first section, general aspects of mathematics learning in a cultural context are discussed with regard to different schools of thought. Is mathematical meaning really a matter under negotiation? Why are social aspects intrinsic to learning mathematics? In the second section, several specific findings and theoretical concepts of the negotiation of mathematical meaning are presented. Why is ambiguity an essential feature of discourse in mathematics lessons? Through which regularities can knowledge be taken to be shared in spite of the teacher's and the students' different background understandings? In the third section, relations between mathematics learning and social interaction are discussed. Is learning mathematics an effect of social regulations or does it occur when overcoming the entanglement in the regulations? In all sections, several classroom scenes and specific findings of ethnographical studies are used to illustrate abstract statements.

Links Between Mathematics, Culture, and Cognition

In several countries, there is a growing body of research demonstrating the relevance of social activities to learning mathematics. In Brazil, Carraher, Carraher raher ,Schliemann and Saxe studied relations between cultural activities and cognitive development by comparing the children's mathematical thinking outside and inside the culture of school. In Great Britain, Bishop, Geoffrey and Walkerdine analyzed the social constitution of mathematical meaning during classroom processes. In France, Balacheff and Laborde developed experimental situations in which students interactively constituted mathematical solutions. In Italy, Bartolini Bussi introduced phases of mathematical discussions into classrooms and explored the learning processes taking place during the discussions. In the United States, Cobb, Wood, and Yackel analyzed how the change of social norms in the classroom affected the students' learning. In Germany, Bauersfeld, Krummheuer and Voigt investigated relations between social characteristics of interaction processes and the students' or teacher's thinking.

Although the list is not complete, it gives an impression of the change of many mathematics educators' foci of attention. In the decades before, in order to understand the individual student's thinking, clinical interviews were preferred. Nowadays cultural and social dimensions are not excluded or neglected, but they are taken into account by undertaking "ethnographical" case studies in order to understand mathematics learning in context. The basic assumption is that cultural and social dimensions are not only peripheral conditions of learning mathematics but are intrinsic to learning mathematics.

This view has to be justified because mathematics is often seen as a domain of rationality which is free of social dynamics and cultural influences. Other reasons against the emphasis on social aspects are given by child-centered conceptions that stress the autonomy of the learner. First, I justify that mathematical meanings are matter under negotiation. Epistemological considerations are emphasized that support the relevance of the concept of negotiation of mathematical meaning. The claim is not declaring what mathematics "really" is. Second, the theoretical focus on the individual child is contrasted with the theoretical focus on the social context. Finally, I give reasons for the decision to go along with the interactionist perspective.

Social Aspects of School Mathematics

Traditional philosophies like platonism or intuitionism assume that mathematics expresses eternal relationships between objects that are intuitive as well as objective. Tymoczko called such theories "private theories" because, in the ideal situation, a single isolated mathematician discovers or creates mathematical knowledge. Diverging from these perspectives, other philosophers, such as Lakatos and Wittgenstein, considered mathematics to be also a product of social processes. Using the literary form of classroom discussions, Lakatos described how mathematical concepts are stabilized or changed over time through processes of agreement and refutation. From this philosophical point of view, the truth of mathematical statements is not absolute. The statements are only (justified) conjectures, which can fail in the future when new problems are created.

Wittgenstein explained the inexorableness of mathematical argumentation in our experience by his concept of "language game."

> *The indelible nature of numbers and figures and the certainty of proving procedures are not expressions of the ideal existence of mathematical objects nor of the absolute validity of the procedures. Because we needed such a rigid language game for various purposes we invented it along with its grammar and its dovetailing with practice. The mathematician is an inventor not a discoverer.*

The image of the mathematician as an inventor corresponds to the statement that mathematics is a product of social processes because individual inventions have to be accepted in order to become official mathematics.

The dispute is very old: Is mathematics invented, and thus man-made, or is mathematics discovered, and thus pre given? Although philosophers can make rigid and universal assumptions about "the nature of mathematics," it seems to be helpful here to make distinctions between different components of mathematics. In his dialogues about mathematics, the mathematician Renyi offered a distinction—the mathematician invents concepts and discovers theorems. Rényi compared the mathematical researcher with a seafarer who discovers unknown islands:

> *If a seafarer intends to sail into a region into which nobody before has sailed he has to be also an inventor. The seafarer has to construct a ship that is more storm proof than the ships of his predecessors. I would like to say that the new concepts which a mathematician puts forward are like ships of a new type. These ships take the seafarer who is out for discoveries faster and faster over the stormy sea into new regions.*

By using epistemological arguments, Burscheid and Struve came to a similar conclusion. The learning of "theoretical concepts" in school cannot be explained sufficiently by focusing on the individual learner who would discover concepts. Burscheid and Struve emphasized the necessity of "social impulses" in school so that the learner constructs theoretical concepts as wanted.

Working at the forefront of research, the mathematician has a relative freedom to invent concepts or to change concepts given. However, the learner is not as free to introduce new concepts into the discipline. In Protocol 1, two students extended the concept of an even number to fractions. Although the construction fits several mathematical inferences, it is excluded by definition in regular mathematics.

Protocol 1

David: Fifteen's odd and a half's even

Interviewer: Fifteen's odd and a half's even? Is it?

David: Yes.

Interviewer: Why is half even?

David: Because, erm, a quarter's odd and a half must be even.

Interviewer: Why is a quarter odd?

David: Because it's only three.

Interviewer: What's only three?

David: A quarter.

Interviewer: A quarter's only three?

David: That's what I did in my division.

Robert: Yes, there's three parts in a quarter like on a clock. It goes five, ten, fifteen.

Interviewer: Oh, I see.

Robert: There's only three parts in it.

The pupils had possibly learned that every whole number is odd or even. Later on, they learned that fractions are numbers, too. Also, the students drew the conclusion correctly that the sum of two odd numbers is an even number. Now, there is the need of negotiation of meaning so that, on the one hand, the students confirm their correct inferences and, on the other hand, are supported in imaging the contradictions evoked by their extension of the definition of oddness. (For example, the teacher may puzzle the students by stating that the addition of two halves makes one, an odd number.)

In the following, I want to argue against the assumption that social interaction is not intrinsic for the learning of mathematics because single mathematical meanings would be given self-referentially through their interrelations in a mathematical theory. Mathematics is often understood as a body of knowledge that is relatively autonomous. It is often viewed as a closed system that is not mixed up by meanings from other domains of experience (except in application of mathematics).

In the scene described, the students make sense of oddness and evenness of fractions by links to units of time represented on clocks. In school, it is typical that mathematical meanings are related to domains of experience outside pure mathematics. Although the modern mathematician considers concepts to be variables whose meanings are given self-referentially through the system of the mathematical theory (especially through the network of concepts), the epistemological status of school mathematics is not so definite. Struve analyzed several domains of school mathematics by epistemological means. He summarizes his findings as follows: "Mathematical knowledge taught in school does not consist of clear-cut mathematical facts but of rather complex structures of different epistemological status, viz. of empirical and normative character" In the classroom, mathematical knowledge is intertwined with meanings of objects outside "pure" mathematics.

For example, in elementary classrooms, the validity of the statement $3 + 4 = 7$ is not explained by inferences from Peano's axioms. At first, adults regulate the children's use of fingers or chips coordinated with sequences of words. Addition is explained as counting forward or as increasing the number of concrete things. Later, sophisticated argumentation come nearer to the autonomous characteristics of mathematical activities, for example, "3 + 4 = 7, therefore 13 + 4 has to be 17." During introduction to negative numbers, addition can not successfully be interpreted as synonymous with increasing the amount of concrete things like apples: Addition should become an operation with more abstract objects.

In classroom life, the meanings of mathematical concepts and the validity of mathematical statements are socially accomplished. Only when the mathematical meanings are enriched so that they mutually support each other as a system, does the socially regulated "borrowing" of experience from outside mathematics become less important for further learning; for example, then the student handles negative numbers by thinking of mathematical interrelations of numbers rather than imagining (missing) apples.

Nevertheless, whereas the expert can experience an element of the topic as an element to be discovered by reasoning, the learner cannot experience "it" if the learner does not realize at least the outlines of the expert's theory. There is the need of negotiation of meaning if the topic of discourse is to be meaningful for the learner and if the learner is to avoid confusing mathematical meanings with divergent everyday meanings of clocks, fingers, apples, and so forth. My claim is not that students should learn mathematics in Hilbert's sense. My point is that, especially in introductory situations, we cannot presume that the learner would ascribe specific meanings to the topic by themselves—meanings that are compatible with the mathematical meanings the teacher wants the student to learn.

The Focus on the Individual

Up to this point, in my use of the term "mathematical meaning," I have mixed the observer's point of view with the sense-making of the individual observed. In this, there is the danger of identifying objective validity with subjective conviction. The ambiguous meaning of "mathematical meaning" arises from the fact that it can be understood with regard to an epistemological theory of mathematics as well as with regard to a psychological theory of subjective sense-making processes. The following discussion restricts the meaning of meaning to the latter issue.

For a long period of time, research in mathematics education has been profoundly influenced by Piaget's genetic epistemology and developmental psychology. Many researchers focused their attention on the cognitive development of individual children. The child's mathematical knowledge is viewed as the product of the individual's conceptual operations. Nowadays, this perspective is well known as radical constructivism. From this point of view, the individual's knowledge can be at best viable; that is, if the student's knowledge is compatible with new experiences subjectively interpreted, the student's knowledge is confirmed without necessarily being true or intended by the teacher. In this perspective, there is no place for the idea of transmission of knowledge from the teacher to the student or for the idea of reading reality as it is.

In Protocol 2, the students construct meanings of sequences of numbers. Although the teacher poses questions in order to elicit definite meanings that he intends, the students interpret the problem differently. The students (aged 13 to 14) experience their first lesson in probability. In a preparatory situation, several students had thrown a die each 100 times. The outcomes of the casts are written on the blackboard.

1	2	3	4	5	6
15	13	19	14	19	17
23	15	18	12	12	20
14	14	13	19	18	22
20	15	11	21	20	13
18	21	15	18	10	18
15	15	15	20	15	20
19	15	14	15	14	21

The teacher wants the students to look at the outcomes, to see the variations of the outcomes, and to trace the variations to the concept of randomness.

Protocol 2

Teacher: What do you notice about these outcomes? Martina.

Martina: The outcomes are all above ten.

Teacher: (drawling way of speaking) Yes, Achim.

Achim: I wanted to say it, too.

Teacher: Does anybody notice something else? Michael.

Michael: It's obvious that the outcomes are different.

Teacher: Why didn't you expect that all outcomes are the same?

Michael: 100 cannot be divided by 6. [The teacher shows surprise.]

Nothing of the table is conspicuous by itself. Realizing something in the givens, that is not readily apparent, depends on corresponding expectations. Presumably, the students' actual constructions of meaning are influenced by their previous experiences in situations in which similarities of numbers or calculations were relevant. In contrast to it, the teacher's intention (fixed introduction in probability) influences his construction of meaning of the table as well as his interpretation of Michael's thinking. Presumably, the teacher sees Michael on the right track toward the meaning of randomness. Later on, the teacher will give a suggestive hint so that the students offer the catchword "random."

The problem of misunderstanding between the adult and the student can be reconstructed not only during frontal teaching but also during clinical interviews. Varying Piagetian experiments, Donaldson and Hundeide showed that a student's ability displayed in an interview can depend on the interview situation. Neglecting the relevance of the social and empirical context supports the illusion that the subject's thinking can be explained sufficiently by developmental processes inside the person.

Although the sociological aspects in Piaget's research are under specified, Piaget remarked that "social interaction is a necessary condition for the development of logic". In Geneve, Piaget's followers took Piaget's developmental psychology as a basis of their work, and they explored social interactions between children and conflicts between the children's perspectives as conditions of mental reorganizations. However, they conceptualized social interaction as an external variable with regard to developmental processes inside the learner. Solomon criticized this extension of Piaget's work because only the learning of knowledge and not the knowledge itself is viewed as socially conditioned. If we do not assume innate organizers, how can we think of inter-subjective meanings when each individual constructs his or her own meanings? The cultural aspects of mathematical practices in school have to be taken into account. "Acculturation and the institutionalisation of mathematical practices are . . . a necessary aspect of children's mathematics education. Analyses that focus solely on individual children's construction of mathematical knowledge tell only half of a good story".

The Focus on Culture

Bruner is well known for emphasizing children's discoveries and for criticizing the teacher's guidance. In 1986, he remarked on a development in his own work: "I have come increasingly to recognize that most learning in most settings is a communal activity, a sharing of the culture". As early as during the dispute about the concept of discovery, Bruner stated: "Culture, thus, is not discovered; it is passed on or forgotten. All this suggests to me that we have better to be cautions in talking about the method of discovery, or discovery as the principal vehicle of education". Edwards and Mercer increased the importance of culture as the point of reference in educational research: "The child-centered ideology needs to be replaced with one that emphasizes the socio-cultural and discursive bases of knowledge and learning". Instead of the individual person, now, the social group is the basic element of interest. Before the appropriateness of this change is discussed, the implications of a one-sided concentration on culture are roughly outlined.

In contrast to locating rational argumentation in the private realms of individual experience, Harre understood rationality as "a feature of public collective discourses to which there may have been several individual contributions". "To say that someone is rational is not to congratulate them on their private cognitive processes but to praise them for their contributions to the collective discourse". Like Wittgenstein, Harre and other social constructivists looked for the roots of (mathematical) competence in social activities. Correspondingly, Solomon claimed that cognitive development is "the progressive socialization of the child's judgements". In mathematics lessons, "learning is the initiation into a social tradition".

Many researchers are inspired by Vygotsky work when they are studying social events in order to explore links between culture and cognition. Vygotsky assumed that the characteristics of adult-guided interactions are internalized by the learner during the learner's development: "Any function in the child's cultural development appears twice, or on two planes. First it appears on the social plane, and then on the psychological plane. First it appears between people as an interpsychological category, and then within the child as an intrapsychological category. All higher mental functions are internalized social relationships". Vygotsky characterized the learner's development in terms of shifts in control or responsibility. The possibility of shifts is given in the "zone of proximal development," that is, the difference between a learner's actual development as determined by independent problem solving and the higher level of "potential development as determined through problem solving under adult guidance or in collaboration with more capable peers". The more competent participants guide the interactions so that the learners can participate in activities that they could not manage by themselves. More and more, in these interactions learners increase their control and responsibility.

In comparison to the emphasis on the autonomy of the individual's cognitive processes, theories inspired by Vygotsky tend to take the student as an object of the teacher's activities or as a rather passive participant of the classroom processes. The classroom culture seems to be pregiven, the students' unusual and unexpected actions could be evaluated as mere deviations, and differences among individuals' developments are rather unexplained. However, the learner's active role in the constitution of a classroom culture becomes more relevant if micro-processes of classroom discourse are investigated.

The Focus on Interaction—A Chance of Mediating Between the Foci on the Subject and on Culture?

Several theoretical approaches with regard to mathematics learning through interaction have already been mentioned. Roughly compared, two antithetical strands can be reconstructed: individualism versus collectivism. With reference to Piaget, learning mathematics is viewed as structured by the individual's attempts to resolve what he or she finds problematic in the world of his or her experience. With reference to Vygotsky, the environment given seems to direct the individual's learning of mathematics. On the one hand, the individual is the actor ("subject"), and mathematical knowledge is constructed by it. On the other hand, the subject is the object of cultural practices, and mathematical knowledge given is internalized. I think it does not happen by chance that the former school of thought has been established as prominent in the Western part of the world, whereas the latter school is rooted in the Eastern part.

Of course, the comparison gives a crude contrast of opposing tendencies. Either school has produced sophisticated ideas to answer questions posed from the other side. But which basic alternatives should a mathematics educator pursue? The statement that we should follow both orientations is avoiding an answer even though one perspective is more appropriate to the microlevel of classroom processes and the other to the macrolevel of school culture. Bauersfeld and Cobb stressed the complementary character of the theories. If mixing incompatible theories is unsatisfactory and if the juxtaposition of theories shifts the problem of integration to the practitioner, normative considerations may help.

Personally, I take the emphasis on the subject as the starting point in order to understand the negotiation of meaning and the learning of mathematics in classrooms. The main reason is that concepts like "socialization," "internalization," "initiation into a social tradition," and so forth do not (directly) explain what I think is the most important objective of mathematics education: Bildung. Bildung is a main claim in the German tradition of thinking about education. Immanuel Kant, the German philosopher of Enlightenment, criticized what appeared to be habitual or natural. The individual should act on rational grounds in the individual's mind without relying on the other's guidance. (Today, we would comment that reason is not innate but emerges when the subject becomes a member of our culture.) The prominent objective of mathematics education is not that the students produce objectively solutions to mathematical problems but that they do it insightfully and by reasonably thinking. What on the behavioral level does in fact not make a difference should be an important subjective difference. Do the students act as desired because they intend to fulfill the teacher's expectations in order to participate successfully, or because they draw conclusions in order to solve a mathematical problem in their experiential world?

Accordingly, the following discussion about social interaction stresses the reasoning and sense-making processes of subjects that interactively constitute mathematical meanings. An interactionist approach is preferred because it emphasizes the individual's sense-making processes as well as the interaction processes. It does not deduce the individual's learning from the social interaction as suggested by theories of socialization and of internationalization. From the interactionist point of view, social interaction does not function as a vehicle that transforms "objective" knowledge into subjective knowledge. But social interaction makes possible that subjective ideas become compatible with culture and with inter-subjective knowledge like mathematics.

In the following section, a network of theoretical concepts is outlined. First, a possible conflict between the reader's expectation and the author's intention should be taken into account. The term negotiation of mathematical meanings is used with regard to a theoretical perspective on mathematics classrooms. Its use could be misunderstood in a normative sense, as if negotiation of meaning happens only in a liberal classroom culture. From the theoretical point of view of symbolic interactionism, negotiation of meanings happens in every social interaction. Of course, in a specific classroom situation, the negotiation could be more explicit or implicit. The application of the theoretical concept to a specific classroom situation could be more or less helpful in order to understand what happens in the classroom. Nevertheless, in this chapter, theoretical considerations give reasons for the relevance of the concept.

Negotiation of Mathematical Meanings

This section presents an interactional approach to classroom processes. The approach is based on microsociology; it is particularly influenced by symbolic interactionism and ethnomethodology. However, the sociological concepts have been modified in order to deal with teaching and learning of mathematics.

Ambiguity and Interpretation

According to folk beliefs, the tasks, the questions, the signs, and so on of mathematics lessons have definite, clear-cut meanings. These beliefs have to be questioned in order to realize the relevance of negotiation. Of course, for the reader I am charging an open door. If one looks at microprocesses in the classroom carefully, things seem to be ambiguous and call for interpretation. What is the meaning of "5" to young children in a specific situation? Is the meaning bound to concrete things (e.g., "the little finger of my left hand"), does the sign remind the student of previous activities (e.g., "a difficult number to write"), does it evoke specific emotions (e.g., "my favourite number"), is its meaning related to other numbers (e.g., "equal to 2 plus 3, 1 and 4, 0 and 5"), and so on?

Another example is given by the interpretations of a picture which is presented as a supposed unambiguous task in a regular German schoolbook for first graders. Several children were asked to give the correct number sentence. Solutions are:

2 + 3 = 5	("sum of the bananas")
5 - 2 = 3	("the keeper gives two bananas to the ape")
1 + 1 = 2	("the keeper and the ape")
3 - 2 = 1	("the keeper has one banana more than the ape")
5 - 4 = 1	("one banana more than hands, the keeper will lose the middle one")

One of the findings of a research project was that, in principle, such pictures, text problems, games, and stories have multiple meanings if the interpreting children are not familiar with the specific type of the task. Nevertheless, many textbook authors and mathematics teachers, as well as the students, assume that these pictures have unambiguous meanings with respect to solutions. The processes of mathematicization taken for granted turn out to be problematic when the situations are interpreted by subjects who are (still) not members of the classroom culture.

According to one of the interactionist assumptions, every object or event in human interaction is plurisemantic. In order to make sense of it, the subject uses a background knowledge and forms a context of sense for interpreting the object. For example, a first grader can interpret the picture as the invitation to tell a personal experience of a zoo; or, the teacher can take the picture as the opportunity for motivating students to apply subtraction. The subject does not necessarily experience the ambiguous object as plurisemantic but as factual if the background understanding is taken for granted. With reference to Goffman's frame analysis, Krummheuer reconstructed different background understandings ("framings") between the teacher and the students of an algebra class over a longer period of time. Comparing the interactions during collaborative learning with the interactions during frontal class teaching, he demonstrated that "misunderstandings" between the teacher and the students are quite usual without the participants being aware of it. Steinbring's epistemological study explained why the disparity between the teacher's and the students' background understandings exists necessarily. In order to learn new mathematical concepts that the teacher introduces, the students change their background understandings.

The ambiguity of tasks, question, and so forth does not have to be evaluated as a disaster so that we would try to minimize it. The following problem situation makes explicit use of different possibilities of interpreting a problem. The teacher announces the sum of the spots: __ + __ + __ = 11. The students have to jointly ascertain the number of spots of each die. In the classroom discourse the students are free to ask clever questions, to guess, to consider the probability of singular outcomes (if the sum is very small or large), or to calculate. Thus, there are more or less advanced ways to interpret the problem depending on the students 's dispositions. The matter of interaction needs attention if we consider reactions to students who are always guessing even though the first two numbers of spots are known.

Social Interaction

From the point of view of symbolic interactionism, interaction is more than a sequence of actions and reactions. A participant of an interaction monitors his action in accordance with what he assumes to be the other participants' background understandings, expectations, and so on, whereas the other participants make sense of the action adopting what they believe to be the actor's background understandings, intentions, and so on. The following actions of the other participants are interpreted by the former actor with regard to his expectations and can prompt a reconsideration, and so on. For example, the student can interpret the teacher's reaction as a specific evaluation of his own thinking even though the teacher's reaction might have been only the expression of amusement at a particular moment during the student's action. Using his background knowledge of the teacher's supposed emotion and being ashamed, the student might search for more advanced ways to interpret the problem at hand and to solve it. Experiencing a similar situation, another student might cope by pleasing the teacher superficially. Of course, the teacher could react differently according to his background knowledge of the two students' different dispositions. It is not only important that the teacher and the students attempt to understand each other. A third thing, the accomplishment of inter-subjective meanings taken as mathematical ones, is essential in mathematics teaching and learning. The point is not that teacher and students "share knowledge." From the symbolic interactionist and the radical constructivist point of view, only mathematical meanings "taken to be shared" can be produced through negotiation. The participants take meanings to be shared if they neglect that they could interpret the signs differently. Krummheuer and Cobb used the terms working interim and consensual domain, respectively, in order to describe that the participants interact as if they interpret the mathematical topic of their discourse equally. However, one can never be sure that two persons are thinking the same even if they collaborate without conflict, especially if they agree about formal statements and processes. One of the characteristics of formal mathematics is that people can coordinate their actions smoothly while they are actually ascribing different meanings to the objects. Cobb, Wood, and Yackel documented the following scene in a classroom teaching experiment. The students Josh and Joey are solving several tasks:

1. 50 - 9 = 41
2. 60 - 9 = 51
3. 60 - 19 = 41
4. 41 + 19 = 60
5. 31 + 29 = 60
6. 31 + 19 = 50
7. 32 + 18 = __

We don't know how both students solved the first six tasks because the videotape begins when the students are solving the seventh task. In the classroom a variety of ways of solving was allowed, such as counting by ones, using the hundreds board, or relating a new problem to a previously solved one.

The videotape begins when Josh makes a statement.

Protocol 3

Josh: Uh-huh, that's 18, not 19.

Joey: Yeah, but that's 32 not 31.

Josh: Oh yeah!

Joey: They're the same thing.

Project member: What's the same thing?

Joey: These two [points to 31 + 19 = 50 and 32 + 18 = __].

Project member: Hang on, I was asking Josh. Which ones? We've got 31 and 19.

Josh: Makes 50.

Project member: Yeah.

Josh: And, look 32 and 18. See, it's just one more than that [points to the tasks], and that's one higher than that.

Later on in the interview, Josh and Joey indicated that they solved the fifth task by adding the tens and the ones 31 + 29 = 30 + 20 + 1 + 9 = 50 + 10 = 60. The sixth task was solved by comparing the second summands of the sixth and the fifth task. So the students were able to combine two tasks that did not differ in one summand. But the fifth task, which differs in both summands from the preceding task, was solved as an isolated one.

When the students solve the seventh task a new way of solving emerges in the course of interaction. From the interactionist point of view, the meaning of this task is interactively constituted as one in which the increase of one number compensates the decrease of the other. At the beginning, either of the students focused his attention to the change of one summand and points to it. Either alters his attention stimulated by his partner and accepts the partner's statement. The students gain a tacit agreement without checking whether they "share" a common knowledge in fact. Through this negotiation, a meaning of the task is constituted, without which we have to suppose that one student would have constructed this meaning if working alone or that one student would take over the responsibility for the solution alone.

In the classroom, the participants interactively constitute taken-to-be-shared meanings. What is referred to taken-to-be-shared meaning emerges during processes of negotiation. From the observer's point of view, the meaning of "taken to-be-shared" is not a partial match of individuals' constructions, nor is it a cognitive element. Instead, it exists at the level of interaction. "Symbolic interactionism views meaning as arising in the process of interaction between people. The meaning of a thing grows out of the ways in which other persons act toward the person with regard to the thing. Symbolic interactionism sees meanings as social products". In the scene just described, the meaning of the seventh task emerges when the students interact. The task is taken as the "same thing" compared with the sixth task. When the project member and the students interact, this meaning is stabilized between them.

In the course of negotiation, the teacher and the students (or the students among themselves) accomplish relationships of mathematical meanings taken to be shared. From the observer's point of view, I call these relationships of meanings a mathematical theme. In the scene described, the theme is the comparison of two tasks because the participants seem to pay attention to differences and correspondences of the tasks.

During frontal teaching, the students can originally contribute to the theme. Thus, the theme may not be a representation of the mathematical content which the teacher intended to establish. Realizing his or her intentions, the teacher is dependent on the students' indications of understanding and, reciprocally, the students are dependent on the teacher's acceptance of their contributions. Thus, the theme is not a fixed body of knowledge. As the topic of discourse, it is interactively constituted and it is changed through the negotiation of meaning.

If the teacher does not direct and evaluate the students rigidly, step by step, and if a dialogue is not established in the old normative sense, the theme can be described as a river that produces its own bed. The result of the dialogue is not clear in advance. In the scene described, Joey and Josh are not forced to solve the task using a compensation strategy. But if they solved several tasks in a similar way and if they justified this way successfully, the observer might expect that the comparison of tasks will be a common theme between Josh and Joey in future problems.

Because people usually are obliged to take care of the thematic coherence of discourse (except small talk) and because mathematical discussions are constrained by specific rigid obligations, the theme gains stability often as time is spent in a discussion. In cases of conflict, the participants clarify what is taken as the theme. A participant could be accused of straying from the theme or could be forced to justify the relevance of his or her divergent contribution, or a change in the theme may need metacommunicative remarks or markers.

From an epistemological point of view, the stability of a theme corresponds to the self-reference of mathematical knowledge. For example, an observer could state that Josh's and Joey's way of solving expresses the use or the discovery of mathematical laws in a theory of numbers. The fit of this description to the students' sense-making processes can be clarified if we interview them about their reasoning or if we ask them whether subtraction tasks can be solved analogously: 31 - 19 * 32 - 18.

Provisionally summarized, in the classroom situation, objects are ambiguous. But the individuals experience the objects as unambiguous by using a back- ground understanding taken for granted. The objective appearance of the individual's knowledge is the accomplishment of subjective activity. Because of the disparity of their background knowledge, the teacher and the students have to negotiate mathematical meanings. When constituted, the relations between meanings form a theme.

In the following, the objective appearance of the taken-to-be-shared knowledge is described as the accomplishment of the interaction between individuals.

Stability and Regulations of the Negotiation of Meaning

In time, the negotiation of meaning forms commitments between the participants with respect to stable expectations on the individual's side. In smooth interactions a background knowledge is taken to be shared. What was before constituted explicitly, now remains implicit. Cobb called this process the institutionalization of knowledge. Studying everyday life, ethnomethodologists point out that knowledge is to be shared and to be given using descriptive "accounting practices": "The stories that people are continually telling are descriptive accounts. To construct an account is to make an object or event (past or present) observable and understandable to oneself or to someone else. To make an object or event observable and understandable is to endow it with the status of an inter-subjective object". In the scene described earlier, Joey and Josh made the compensation observable and understandable between themselves; they took for granted that the results of the sixth and the seventh task are the same. They endowed their solution with the status of inter-subjectivity, which has to be established once more when the project member joins them.

The ambiguity of a single object is reduced by relating its meaning to a context that is taken to be shared. At the same time, the context is confirmed by constituting the meaning of the single object. The context and the singular meaning elaborate each other. From the ethno-methodological point of view, meanings are not given by the context (of school mathematics or of the classroom culture), which would exist independently of the negotiation of meaning, but the context is continually constituted. Ethno-methodologists call this relationship reflexivity. For example, first graders experience that apples, coloured blocks, chips, and so forth are used differently in the mathematics classroom than at home. The members of the classroom ascribe mathematical meanings to the things. At the same time, the meaning of what is called "math" becomes clearer to the first graders. One has to compare apples and other things numerically.

If the observer looks at the classroom life as an ethnographer who investigates a strange culture, the observer may be surprised by what is taken for granted by the participants: The use of fingers is taken as an explanation, a picture is taken as a calculation task, and so on. However, in the treadmill of everyday life, the participants would say that they know what mathematics or the classroom practice really is. In everyday classroom situations, the teacher and the students often constitute the context routinely, without being aware of this ongoing accomplishment, so that the context seems to be pregiven. In everyday classroom practice, the teacher and the students assume that the context is known, but it is in fact taken to be shared, diffuse, and vague.

For example, describing a specific method of solving as "simple" does not only ascribe meaning to the method but at the same time gives meaning to the context of mathematical argumentation. In the classroom mentioned earlier, the participants use the term "simple" in the sense of "mathematically elegant" (and not as cognitively easy). For example, Josh's and Joey's way would be evaluated as simple. This positive evaluation supports the students in orienting their activities toward this advanced mathematical argumentation. The students can be assured that the construction and use of complex thinking strategies and abstract considerations are characteristics of mathematics classrooms. Nevertheless, from a distance, the ethnographer can think of traditional classrooms with different characteristics. In traditional classrooms, the teacher sets a standard how to solve a task; the students have to obey step by step.

To close this section, I would like to sketch several findings of micro ethnographical projects that explore hidden regularities of interaction in mathematics classrooms. In Germany, educational reformers have been disappointed when comparing their ideal conceptions with the usual teaching styles. Disillusionment about the period of educational reform in the 1960s and 1970s has provided a motive for understanding the stability of the regularities of everyday classroom life.

Because of the ambiguity and different background understandings in the classroom, on principle, the negotiation of meaning in the micro situation is fragile. There is a permanent risk of collapse and disorganization of the interactive process, but "routines" function to minimize this risk. In several case studies, teachers' and students' routines, through which a smooth functioning of the classroom discourse proceeds and through which mathematical meanings are interactively constituted, have been reconstructed the teacher's "open" questions to which one definite answer is expected, the suggestive hint, the decomposing of a solving process in small pieces of subsequent actions, the student's routine of verbal reduction, i.e., restricting utterances to numbers or catchwords, the trial and-error routine in order to meet the teacher's expectation, etc..

The routines are connected by interactional "obligations." The obligations become more obvious in cases of conflict. In the following scene, a student violates an obligation and the teacher takes care to maintain the sense of normality and the image of the classroom orientated toward the folk ideal of discovery learning. The conflict happens in the probability class from which another scene was taken earlier ("100 cannot be divided by six"):

Protocol 4

Teacher: That is enough for the moment. We cannot write down all the results, don't you think. Does anybody notice anything?

Student: What am I supposed to notice?

Teacher: What are you supposed to notice? That's something you ought to know yourself. Born, have you noticed anything?

The teacher's activities are also under obligations. For example, in traditional classrooms, the students often expect the teacher to present an official algorithm of solving "problems" step by step without the need for reflection ("What to do next?"). So the students are not only the "victims" of the micro-culture but are also the "culprits." The network of routines and obligations can be described as "patterns of interaction". The patterns of interaction are considered as regularities interactively constituted by the teacher and the students: "What is presented is a level on which processes remain processes and do not coagulate into entities, to which the very process from which they were abstracted is assigned to as effect". For example, the "elicitation pattern" hints at the contradictory combination of two claims. The idea of eliciting a clear-cut body of mathematical knowledge is juxtaposed with the claims of a liberal and child-centered classroom. In the pattern, three phases can be distinguished:

- The teacher proposes an ambiguous task, and the students offer different answers or solutions, which the teacher evaluates.
- If the students' contributions are too divergent the teacher guides the students toward one definite argument, solution, and so forth. Believing that it will help the students, the teacher poses small questions and elicits bits of knowledge.
- The teacher and the students reflect and evaluate what has been done.

Jungwirth reconstructed gender-specific routines by which boys contribute to the elicitation pattern and activities by which girls modify the ordinary pattern. In the classrooms analyzed, the boys participated more successfully in the smcoth accomplishment of the pattern. Therefore, they might (erroneously) appear to the teachers to be more mathematically competent.

When educators study classroom processes by micro-ethnographical means, the stability of traditional regularities is astonishing. Expected to be structured by rational argumentation, the mathematical discourse comes out to be highly socially structured. Even in classroom situations that are expected to be designed with regard to modern educational claims, traditional patterns are reconstructed. For example, students' group work is realized in order to overcome the bad features of frontal teaching. Bauersfeld used the concept habitus in order to explain the persistence of students' routines during group work. He demonstrated that, in one group, the students constituted patterns and ways of solving the mathematical problem that partly appeared as copies of traditional frontal teaching. The change of the formal social organization of classroom life (replacing frontal teaching by group work) does not guarantee the immediate change of hidden and stable regularities in the microprocesses. The resistance of the regularities to change has to be taken into account when changing the microculture of mathematics classrooms.

Voigt pointed out that teachers do not realize that traditional patterns of interaction are still alive in their classrooms and that they contradict the teachers' intentions. The tradition of "Socratic catechism" still has an effect in the microculture today. In context of preservice teacher training, examined "under the microscope," ideal teaching styles in part merely seem to be staged in "holiday lessons". Presumably, in everyday classroom processes, teachers reproduce routines and background understandings that have been developed during their schooldays and behind the back of their intentional orientation.

Therefore, Yackel, Cobb, Wood, Wheatley and Merkel influenced classroom life, for example, by encouraging teachers to change specific social norms in the classroom discourse. Voigt developed teacher training courses where teachers videotape their own teaching and analyze the tapes. Nevertheless, it must be taken into account that in everyday classroom life routines and patterns cannot all be eliminated. Because of the permanent ambiguity we want assurance, relief, implicit orientation, and reliability. "We like to settle down like in a familiar nest, the nest of everyday life".

At the beginning of the section on negotiation of mathematical meanings, an ambiguous illustration was presented (ape, keeper, and bananas). With regard to such a picture, it was typical of the observed elementary class that a definite solution was established step by step. When the teacher was confronted with divergent interpretations ("one more banana" or "you have to add," etc.) the teacher asked a sequence of questions: How many bananas has the keeper brought ("5")? Which sign has to be written if something is taken away ("-")? How many bananas does the keeper give to the ape ("2")? How many bananas does the keeper have left over ("3")? Through this procedure, the picture comes out to be a specific arithmetical task, and a "number sentence" comes out to be the solution. Details of the picture are clearly related to mathematical signs. The sequence of questions goes along with writing the sentence. Accordingly, nearly all pictures of the textbook are so stereotyped that a subtraction intended is indicated by the picture of persons or things leaving the picture at the right-hand side. In the course of lessons, the students learn so that they mathematize such pictures as expected.

This procedure is an example of a pattern of interaction that I name direct mathematization. The pattern of direct mathematization is a "thematic pattern (procedure)" because it is specific to mathematics classrooms. Producing a thematic pattern, the teacher and the students constitute the theme routinely. The variety of options on how to continue the theme is reduced by specific conventions. If a thematic pattern is ritualized as in the presented case there is the danger that the students learn to participate effectively in complying with didactical conventions without realizing the mathematical coherence. For example, if the last question of the sequence is replaced by "How many more bananas does the keeper have than the ape?" the student might answer all questions correctly but contribute a mathematically incorrect statement: $5 - 2 = 1$.

Although the (thematic) patterns of interaction take over functions for the institution of school (e.g., definiteness for examinations), they are not pre-given but constituted by the participants. Therefore, the regularities could change at every moment. The following event may serve as an example.

In an elementary classroom observed, the negotiation of meaning of multiplication has run into conflict when the discussion has focussed on mathematical signs. The teacher feels herself under the obligation to relate the meaning of multiplication to concrete materials, which seem to stand for the rock bottom of the knowledge taken to be shared. She holds up three packs each containing ten pens. In the lessons before, arithmetical pattern was established so that these materials definitely implied "3 times 10."

Protocol 5

Teacher: To these packs, please, find a multiplication task.

Natalie: 10 times 3.

[The students become noisy, the teacher calls them to order.]

Teacher: Yeah, but, is this really correct?

Student A: No!

Teacher: Do you all agree?

Student B: No.

Student C: That's the same like a swap task. [known by the student in the context of addition, e.g., 3 + 4 = 4 + 3]

Teacher: That's a swap task. If I empty the packs and if I line them up in threes, then this is 30, too. In lines of three! But to these packs (points to the three original packs) you would really have to write 3 times 10 . And then you have the same amount of all pens.

Natalie at first does not fulfill the teacher's expectation of the mathematization, that the first factor represents the amounts of packs. Presumably, Natalie's mental representation conflicts with the official mathematization constituted in the lesson before. The teacher seems to elicit a negative evaluation of Natalie's answer from the students. Considering the "weaker" students, perhaps, the teacher wants to avoid the risk of ambiguity. However, Student C hints at the mathematical identity of the different forms and the teacher is now under the obligation to consider the swap task that implies the commutative law. She mentions that the difference between the orders of pens does not affect the total amount. Implicitly, the teacher points out that, at the level of the concrete things, the different terms have something in common. The obligation, that the students undertake only a specific mathematization, seems to be weakened. Also, the teacher uses the subjunctive mood "irrealis" –

that is, the German phrase "müßtet ihr eigentlich schreiben" is sometimes used to express an expectation on which one does not insist any longer. The former thematic pattern implied that each number of a product is represented unambiguously by specific materials. But in this scene, the mathematization is not rigid but open to change because a child introduces a level of argumentation that the teacher didn't expect but accepts.

The theoretical considerations of this section can be summarized as follows. In the negotiation of mathematical meaning, the single meaning and the context of meaning elaborate each other. The potential conflicts of the negotiation are minimized through routines and obligations. As they are constituted, the relations between routines and obligations form (thematic) patterns of interaction. Through the (thematic) patterns, the teacher and the students arrive at mathematical meanings taken to be shared. In everyday classroom life, there is the danger that the processes degenerate into poor rituals. However, on the microlevel, the regularities are not pre-given, and the negotiation could be improvised by the participants themselves.

Indirect Relations Between Social Interaction and Mathematics Learning

Before proceeding further, I would like to stress that the interactionist does not view relations between interaction and learning as relations between variables in the technological sense. Using ethnographical methods and examining individual's sense-making as closely as possible, the interactionist constructs more and more interpretations of what the student is actually thinking. Maier described this experience the interpreter has as a hermeneutical "uncertainty relation." Also, using interview methods, the interactionist's attention is caught by the interviewer's influences on the individual interviewed, so there is no clear access to the privacy of the individual's thinking and learning. Furthermore, in classroom discourses, the mutual influences between the teacher and the students have become more subtle through their history. Comparing detailed reports of classroom processes of the last centuries with transcripts of present mathematics classroom, Maier and Voigt realized that today the interactional regularities seem to be more hidden and complex. The regularities of microprocesses are not methods that the participants would intentionally apply. Taking the modern educational claims of the autonomy of the learner into account, Luhmann and Schorr gave reasons for the fact that, in education, there exists a "deficit" of technology on principle. That is, there is no hope to find methods that "make" the students learn.

Several approaches to the relation between interaction and learning have been mentioned earlier. One chain of thought assumes that some aspects of the social interaction are transformed into the learner's mind when learning occurs. Bruner and Vygotsky described how other-regulation results in self-regulation. Referring to Bruner, Krummheuer analyzed mathematics classrooms. He reconstructed specific patterns of interaction, "formats of argumentation," which are initiated by the teacher and which imply obligations for the students. The more the students participate successfully in the formats, the more the teacher lets the students take responsibility, so that, at the end, the students gain the ability to argue independently.

Another line of theories stresses the individual's sense-making processes. Saxe, Guberman and Gearhart criticized the Vygotskian studies in that sufficient attention is not given to the learner's point of view and to the learner's active role as a participant in social interaction. The basic assumption is that learners construct mathematical understandings in their efforts to achieve mathematical goals; these goals emerge partly through adjustments of the participants to each other in the interaction. In empirical studies of the practice of street-vending and of mother-child interaction, the learner's goals are reconstructed by a developmental analysis, the official goals are reconstructed by a cultural analysis, and the shifts and emerging of goals are reconstructed by a social interactional analysis.

Furthermore, several researchers take interactional conflicts as a condition of learning. For example, learning is viewed as arising from the learner's attempts to resolve conflicting points of view. The conflicts are indicated as contradictions between arguments in the interaction between individuals. These socioconflicts result in a contradiction of oneself, which leads to mental reorganization. Also, Kumagai stressed that the differences of perspectives between the interacting individuals form a helpful prerequisite of learning mathematics. Because the observer's realization of an interactional conflict does not suffice to engender a learning process, Balacheff suggested considering an existing contradiction between persons as essential if the learner could experience it.

From the interactionist point of view, the negotiation between the teacher and the students is a fascinating unit of analysis because of the differences between the participants. The teacher represents mathematical claims and the tradition of mathematics education, whereas the student has a different background knowledge. The negotiation of meaning is a necessary condition of learning if the students' background knowledge differs from the knowledge the teacher wants the students to gain. The difference (no deficit) of knowledge characterizes discourses especially with ambiguous topics where the students erroneously assume that they understand mathematically according to the teacher's intentions. "Thus, instead of making entries on a blank slate, teaching in school seems to be involved in erasing entries from a too full slate".

Nevertheless, the student is not a minor partner at all. In Protocol 5, for example, Student C proposed a solution to a conflict between interpretations by using a mathematical argument. Opposed to it, the teacher stated arguments in a very concrete domain of meanings. If mathematics teachers have the opportunity to look at videotapes of their lessons and to analyze the students' contributions in a leisurely way, there is the chance that the teachers can experience their students as being more knowledgeable than expected and as influencing the teacher's activities more than experienced during teaching. Thus the students' contributions to the mathematical theme have to be considered as an essential aspect in the theory: The student's thinking and the mathematical theme develop reflexively, and the student's learning contributes to the evolution of the theme that contributes to the student's learning.

Cobb, Wood and Yackel conducted an year-long teaching experiment in which the mathematical themes were highly influenced by the students. The students worked on tasks that could be solved in very different ways. The students had to work in pairs, and they knew that they were expected to attempt to understand each other's thoughts and to make themselves understandable. The students were obliged to explain and to justify their ways of solving to the partner and to the whole class. These conditions contributed to classroom situations in which the students constituted themes by themselves.

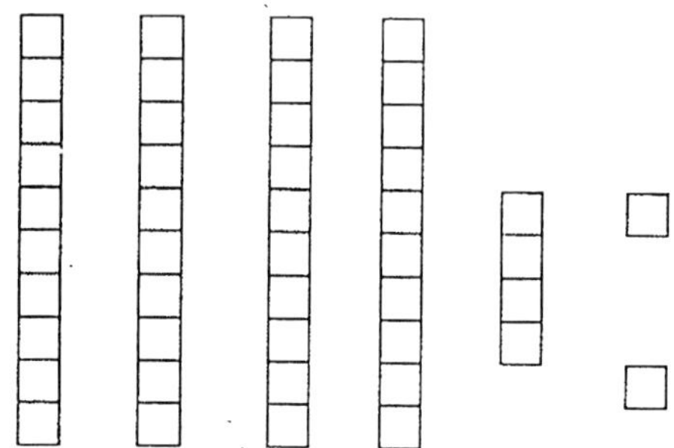

Fig. 2.1. Strips-and-squares task corresponding to 46 + __ = 73

The students know that the strips and squares are representations of multilinks and that they can use the concrete materials to solve the task. Analyzing several lessons I reconstructed two relatively stable tiematic patterns:

Thematic pattern of counting materials (T1)	*Thematic pattern of calculation with two-digit numbers (T2).*
Working together some students interpret the signs as representations of concrete materials. They compare the bars and cubes separately. A typical solution would be: Add 3 barrs and take away 3 ones.	Working together some students interpret the signs as representations of numbers. The difference is calculated within a system of numbers. A typical solution would be: 46, 56, 66 are 20, and 4, and 3, it's 27.
Quantities of materials are mathematized.	The application of arithmetical rules is mathematized.

In the classroom, the participation in a thematic pattern facilitates the cognitive development of a corresponding aspect of the concept of number, and vice versa. Moreover, in the classroom, several occasions have been reconstructed in which the patterns are not constituted purely. In these situations, the theme is improvised: In some cases, the teacher transforms the statements from the students' comparison of material objects to the calculation with numerals, and vice versa. In other cases, the students make contributions that the observer can take as relations between the different domains of meaning, such as "but 20 take away 3 more is 17." By these improvisations, different aspects of the number concept are combined. The improvisations offer the opportunity for students to change their individual interpretation of the task. The dealing with squares and bars is combined with the calculation of two-digit numbers. From a developmental point of view, the thematic transition from T_1 to T_2 supports the students' construction of numbers as "abstract composite units" and not longer as figurative objects.

Although the students' participation in the thematic pattern can facilitate the students' learning, the inference is problematic that the teacher should force the students to participate in specific patterns because the students can bypass the regulations enforced by the teacher.

In the diagram, 8 should be split up into 3 (in order to fill 7 up to 10) and 5. The students are expected to fill the diagram out, marking the left array with "+ 3" and the right array with "+ 5" and noting the solution at last. Instead, many students solve the arithmetical task by own methods in their head, and they fill out the right square. Then they mark the arrays because they know that the teacher wants them to do so.

Mead described the subject's identity as a dynamic balance between the "I" and the "Me." The student has to keep a balance between what she experiences as expected to do, what she wants to do, what she can do, and what she experiences the others do. As in the last example, there can be a difference between the student's private sense-making and the student's causes for doing something. Therefore, the emphasis on the negotiation of mathematical meaning seems to be more promising than the tradition of ritualized classroom interaction controlled by the teacher step by step.

Up to this point, interactional regularities as well as the subject's creativity have been described as prerequisites of learning mathematics. "So, what we have here are neither automatic rituals—repeated endlessly and mechanically, nor instantaneous creations,—emerging uniquely upon each occasion of interaction. These are negotiated conventions—spontaneous improvisations on basic patterns of interaction".

On the one hand, the conventions are useful insofar as they enable the participants to collaborate even if the individual backgrounds of knowledge differ. In analyzing mathematical discussions, Walther and Lampert took the conventions as means of negotiation of mathematical meaning. Both authors described how teachers took care of conventions constituted upon the students' contributions. Here, the teacher acts as a mediator between students' individual knowledge and school mathematics.

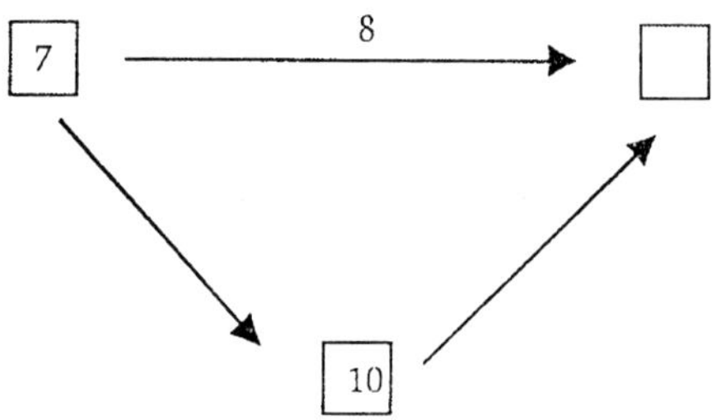

Fig. 2.2. Schematic representation of crossing the ten

On the other hand, unnoticed conventions of school mathematics could be established incidentally and could become a burden on the learner. In an elementary class observed, first graders experienced that the numbers always stand for the amounts of several things or persons. Some months later, the teacher presented several columns filled with different stickers, with uniform stickers in each column. At the top of each column the price of one sticker is written, for example "4¢." The teacher wants the students to fictitiously buy several stickers in order to arrive at addition problems. However, the students protest vehemently. They call for a change of the numbers at the top of the columns. They argue that a number written has to correspond to the quantity of stickers of the column. Although the teacher explains her intention, a student engages in a long and excited negotiation of meaning. If a student really went shopping one would not expect a similar conflict.

Students have to learn to distinguish between mathematical arguments and those conventions that are established in order to make the negotiation of mathematical meaning easier. This is a difficult point, because mathematics itself is full of conventions invented to make mathematical communication easier.

Nevertheless, in school mathematics there are many conventions that educators developed because of didactical reasons and that have a short life during teaching mathematics. Thus, the student's skeptical attitude toward the routine participation in regularities is reasonable. The student should share the responsibility to negotiate mathematical meanings of the objects of the classroom discourse.

The arguments of this section have been developed starting from theories that take learning as the effect of interaction and moving to an interactionist view that takes the student as an actor who orientates himself instead of merely being regulated. In order to describe a relation between the student's self-orientation and interaction, a final case is presented. Working in pairs, the students solved the following tasks:

27 + 9 = 37 + 9 = 47 + 9 = 47 + 19 = 48 + 18 = 49 + 17 = etc.

Many students solved the tasks by using fingers, tally marks, multi links, or the hundreds board. Some students compared the tasks and made use of previous solutions in order to solve the next ones. Next, during a whole class discussion, different ways of solving were compared. The teacher accepted all correct explanations. It is important to note that the teacher evaluated the correct explanations differently. If the offered way of solving seemed to be demanding (e.g., use of the compensation strategy), the teacher outlined the mathematical structure or she asked the students to explain their methods while requesting the other students to listen. Furthermore, the teacher explicitly characterized the way as an insightful way one or she expressed delight ("Aha!").

By her evaluations, the teacher indicated mathematical claims implicitly. It was up to the students to decide whether or not they would orientation their activities toward these claims. Usually, the students expect the teacher to represent the culture of the mathematical discipline. In the classroom observed, several students accepted the intellectual challenge. Looking at the fourth, fifth, and sixth tasks, Jonathan said, "I made two discoveries the beginning numbers go 47, 48, and 49 . . . then it was 17 the bottom one then 18 . . . 19 . . . so it's all the same answer." And Matt, who realized that the fourth solution has to be 10 more than the third one, announced, "I found a discovery." In this lesson, the students' contributions form the basis of the theme. The teacher influences the development of the theme so that the students can orientate their activities toward more advanced mathematical arguments.

Stressing the negotiation of mathematical meaning in classroom processes, I have attempted to relate theoretical ideas to concrete examples. But I did not present concrete proposals to tell teachers what to do. Rather, I have tried to build an appreciation of problems with regard to the micro culture of the classroom. Hopefully, the considerations form a contribution to the understanding of what we want to improve.

3

PLANNING

Introduction

Teaching is not simply standing in front of a group of kids and telling them how to do things. Teaching is not merely having students read information out of a book. Teaching mathematics is more than simply checking answers on tests or homework. We hope you are aware that becoming an effective teacher of mathematics involves much more. Teaching is not easy. It takes tremendous time, energy, dedication, and resilience. You need to:

- Provide examples of where the information being covered will be used.
- Motivate the students to want to learn.
- Patiently explain again for those who did not comprehend the initial coverage of the topic.
- Deal with a variety of learning modalities and capabilities.
- Discipline.
- Assess progress (both yours and the students).
- Grow personally.
- Be enthusiastic.

Teaching is selling. What would you think of a Ford salesperson who drove a Chevrolet? The teacher of mathematics must be an advocate of the field. Belief, excitement, and enthusiasm about what is being covered are mandatory. If the teacher does not seem interested in what is going on in class, why should the students be interested? Good classes do not just happen. They are carefully planned and orchestrated. Certainly, there are deviations from the plan, depending on happenings during the class, but the framework is laid out well ahead of time. Here are three axioms a teacher of mathematics should consider:

1. Know the content being presented.
2. Know more than the content being presented.
3. Teach from the overflow of knowledge.

Knowing the content, and more, and teaching from the overflow of knowledge implies careful planning and organization. Prior to teaching, it is imperative that the topics covered be carefully contemplated and organized. This thinking and organizing needs to be done well in advance to allow time for the ideas to germinate and blend in your subconscious. The advanced planning also provides the opportunity to connect topics from different lessons throughout the course.

Need of Planning

This is an easy question to answer, and yet the production of the answer is very difficult. Teachers generally have little input into the curriculum for a given course. The broad course objectives are dictated at the federal, state, district, school, and even department levels. Some schools and districts mandate that a given course be covered in lockstep fashion. All classes are given the same objective to be completed within a given time frame. Even with constraints such as these, there is opportunity for individualization by the teacher. Variation of presentation styles, relating the subject matter to background material, calling on student strengths established earlier in the curriculum, and use of technology can all provide extra time that permits some flexibility for teaching. Individual teachers, unless they are in a lockstep setting that dictates the topic to be covered, can vary their curriculum in a manner that will best meet the needs of all students. This mandates that the teacher look at the full year and establish an outline that covers the topics and builds needed strengths that will enhance later learning, determine a sequence in which the concepts will be covered, and establish an evaluation plan. The goals and statements here will be broad and general, but they provide a basic skeleton from which to work. Often this framework is dictated by the textbook, something that is not necessarily the best move. Textbooks are written to meet the needs of a wide variety of students. Your class may or may not be representative of the sample the authors had in mind. It may be the case that you will need to alter the sequence in which topics are placed before students. There is nothing wrong with that, as long as appropriate readiness and background are considered. Once the long-range plan has been established, more careful consideration should be given to smaller, but still sizable, chunks of information. Often these topics are determined by chapters in the textbook. Again, this is not necessarily bad. However, you need to reserve the right to delay sections of a chapter, or a whole chapter, until it is more suitable for your class. You may need to alter the sequence of the chapters and, perhaps, supplement the information in the text with material from other sources. Certainly, each daily lesson must be carefully prepared and set forth. Pressures or time constraints often hinder the development of well-planned lessons. Consider the person who is about to discuss addition of fractions with a class. Suppose the specific objective is to cover how to add two non-unit fractions with denominators that are relatively prime. Consider a teacher who did not plan, but did skim the text for a few seconds prior to class thinking, "OK, I know how to do that." Class begins and the teacher says something like "Today we are going to add fractions; you know, something like 4/7 + 9/13." while writing the two fractions on the board. Then there is a short pause and the teacher asks a series of questions like the following, with the class providing appropriate responses before going on to the next question.

- "What is a fraction?"
- "Define numerator."
- "The denominator of a fraction tells . . .?"
- "In 4/7, the numerator is . . .?"
- "And the denominator is . . .?"
- "When we add things, basically what do we do?"

And so on.

What is the teacher doing? These answers are all things the class should know. If they do not, how can the teacher justify dealing with the topic at hand? Ask a class of students what the teacher is doing and they will tell you the teacher is stalling. The teacher, for whatever reason, momentarily forgot how to add fractions. While each of those mundane questions was being asked, the teacher was probing memory banks, trying to recall how to do the problem; how to organize thoughts; and attempting to devise a coherent explanation. Most of us are very quick to say that would never happen to us. Many of us would be quick to say that we would not draw a blank on something as simple as that. Maybe, or maybe not. The real issue is not whether or not it will happen. The question is, when? The solution to the dilemma is so simple. All planning requires time for ideas to germinate. Certainly the yearly plans need to be established at the beginning of the course. These may or may not be altered throughout the year. Units, more likely, will be changed some—perhaps not by interchanging one unit with another, but at least by increasing or decreasing emphasis on topics, or switching the order in which concepts are presented. Decisions that would influence such alterations would be based on information gleaned from students in the class: readiness, background knowledge, the need for a change of pace, adjustment in the degree of difficulty of ideas, to name a few. Daily lesson plans need that germination time. Doing daily plans at least a week ahead allows time to adjust presentations and relate current information to prior or future work.

Daily Lesson Plans

A "rule of thumb" for planning is to formulate ideas weeks before they are to be delivered, look the plan over a few times between development and delivery, and take time to review it the day before it happens. This procedure enhances the connections between different plans, stimulates thoughts, and amplifies needed changes. Even with all that, there will still be many times when changes will be made right before or during the class. The amount of time this takes is understood, but it is a part of being a professional in the beginning stages of your career. It is also part of the process of building the background that becomes overflow. As time progresses, the preparations will take less time and you will find yourself struggling to select from among the many ideas you have, that special one that will be best for a given class. Even if nothing happens that specifically causes you to be more cognizant of the plan, you should look at it periodically between the time it is prepared and when it is to be delivered. That is, 2 days after you prepare a lesson, skim through it, thinking about what you will be presenting. Do the same thing 5 days after you prepare it and then, finally, glance at it the day you will be teaching it. This process helps cement the overall scheme of presentation into your mind at a level that allows you to deliver a very natural presentation. That lesson has become a part of you. Because of your intimate understanding of the material to be covered, you should be able to adjust things quickly and naturally. However, this will not happen unless you organize your teaching so that you consistently prepare daily lesson plans at least a week before they are to be taught. Many factors impact your plans:

- Students
- Ability levels
- Administrative decisions
- Departmental procedures
- Personal bias
- Departmental policy
- Textbook
- Homework policies
- Testing practices
- Available class time

Some of the items listed, along with others, are beyond your control. The teacher does have the power to influence some factors. Frequently, the textbook is handed to you for a class. You may or may not have participated in the selection. Either way, nothing mandates that the text sequence must be followed page by page.

Teachers, in general, tend to rely heavily on textbooks in their day-to-day teaching. Typically this is even more common with the teaching of mathematics. Most decisions about what to teach, how to teach it, when to teach it, and the associated exercises are based largely on what is in the textbook adopted for the course. Some people are concerned about the quality of textbooks, the way they are written and the tremendous influence they have in determining what students learn. You can alter how things are done.

American education utilizes a spiral curriculum approach. It is not uncommon for a topic to be encountered more than once in a textbook. If encounters after the first add nothing new to the knowledge base, why bother with it? *If*, and note that is a big "if," the material is learned the first time, there should be no need for repetition. If these subsequent encounters with a topic do add to the knowledge base, how much time is necessary to review the prior material? Again, *if* the material was learned the first time, there is no need for the review, with the possible exception of a few minutes to relate the new topic to the earlier work and orient the student. Still, it is rather common for the text to provide more review than is necessary. Blindly following the text without consideration for the development and needs of students can lead to more repetition than is necessary.

Before dealing with the specifics of a daily lesson plan, one more issue needs to be visited. Homework is a part of the learning environment. Typically, a topic is covered in class, usually involving determination of how to do a problem type, and then an assignment is given in which the students practice the newly learned skill. Characteristically, a selection of odd or even-numbered problems is then assigned. Some teachers like the students to have the answers available whereas others do not; and because some texts list answers for only the odd- or even-numbered problems, the text again becomes a decision-making factor. More significant is consideration of the problem types assigned. Suppose the topic of the day deals with solving proportions for an unknown variable, which typically occurs at several places in the middle-school curriculum and also in algebra.

Examination of assignment sections shows this is frequently not the case. The partitioning is not equal; in most cases, there are far fewer examples having the variable in locations other than top left. Furthermore, it sometimes happens that doing only the odd or even problems will eliminate one of the four possible settings where the variable could be located. How appropriate is this for the student learning process?

Since that time, some other publishers have adopted similar procedures. Assume there are 20 homework problems listed. The first 2 are from today's lesson and often are exactly the same problems discussed in the example section of the lesson. If a student encounters difficulty recalling how to do the problem, the sample is available for review. Because only 2 problems in the homework assignment deal with today's lesson, the opportunity to seek additional clarification will also be available before more problems of this type are done. The second 2 problems in the homework assignment would relate to yesterday's lesson. They would be slightly different from the examples. Again, if the student needs help in working the problem, it might be available through the examples found with yesterday's lesson because they are similar. Each problem pair increases in degree of difficulty and relates to lessons from prior days. In a set of 20 problems, as many as 10 different lessons could be encountered. Spaced review, or incremental encounters and the opportunity for clarification, are strong arguments for such a homework policy. It provides time to learn the topic before inundating the students with problems based on knowledge they may not have.

One final note relating to homework is that an argument can be made for having you, the teacher, do the homework problems you assign *before* the assignment is made. This can be quite time-consuming, but there are reasons for it. First, you are not asking the students to do something you have not done yourself. That is a minor point, but it is significant in the eyes of some students. Second, you become aware of any problem-type specialisations or omissions, like the one noted when discussing solving proportions earlier. Third, as you work through the problems, you are strengthening your ability to reflexively deal with the topic at hand when it is covered in class. In a sense you are reviewing the lesson plan you prepared. You might become aware of a better way for the students to learn the material or some useful shortcut that would help them. Finally, by doing the problems and recording your work in a manner similar to that expected of the students, you provide yourself with a teaching tool that can prove invaluable.

Suppose, for the sake of this discussion, that the class we are talking about has three distinct ability groups within it: fast, average, and slow. Generally speaking, the fast students understand the initial coverage of the content and do not need much help with homework assignments. Average students may need some help. If your solutions are available for student inspection, during seatwork time in class, many average students will be able to look at your solution and figure out what to do. Thus, you are free to deal with the slower students who are most in need of your additional attention. Adopting such a practice demands some ground rules on how your notes are to be used, but that can be handled.

Constitution of A Daily Lesson Plan

A completed daily lesson plan should contain the following:

1. Topic
2. Goal statement(s): the purpose, concepts, or knowledge that the student will learn
3. Objective statement(s): activities used to assist the learner in achieving the goal(s)
   a. Concept objective(s) when appropriate
   b. Skill/attitude objective(s) when appropriate
4. Materials required (instructional and learning)
5. Procedures
   a. Set: how you introduce the lesson
   b. Instructional outline
   c. Examples (and nonexamples) of concepts
   d. Upper level questions
   e. Review/closure/bridge to next lesson
   f. Assessment/evaluation procedures

Initially there needs to be an objective for the lesson. Why is this topic being covered? As you rationalize why a topic is being taught, you must remember to look at it from the world of the students. You, as an adult, might see applications of the topic in future mathematical arenas, but the students want to know where they can use it today. Objectives are a must for any lesson plan. Some administrators may insist that objectives are behaviorally stated with percentages included for how many students will perform at what level. For example, 80% of the students will correctly find the sum of 90% of two non-unit fractions with relatively prime denominators 95% of the time. There is a segment of the profession that takes issue with these percentages, claiming that they are fictitious numbers. You eventually will have to establish your own style for writing objectives. The important point is that objectives are necessary for a lesson plan. There must be a reason you are requiring your class to learn this material. What is it? It is also assumed that the focus is on the students being able to perform tasks they could not do prior to the lesson. For example, suppose you are going to teach someone to bake banana nut muffins. This will be the first time the person will have done such a thing. You say:

- "Get the mix."
- "Get a big bowl."
- "Get a spoon."
- "Get one egg."
- "Get the milk."
- "Get the measuring cup."
- "Get the muffin pan."
- "Put a paper baking cup in each hole in the pan."

At this point, you proceed to do the following:

- Turn the oven on to preheat to 400.
- Empty the mix into the bowl.
- Measure a third of a cup of milk.
- Pour the milk into the bowl with the mix. Break the egg and put it into the bowl.
- Blend the ingredients.
- Fill each muffin cup until it is half full.
- Bake 13 to 15 minutes or until golden brown.
- Remove the muffin pan from the oven.
- Let the muffins cool.
- Now, you say to the person:
- "We baked muffins."

You did not let the person measure the milk because of potential spills or, perhaps, an inability to deal with a third of a cup. You did not let the learner break the egg because of the possibility of shells getting into the mix. Similar excuses can be made for other events that would occur during the making of the muffins. Assessment of the muffin example shows that "we" did not make muffins. You did. You used the individual as a "gofer" by saying "Go for this" or "Go for that." The objective in this case was to make muffins. Clearly, the objective was not that the learner would make the muffins. If the objective had been behaviorally stated and learner-oriented, the instructions would have had the learner doing each of the steps, or at least most of them. As lessons are considered in the context of this text and the mathematics classrooms described, it is assumed that they will be behaviorally oriented even if they are not so stated. It must be that way. Otherwise you, the teacher, become a dispenser of information paying no attention to whether or not it is received. More significantly, you run the risk of having a learning environment where the students are not active participants. The ability to process information brings out the second of the five essential ingredients to a lesson plan: Assessment. You need to determine how successfully you created an environment in which the students could learn the material, and you need to determine whether or not the class understood what was covered. Deciding how well you did is not always easy. Some of us tend to be supercritical of ourselves. Others are quite lenient when it comes to self-examination and decide that it had to be good because "I" did it. Somewhere between those two extremes is probably where most of us will lie. A few moments for reflection can be very revealing:

- Were the examples clear and pertinent?
- Did the students ask similar questions repeatedly?
- How were the questions I asked answered?
- Did the students show reflection and thought?
- Were the students able to relate the topic to prior work?
- Were the applications clear to the students?
- Could the students see the relevance of the topic?
- Did I act excited and interested as the lesson was taking place?
- Where could the presentation be improved?
- Would this lesson be effective with another class?

This is not an exhaustive list of questions to ask as you go over your self-evaluation, but it is a start. Video- or audio taping a class can prove quite revealing.

Information about teacher effectiveness can be derived by asking students to supply you with anonymous one- or two-word evaluations of the class. You could present this idea under the guise of the student writing to a friend who had asked for a one-or two-word description of how the class went. Another option would be to suggest to students that they have another person call you and talk with you about your class. This third party individual would be unknown to you. Alternatively, if a class seems to be totally off track, you could appoint a chair for the group and go outside for a few minutes. Clearly, this option could be used in some settings and not others – another place where you have to make a decision. The class would then have an open discussion about what was going on and how things could be reoriented. Finally, students could pair up and write thoughts about the lesson. That summary could be rewritten by a third person so there is no way the submitting individuals can be identified. This would be a summary of what needs to be done to create a more productive learning environment. Student assessment is more straightforward. You can give a homework assignment and then check it to see if the subject has been mastered. Quizzes, tests, portfolios, group work, reports, individual projects, and software programs can all be used to provide insight into the progress of students. Each of these methods has strengths and weaknesses that you need to become aware of. The NCTM *Assessment Standards for School Mathematics* lists six tenets about valid assessments:

- Reflect the mathematics that all students need to know and be able to do.
- Enhance mathematics learning.
- Promote equity.
- Be an open process.
- Promote valid inferences about mathematics learning.
- Be a coherent process.

This list is only a beginning, but it is something you need to study and integrate into your teaching process.

Questions and questioning techniques are crucial to a good lesson plan. Remember, you are trying to stimulate thought in your students as they are active learners in class. Consider the level of questions you are asking. If your questions are all on the knowledge level, there is little or no thought involved, because the student is merely regurgitating information previously encountered. The questions included in your lesson plans should be upper level. *Higher order questions* are generally defined as anything more complex than knowledge level, using Bloom's taxonomy of knowledge, comprehension, application, analysis, synthesis, and evaluation. Upper level questions usually cannot be generated "off the top of your head," although it does become easier and more reflexive as you mature within your career development. They require careful thought in advance of the class. Listing upper level questions in your plans shows that you have given them appropriate consideration. Do not worry about including exact wording in your plans. You will be able to phrase the idea within the context of the class as long as you have the idea in the plans.

Questioning is not easy. Asking for an answer to a given problem is not the type of question to be considered as a part of the basic plan. A knowledge-level question, although still important, should be fairly reflexive. Similarly, when planning for questions, it is not necessary to state in the plans the name of the student who will be called on to respond. It is assumed you will distribute participation throughout the class. Higher order questions are designed to make students think and reflect about what they are learning. Upper level questions strengthen students' reasoning ability and communication skills.

Usually questions requiring thought are not easy for students to answer. "How?" and "Why?" can be upper level questions when connected to a response given by a student. Research shows that up to 80% of all questions asked in a classroom are lower level. Probably the most likely reason for the preponderance of lower level questions is that higher order questions are difficult to create extemporaneously in front of a class. Planning becomes important for the development of upper level questions.

Embarking on a course of designing upper level questions is challenging. The questions themselves require careful thought and organization. As a question is asked, you have to decide if it is realistic for students to answer. Certainly, asking the right question can pique the interest of students. Suppose you prepare a lesson dealing with the impact of changing A in the equation $y = A \sin(x)$. If your first question is "What happens if A is changed in the equation y = A sin(x)?" and students can answer it, you have fallen into a basic trap. The students' ability to answer that question indicates the information has been covered before. Depending on the setting, you could be planning on covering information the students have already mastered. If the question is asked to establish a starting point for a new topic, then it is an acceptable question.

On the other hand, if students have never encountered this topic before, the question is impossible for them to answer at this point. Perhaps the question could motivate them to investigate the situation and, in the process, they will derive a solution. You have prodded the students to seek an answer. The prodding and investigation lead them along a path that ends with an acceptable solution.

Often, questions that are lower level can be restructured to become upper level. Some examples are given here:

Lower Level?	*Recorded to Upper Level?*
Find the area of a rectangle with dimensions 4 × 6 feet.	What is the maximum area of a 20 perimeter Rectangle?
Round 3.87 to tenths.	What numbers round to 3.9?
How would you cut a pizza with 5 straight cuts to get 16 pieces?	What is the greatest number of pieces you can get if you cut a pizza with
5 straight cuts?	
What is the sum of the measures of supplementary angles?	What are the possible Measures of 2 Supplementary angles?

Jim Wilson created questions that could be used to provide some direction. The questions can be classified using Wilson's format. His work focused on providing possible responses for particular questions at each level of Bloom's taxonomy. Because we are concentrating on classroom discussion, the answers supplied by Wilson are omitted in most examples.

Knowledge Examples

Knowledge of Specific Facts

"Which of the following is not a whole number?".

"State the addition algorithm for rational numbers".

"The slope of a horizontal line is _____".

Knowledge of Terminology

"The set with no elements is called the _____ set."

"5! equals _____".

"The absolute value of any number is written as _____".

Comprehension Examples

Knowledge of Concepts

"In what way does the set of whole numbers differ from the set of natural numbers?".

"Given the complex number 5 + 3i, its conjugate is _____".

"Suppose A and B are two acute angles of p° and q°, respectively. A and B are complementary angles if and only if _____".

Knowledge of Principles, Rules, and Generalizations

"If three fractions have denominators that are relatively prime, the least common denominator is equal to _____".

"If the decimal point in a number is moved three places to the right, we are _____".

"If the intersection of two different planes is not empty, then the intersection is _____".

Knowledge of Mathematical Structure

"If $(N + 68)^2 = 654{,}481$, then $(N + 58)(N + 78) = (?)$".

"For what number n does $47 \times 52 = (47 \times n) + (47 \times 2)$?"

"If $a \cdot b = 0$, then _____".

Application Examples

Ability to Solve Routine Problems

"Which of the following numbers, expressed in base 7 numeration, is both prime and odd?".

"Given $\log_b 2 = 0.693$ and $\log_b 3 = 1.099$, find $\log_b 12$.".

"A piece of wire 36 inches long is bent into the form of a right triangle. If one of the legs is 12 inches long, find the length of the other leg.".

Ability to Make Comparisons

"The difference in the circumference between the larger and smaller of two balls is 3 inches. Which of the following is the best estimate of the difference in their diameters?".

"Two different savings plans are available to you. At the bank, your savings will earn 5 percent compounded quarterly. The Savings and Loan Association pays 5.25 percent compounded annually. Where should you place your money to earn the maximum interest?.

"Ten objects are numbered from 1 through 10 and distributed into bags. If it is known that 1, 4, and 7 are in the same bag, the pair 2 and 10 are in the same bag, and similarly, for the pairs 3 and 6, 1 and 5, 3 and 8, 7 and 9, and 2 and 6, what is the largest number of bags that can contain at least one object?".

Ability to Analyze Data

"Five spelling tests are to be given to John's class. Each test has a value of 25 points. John's average for the first four tests is 15. What is the lowest score he can get on the fifth test to have an average of at least 16?".

"Harriet wanted 6 pairs of socks. Store X sold them at 2 pairs for $1.25; the same brand sold in store Y at 3 pairs for $1.98. To be economical, what should Harriet do?".

"On the same set of axes, sketch the graphs of y = sin x and y = cos 1/2 x as x varies from 0 to 2B radians. Determine from the graphs the quadrant in which sin x - cos 1/2x is always positive" (Wilson et al., 1968a, p. 679).

Ability to Recognize Patterns, Isomorphisms, and Symmetries

"In an election, 356 people vote to choose one of five candidates. The candidate with most votes is the winner. What is the smallest number of votes the winner could receive?".

"The amount of weight a board of a certain width, depth, and material can support at its midpoint is inversely proportional to the distance between its supports. If the distance between the supports is made three times as great, the weight which can be supported is ______".

"The last digit in 410 is". (This question should be altered to reflect the availability of technology.)

Analysis Examples

"What is the largest rational number which is the sum of two rational numbers each having a numerator of 1 and a whole number for its denominator?".

"Given the set $p = r^2 - t^2$, where p is a prime number, find t if (1) $r = 7$ (2) $r = 157$ (3) $r = 58$".

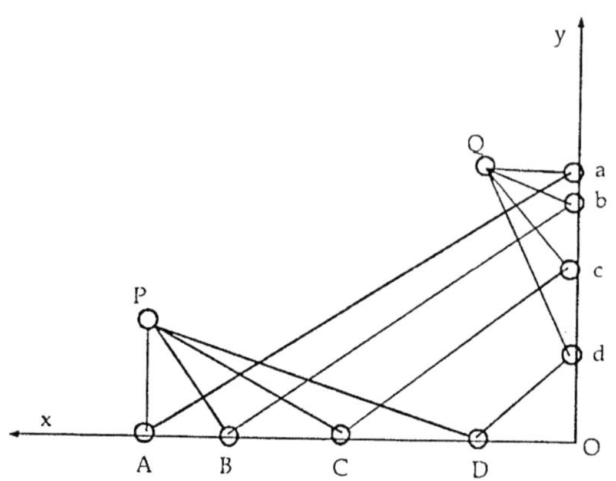

Fig. 3.1. Created with Geometer's Sketchpad

"In Fig. 3.1 what is the shortest path from P to Q which touches both line XO and line OY?".

Ability to Discover Relationships

"The length of a diagonal of a square is $x + y$. Find its area".

"Determine the number of lines obtained by joining n distinct points in the plane, no three of which are collinear".

"Find the number of diagonals in a convex polygon (1) with 5 sides (2) with 25 sides (3) with n sides".

Ability to Criticize Proofs

Let us attempt to prove the following remarkable proposition: *Any two numbers are equal.*

Call the two numbers a and b; call their sum C.

Thus we have the equation

(1) $a + b = c$

From (1) we obtain the equations:

(2) $c - b = a$ and (3) $c - a = b$

Multiply each side of (2) by ^{-}b, and multiply each side of (3) by ^{-}a, to get

(4) $b2 - be = {}^{-}ab$ and (5) $a2 - ac = -ah$

From (4) and (5) we have

(6) $b2 - bc = a2 - ac$

Ability to Formulate and Validate Generalizations

"Without actually making the calculations, write out in detail a step-by-step procedure for determining (1) whether 12,087 is a prime number (2) the largest prime less than 5,000".

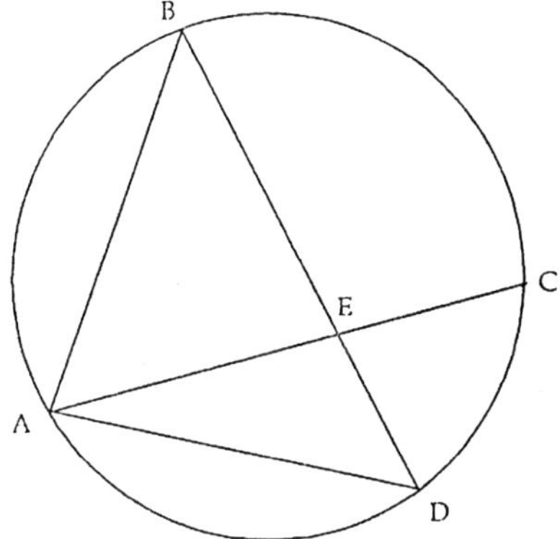

Fig. 3.2. Created with Geometer's Sketchpad

This list of sample questions on the preceding pages is not exhaustive. It has been presented to give you samples of upper level questions that could be used in a classroom setting. These examples should make you aware of the thought needed prior to attempting to use upper level questions. Planning questions is essential.

Most students are curious about things and have questions. At times they need to be trained to ask. A bizarre situation like the following was used by one teacher to stimulate questions. The students entered the classroom to find the teacher sitting on a chair that had been placed on the teacher's desk. The students asked each other what was going on. Some inquired of others whether or not they should call the principal or another teacher. The level of uncertainty and inquisitiveness was quite high. After a few minutes of this, the teacher hopped off the desk and removed the chair, saying to the class, "Isn't it interesting that you had several questions but no one asked me. Since I was the one sitting in the chair, wouldn't it be reasonable to ask me why?" The moral of the story: Know what to ask, and know who to ask.

Examples are equally as important as questions. Specific examples must be carefully thought out as each lesson is planned.

Learning for many individuals is enhanced by investigating specific examples. It is logical to assume that many students learn by observing specific examples. Each new problem type should have one written example in your plans, solved in complete detail, just as you expect your students to do it. This should not be an example worked in the text. You will probably use more than one example in your lesson for each type of problem, but one should be sufficient for your planning. Inserting only one example of each problem type in your plans is adequate, particularly if you do the homework assignments before class.

Plan your examples carefully. If you are talking about factoring trinomials, X2 + 4X + 4 is not a good example. First, there are two 4s in the example. As you discuss what you do with the third term, a student who may not be attending as well as desired might think you are talking about the four of 4X. Furthermore, when factored, X2 + 4X + 4 = (X + 2) (X + 2). Perhaps a student will get the wrong impression that the factors are always duplicates. A trinomial like X2 + 5X + 6 is a better example. It is easy to spot what number is where, and the factors are different. Eventually, both types must be discussed, but care needs to be taken as to when. Saying something like "Forget it for now" will trigger some minds to venture in a different direction. The tangent those students take wondering why they were to forget what was just seen will cause some of them to get lost. In the factoring examples used earlier in this paragraph, it is assumed that concrete exposure that "shows" how factoring occurs would be part of the curricular sequence.

Your lesson notes should reflect the things you will say as a student progresses from a point of not knowing something to a point of knowing. You should initially assume students do not know the material you are about to cover. If they know, why are you teaching it? The notes should be the major points that comprise your discussion or development of the topic. There is no need to give a word-by-word description of what will be said, just the major points. Some form of outline (not necessarily formal) is generally deemed most beneficial. You should be able to quickly skim the outline and determine if all the salient points have been covered by the students. If you plan on discussing some issue, it is wise to elaborate in your outline. What essential points do you expect the students to see? What reactions do you expect them to have? Where is the discussion intended to lead? These matters should be a part of the notes about what is to be covered and the direction to be taken. Otherwise there is a risk that the discussion will become a random talk session with no apparent point or central theme.

Variety of Approaches

Not all students learn the same way. That is why learning modalities are discussed in education classes. You are responsible for knowing your students well enough to determine which is the best method for introducing a topic. Most instruction, even with all the options that are available today, is still done by the lecture method. The teacher tells the students how to do a problem type and the class mimics the model established by the teacher. Little student thought is required in this format. Thinking and flexibility are not highly valued. It basically becomes the teacher saying, "Here is how you do this. Trust me, I would not lie to you. Don't think about it, just do it." That is a sad commentary, but it is a lot closer to the truth than many teachers would like to admit.

You can be a catalyst for change in the secondary classroom. Use technology. Find applications. Create and use models. Insert activities. Establish expectations. You can take a student from an entrance or beginning level to much higher ground. You need to be able to reach that student, and every other student. That is why the variety of approaches is so important. Your college education has provided you the necessary tools. You know the mathematics. You know how students develop and how to teach them mathematics using different methods, at least at an intellectual level. You lack experience in two facets: teaching and creating lessons. Teaching experience comes with time. Your lesson creating skills can be practiced and developed starting right now.

The basics have been discussed as far as establishing a lesson plan. There is another consideration. You have a strong mathematical background. You know more than what you will be teaching. However, your mathematical content is compartmentalized into classes and topics. You need to take the time to reflect on the breadth of mathematical knowledge you have and begin to devise ways to cross between the different compartments. That will create new and stimulating ideas for you.

The "simple halving doubling" method (Russian peasant) for multiplication will show how you can begin taking knowledge out of compartments. Find the product of 47 and 78. One factor will be "halved" repeatedly until the result is one. Each time the first factor is halved, the other is doubled. The row of any even value in the halving column is eliminated from consideration, including the original factors. The remaining values in the doubling column are added. The sum will be the product of the two factors. Students tend to select 78 as the halving value because it is even. However, half of 78 is 39, an odd value. The object is to get the halving column reduced to 1. Logically, starting with the smaller value will achieve that objective faster. In the example 78 × 47,

		Problem Halving	
78	47	23 remainder 1	1 × 20
156	23	11 remainder 1	1 × 21
312	11	5 remainder 1	1 × 22
624	5	2 remainder 1	1 × 23
1248	2	1 remainder 0	0 × 24
2496	1	0 remainder 1	1 × 25

Essentially, the halving factor has been expressed in base 2 numeration, and the problem is re-expressed as $78 \times 101111_2$. That is, 78 × (32 + 8 + 4 + 2 + 1). Sixteen is not considered because there is a zero in the 2^4 place. The product of 78 and 47 is 3666.Somewhere in your career you have worked with bases. Undoubtedly you have investigated multiplication—perhaps not in the form of the "simple halving doubling" method. You are aware of the concept of multiplication. Surely you have been exposed to the idea of proof. Yet, with all that background, each component seems to stay in its own compartment. It is unlikely you have seen this "proof" of why the "simple halving doubling" method of multiplication works. If you decompartmentalize and think about the process, however, the proof is fairly simple. It is impossible to show you all of these intricacies. You must capitalize on your background and develop the connections between the various mathematical exposures you have had.

Exercise 1. In the "simple halving doubling" routine for multiplying two numbers, one situation exists where the halving factor will always be even except for one. Describe the situation and how it occurs.

Classroom Climate

New and stimulating ideas are important to your development. When you teach, you are selling something. If you are not excited about what you are doing, how can you expect your students to be? The Attention, Interest, Desire, and Action (AIDA) method is worth considering as you plan. It is taken from techniques used by many successful sales people for years. Whatever the product, you need to:

- Attract attention
- Create interest
- Establish desire
- Motivate action

Teaching is no different. As you plan, think of ways to apply AIDA.

Think of a coach in any sport. The individual has players doing repetitious tasks day after day. How is it that the coach can get players to perform these tasks, many of which are not a lot of fun? Part of the reason must be the players' desire to do the sport. You need to achieve that same level of desire and cooperativeness in the mathematics classroom, and enthusiasm on your part is one way to begin.

There is no royal road to student discipline. There is no magic answer. Some of the classroom control you exercise will be planned because of established regulations within your class. However, you will frequently "shoot from the hip" and then hope you were right. Coaches are frequently second-guessed by the "Monday morning quarterbacks" (people who discuss what should have been done after the game or play is over). It is easy to criticize and analyze after the play or game is over. However, in the heat of the game, decisions have to be made on the spur of the moment. That is difficult. Many of your discipline decisions will be made on the spot. You make them and then hope you were right. This becomes a part of your discipline plan.

No one can tell you what your discipline plan should be. It has to be created by you, within the parameters you are given. You, and only you, know what you are willing to tolerate. Establish guidelines and make your students aware of them. Be firm and, most of all, be fair. It is much easier to establish strict rules and back off than it is to be congenial and then try to clamp down. Aside from advice such as that, you are on your own. If you are asked to do a postgraduation analysis of your education program, you will likely say you should have been taught how to discipline. In your education program you were probably given broad, general hints about what to do. After that, it is up to you. You need a plan for discipline. Know what is and is not acceptable in your school. Be aware of latitudes provided in your school.

Personal Professional Growth

Just as classroom management is up to you, your professional growth is also. Personal professional growth is critical for your classroom planning and organization. If you are stagnant, you will have difficulty becoming excited about what you are doing. You need to become professionally involved. Join NCTM and take the appropriate publications, being certain to read them. Think of ways the ideas can be applied in your classes. Join your state and local mathematics councils. Go to conferences dealing with the teaching of mathematics at local, state, regional, and national levels. Be willing to present new and innovative ideas to colleagues in your profession. Check the catalogs that come through the mail dealing with books or ideas focusing on the teaching of mathematics. Take classes. Participate in in-service opportunities. Grow. Learn. Stay excited about the teaching of mathematics, and let it show in your planning and actions.

Sample Lesson Plans

These are presented in different formats on purpose. You need to select the style you are most comfortable with. The samples are intended to provide you with ideas. It is assumed you will alter these to fit your style. A. Suppose the objective is for students to become aware of and prove the theorem, "The segment joining the midpoint of two sides of a triangle is parallel to the third side and half the length of that third side." We will assume this is the first encounter these students have had with this idea. The conceptual development will be divided into two parts, which may be covered in one day, if the group moves rapidly enough, or on two successive days.

Part 1 – Informal Development: The activity worksheet/lesson for the students follows. It is purposely open-ended and vague with the intent of having students discover items.

Create triangle ABC.

Determine midpoint D on AC and E on BC.

Place a line segment between D and E.

m(A + B + ¯) = _____

m(D + E + ¯) = _____

m(?ABC) = _____

m(?DEC) = _____

m(?BAC) = _____

m(?EDC) = _____

Describe relations that exist between the measurements.

As the triangle is moved, selecting any vertex, what relations remain constant?

Part 2: This could be developed as a teacher-directed or student-centered lesson. The emphasis would necessarily shift one way or the other, depending on the lesson style selected. The students should have conjectured that "The segment joining the midpoint of two sides of a triangle is parallel to the third side and half the length of that third side" from Part 1. They would be asked to prove that m(D + E + ¯) = 0.5(A + B + ¯) and that segment D + E + ¯ is parallel to segment A + B + ¯. The students should suspect the statements are true because of the investigations from Part 1. The formal proof can be established in a variety of ways, one of which uses coordinate geometry. The triangle can be established so that one vertex, A, lies on the origin and one side lies on the positive x-axis with endpoint B (r, 0). The third vertex, C (s, 2t), would be located somewhere in the first quadrant. The plan for the proof would be:

- The midpoint formula can be used to define D and E.
- Use the distance formula to find m(A + B + ¯) and m (D + E + ¯).

- Use slope formula for the slopes of A + B + ¯ and D + E + ¯.
- State conclusions.

Preference will determine if you want to have the students develop the proof as individuals or as groups. It could be that you will discuss the plan with them, but you might elect to have them develop it on their own. If you do this proof in the format of a teacher-led discussion, perhaps because this is the first coordinate proof they have done, the preceding plan would be expanded to a more complete lesson plan by including calculations that show the distance and slope formulas. This is one of those places where you should know these formulas but you do not want to risk forgetting. If you opt to do a teacher-centered lesson, a few logical extensions that would be student-centered lessons or assignments would be:

- Place the triangle anywhere on the axis system and prove that the segment joining the midpoints of any two sides is parallel to the third side and half its length.
- Show that a quadrilateral with opposite sides parallel has those respective opposite sides of equal length.
- Prove the length of the segment joining the midpoints of the two nonparallel sides of a trapezoid is the average of the lengths of the parallel sides and parallel to them.

B. Suppose you have discussed translating word problems to equations to be solved with your general mathematics class. The practice problems you give them can impact their attitudes. One way this can be accomplished is to use nontraditional wording, like:

1. Jo Cool is 16. This is 1/3 her dad's age. How old is Jo's pop?
2. Dum Diddy's salary is $12,000. This is 1.5 times as much as Q. Cumber's salary. How much does Dum Diddy make? How much does Q. Cumber make?
3. Izzi Zlow types 35 words per minute. This is 0.4 of Ty Pritters speed. How fast does Ty type?
4. Walter Logged's body contains 57 kg of water. This is 2/3 of his weight. How much does Logged weigh?
5. MT and ZT have a combined age of 68 years. If MT is 47, how old is ZT?

C. Suppose you are trying to lead a class to the solution of the thousand-locker problem presented in the problem-solving chapter of this text. The problem states that 1,000 lockers are closed and 1,000 students are going to pass down the row. The first student opens every locker. The second student closes all multiples of 2. The third student changes (opens or closes) all multiples of 3. The fourth student changes all multiples of 4. And so on. Further assume they are not experienced at finding patterns. Have a number of students (it might be advisable to combine classes for this lesson, if possible) stand in front of the group. Suppose you use 18 students. Each student is given a card with a "locker number" on it and they stand in ascending order facing the class, holding their locker number in front of them.In sequential order, starting with one, each student does a 180° turn to indicate that locker has been opened. Then, starting with 2 and in successive order, all multiples of 2 do a 180° turn. Following that, all multiples of 3 do a 180° turn. And so on. After all students have done all their 180° turns, the ones left facing the group will be 1, 4, 9, 16, ... This should help students recognize the pattern. This activity provides a solution for the problem in a concrete manner, as opposed to the two more abstract methods described in the chapter. Once the students know the result through this exposure, they can be led to a discussion about other solutions. They know what the answer is and now can investigate different manners of obtaining it. D. Suppose the task is to add 1/2 and 1/3. Further assume that the students are familiar with Cuisenaire rods, but have never encountered addition of fractions. Most people would agree that this is not the first addition of fractions problem that should be encountered by students. Using the rods, the main task becomes one of determining a unit that can be divided into halves and, at the same time, thirds. The following sequence of questions provides one method for students to find the appropriate unit rod.

- Can White be the unit?
- No. You can't take a half or a third of it.
- Can Red be the unit?
- You can take a half of it (White), but not a third, so no.
- Can Lime be the unit?
- You can take a third of it, but not a half, so no.

- Can Purple be the unit?
- You can take a half of it (Red), but not a third, so no.
- Can Yellow be the unit?
- No. You can't take either a half or a third of it.
- Can Green be the unit?
- Yes. A half is Lime and a third is Red.

Now that the unit is determined, the rest of the problem is relatively simple.

Figure 3.3 shows the result as determined using the Cuisenaire rods. The only remaining task is to interpret what is shown. The assignment was to add a half and a third. Those two addends are represented by Lime and Red, respectively, and their sum is represented by the Red – Lime train. Because Green is the unit, the interpretation becomes one of determining what part of Green the Red – Lime train is. The White rods are shown in Fig. 3.3 to help with that part of the assignment. Green is the same as a 6 White rod train and the Red – Lime train is equivalent to 5 of those White rods, or 5 out of 6 equal pieces, 5 out of 6, J. Notice the language transition in that last sentence, which can help students make the desired connections.

The dashed White rod above and to the right of the Lime in Fig. 3.3 depicts how some students will solve this problem.

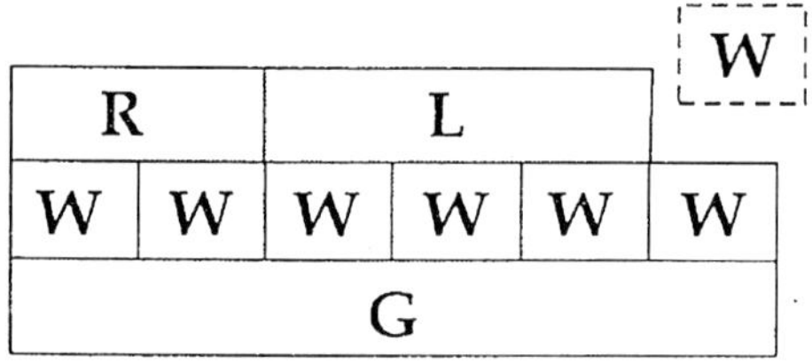

Fig. 3.3. Created with Geometer's Sketchpad

Knowing that Green is equivalent to 6 White rods, some students will notice that the Red – Lime train is only one White short of the unit. They conclude that the result uses all but one of the equal sized pieces. However, all but one of 6 pieces leaves 5 pieces out of 6, or 5/6. This approach is more abstract and is another point that should be classified for future reference if a student uses it.

A carefully developed sequence is needed to have students be able to add any two fractions. The rods could be used to create a string of problems like:

1/2 + 1/3 = 5/6

1/3 + 1/4 = 7/12

1/3 + 1/5 = 8/15

1/2 + 1/7 = 9/14

The generalization here would be that the denominator of the sum is the product of the denominators of the two addends. Many students will quickly conclude that the denominators of the addends are added to give the numerator of the sum. That is a solid foundation from which to build the rules we use to add fractions. The rest of the addition development would follow similar patterns. The students would consider non-unit fractions and "discover" the part of the rule that has the numerator of a fraction multiplied by the missing factor from dividing the LCD (our words, not those of the students) by the denominator of the respective fraction. Again it is important to note that no mention has been made of LCD and yet the students are able to perform the operation with the rods. Then, as generalizations are discussed, the concept of LCD begins to evolve.

E. Solving two equations in two unknowns by addition: Note that the format of this lesson does not include complete sentences. Eliminating complete sentences permits quick scanning of the lesson to determine if an item has been missed or what the next example or question should be. It is assumed that the students have already dealt with solving two equations by graphing and substitution.

Suppose

x + y = 4 (1)

x - y = 6 (2)

Could get either equation to "y =" and substitute.

Recall—Can add same thing to both sides of equation.

Add (2) to (1) using "x - y" on the left and "6" on the right:

(x + y) + (x - y) = 4 + 6

The Vertical method is often easier:

x + y = 4

x - y = 6

$2x = 10$

$x = 5$

In (1),

$5 + y = 4$

$y = {}^{-}1$

Check in (2),

$5 - ({}^{-}1) = ? = 6$

$5 + 1 = ? = 6$, OK

Summarize:

Wrote equations

Lined x under x, y under y, constant under constant

Added to eliminate one variable

Solved

Substituted

Checked

More examples or assignment as needed.

4

Theories of Mathematics Education

Introduction

Throughout this century, there has been a sporadic relationship between theoretical schools in psychology and the emerging field of mathematics education. In the course of this relationship, there has often been tension arising from divergent conceptions of the nature of mathematics and of the aims of mathematics education. To differing degrees, and with honorable exceptions, the psychologists who have worked on mathematics have been open to the charges of viewing mathematics selectively as a convenient domain to supply grist for their theoretical mills, and of having insufficient regard for the implementation of their theories within effective instructional environments.

Progressive exposure of the limitations of behaviorism (dominant as a theoretical school in the United States but much less so elsewhere) culminated in a sequence of events and publications during the second half of the 1950s that Gardner dubbed the "Cognitive Revolution." From the point of view of those involved in mathematics education, this paradigm shift had many positive aspects. The complexity of tasks used in problem-solving research increased, means for dealing with complex knowledge structures were devised, and links between the psychology of learning and school instruction were restored. Moreover, as time went on, there was a swing away from general theories of knowledge processing toward an emphasis on the domain specificity of the knowledge being processed.

During the 1960s and 1970s it looked as if cognitive psychology was in a relatively stable state with a unifying framework provided by the general concept of information processing, represented by a group of approaches bearing a family resemblance to one another, and mostly sharing the following characteristics:

- the analysis of complex task performances in terms of knowledge structures and information-processing steps
- the assumption that mental processes are constrained by human memory architecture
- the allocation of a central role to organizing schemata
- a penchant for the implementation of models as computer simulations

A paradigmatic example of computer-based modeling was the analysis of "buggy algorithms." It is a familiar observation that students' errors in multi digit subtraction are often systematic, one of the most common being to subtract the smaller digit in a column from the larger, regardless of position. A theory to explain the development of such error patterns as "buggy algorithms" was developed by Brown, Burton, and Van Lehn. As well as classifying common errors, the analysis suggests how bugs can be predicted as constructions of the child faced with an impasse when conditions are encountered beyond the scope of currently effective procedures.

This body of work was commended recently by Boden, who singled it out as one of the few examples of a domain modeled in enough detail to be useful to pupils or teachers, adding, "but there is significant scope in principle for pedagogic applications in many different areas" (emphasis added). Even more recently, Newell stated that:

it is critically important to find some cases where cognitive theory can predict long stretches of behavior – long stretches that are relatively unconstrained, during which humans can be assumed to be freely thinking. Even one or two such instances would go a long way toward convincing us of the essential correctness of cognitive theory.

Newell cited the buggy algorithm analysis as a good candidate (along with modeling of solutions of cryptarithmetic puzzles).

The reaction to such work from within the field of mathematics education stands in stark contrast. Thompson asked, "In what way does a detailed understanding of how students perform tasks mindlessly help us to improve mathematics education. Hennessy showed that, in fact, specific "bugs" are very unstable over time and concluded that "the outcome of remediation at a purely syntactic level is the very limited arithmetic competence of a considerable number of both children and adults in our society." This echoes the fundamental criticism made by Cobb in relation to the explanation given by Van Lehn of the choice of children's multi digit subtraction algorithms as a topic for investigation:

Its main advantage, from a psychological point of view, is that it is a virtually meaningless procedure. Most elementary students have only a dim conception of the underlying semantics of subtraction. This isolation is the bane of teachers but a boon to the psychologist. It allows one to study a skill formally without bringing in a whole world's worth of associations.

From this quotation may be inferred a characterization of the goals of mathematics education in terms of skills in symbol manipulation. Kaput made a parallel point in relation to ICAI (intelligent computer-assisted instruction) systems, which, he observed, "were applied to teach the syntax of formal notations—which is the only inherent content of such notations. [They] did not, because they could not, deal with what the formalisms are used to represent and what they evolved to do in the first place. But this competence has come to be pedagogically inappropriate and curricularly superfluous."

More generally, people involved in mathematics education have found information-processing characterizations inadequate to account for the complexity and richness of mathematical activity, unless such characterizations can be reformulated much more widely.

Gardner described the emergence of a multidisciplinary field of study that came to have the label "cognitive science." Among its key features, he included "de-emphasis on affect, context, culture, and history". Moreover, he identified as a central problem the "computational paradox," namely, the insight gained through the use of computational models that "the kind of systematic, logical, rational view of human cognition that pervaded the early literature of cognitive science does not adequately describe much of human thought and behavior".

In reaction to these and other perceived weaknesses, what might be seen as a second wave of the Cognitive Revolution began, the main thrust of which has been to resituate intellectual functioning within a much wider human context. A strong reaction against formalism, in accord with the computational paradox identified by Gardner, has been one of the most salient characteristics of this movement. Prominent examples from the general psychological literature include the description of expert decision making proposed by Dreyfus and the radical changes in theories of categorization initiated by Rosch and others.

In parallel with the attack on what Cobb dubbed "psychological formalism," there have been strong critiques of formalist approaches to the philosophy of mathematics, exemplified by this statement from two mathematicians who have reflected on the practices of their discipline:

> *The definition-theorem-proof approach to mathematics has become almost the sole paradigm of mathematical exposition and advanced instruction. Of course, this is not the way mathematics is created, propagated, or even understood. Mathematics is a human activity, and the formal-logical account is only a fiction.*

Another major theme has been the development of the Piagetian view of cognition as grounded in perception and action, and in human experience in general. In a philosophical analysis, Hamlyn argued that cognitivism inherited from behaviorism the aim of delimiting the subject matter of psychology, and also some of behaviorism's defects. He criticized the concentration on explaining central mental processes while underplaying the complexities of "input" and "output" grounded in the experience, beliefs, and intentions of an agent living in a society.

The first two sections of this book amply testify to the extent to which the de-emphasis on social and cultural contexts identified by Gardner has been addressed. A much richer and more complex view of intellectual functioning has been developed one consequence being that the boundaries of cognitive psychology have become unclear. At one extreme, there are still people working within what Cobb called the "strong information-processing program"; Newell "Unified theories of cognition" is a prime example. On the other hand, Cobb identified others whose positions have radically changed. For example, he pointed to the contrast between Brown's previous work on buggy algorithms and the highly influential paper on situated cognition he co-authored. Contributors to Greer and Verschaffel suggested that information-processing theories might be open to enrichment to address aspects such as affect and intuition. Thus there is likely to be uncertainty and disagreement for some time about how the scope of cognitive psychology should be delimited.

Moreover, in contrast with the period when research in the information processing tradition could be said to have at least approximated to Kuhn idea of "normal science," there is no unifying theoretical framework visible on the horizon. Likewise, current research is characterized by methodological diversity, and a certain lack of agreed conventions and systematically in the communication of experimental findings.

In summary, the current situation is one of complexity as well as excitement, as reflected in this volume. Against this background, my aim is to make the case for the continuing role of cognitive analysis within attempts to construct theories of mathematical education.

Questions of Balance

In the ferment of new ideas, liberalization of methodology, and openness to concepts from many disciplines, there are risks of losing balance through over- compensation. Comments by Cobb on the complementarity rather than opposition of constructivist and sociocultural perspectives have general applicability, as he suggests that "claims that one perspective or the other captures the essence of people and communities should be rejected in favor of pragmatic justifications that consider the relevance and usefulness of a perspective for the issues and purposes at hand".

Clarification of Constructivism

Constructivists have been particularly prominent and effective in the critique of the first wave of cognitive theories and in the ongoing attempts to reformulate the philosophical and epistemological bases of mathematics education. However, comparable contributions have been made by others coming from positions not identified as constructivist, such as Freudenthal and his successors at the Freudenthal Institute. Likewise, Goldin, endorsing a set of ideas on teaching mathematics that are widely identified with constructivism, argued that precisely the same principles could be derived from an empiricist epistemology. Moreover, constructivism does not offer clear guidelines at the detailed level of instructional design; indeed, according to Janvier, constructivism is not concerned with teaching.

Constructivist analysis raises the question of the balance between guidance by the teacher and reinvention by the student. Freudenthal suggested that the learner does not have to repeat in full the learning process of mankind-indeed, it seems implausible that this would ever be possible if advanced mathematics is to be reached. Freudenthal recommended that "the learner should reinvent mathematising rather than mathematics; abstracting rather than abstractions; schematising rather than schemes; formalising rather than formulas; algorithmising rather than algorithms; verbalising rather than language." This key shift to process as what needs to be reconstructed legitimizes the idea that mathematical content may be transmitted—subject to the qualifications set out by Hatano, namely, that what is transmitted is merely the "raw data" for interpretation by the student. The point is that a student with a good understanding of what it means to algorithmize, say, is thereby well equipped to assimilate information about algorithms. More generally, I feel that constructivists have overcompensated in reaction to simplistic theories of language, meaning, and communication; it is noticeable that the limitations of language do not inhibit them from promoting their theoretical position, at length, through writing and speaking.

A major area of theoretical dispute between constructivist theorists and cognitive psychologists has concerned the concept of representation. Goldin and Kaput address these criticisms and argue that the notion of representation is theoretically useful in attempts to organize and explain observations of student behavior. It is not clear that this is incompatible with the view that the teacher or experimenter must build up a model of the student's conceptual world. In the construction of such models, we must have some conceptual tools to work with, and the elaborated view of representations in mathematical cognition offered by Goldin and Kaput must remain a major candidate, in the absence of strong competition.

Only a few issues have been briefly touched on here in order to point to the need for continuing debate and clarification of constructivism, its implications for mathematics education, and its relation to other perspectives. In particular, a major debate, to which I now turn, concerns the balance between individual and social construction of mathematical knowledge.

Individual Cognition and Social Interaction

Voigt outlines the antithesis between two theoretical traditions. The first, largely founded on Piaget's theory and developed as radical constructivism, focuses on the individual as the constructor of knowledge. The second, which emphasizes the social and cultural origins of knowledge, has been very strongly influenced by Vygotsky and his successors. Voigt proposes an interactive synthesis.

As Voigt points out, the influence of Piaget was such that, for a long time, most research addressed the cognitive development of individual children, often using the methodology of clinical interviews. Piaget has been criticized for paying insufficient attention to social, cultural, and educational (in the broad est sense) factors. Even Youniss and Damon, in arguing that ideas about social construction are essential to Piaget's genetic epistemology, admitted that there is some justification for the caricature of a Piagetian "apocryphal child who discovers formal properties of things, such as number, while playing alone with pebbles on the beach".

Attacks from numerous quarters have undermined the characterization of cognitive development in terms of universal, context-independent structures within individual minds. For example, anticipating recent emphasis on situated cognition, Donaldson effectively critiqued Piaget's focus on "disembedded" rather than "embedded" thinking in children. As Hatano points out, evidence suggests that cognitive competencies are not content independent; children with extensive knowledge of a particular domain demonstrate more advanced forms of reasoning within that area of expertise. Likewise, Crawford argues that knowledge is culturally relative. A further considerable body of criticisms of Piagetian theory relates to interpretations of interactions with children, such as clinical interviews, which fail to take account of the child's construal of the social situation within which the interaction takes place.

In recent years, often under the influence of Vygotskian ideas, the emphasis has shifted dramatically. Manifestations of this trend include reconceptualizations of cognition as situated and distributed, and of cognitive development as enculturation within a mathematical community. The parallel methodological shift in research on mathematics education has been to the observation of classroom interactions.

No doubt these shifts represent an appropriate reaction to previous concentration on the individual cognizer, but there is a danger of overreaction. For example, Salomon described the idea of distributed cognition as novel and provocative, but warned that, like many other newly coined terms, it "strongly illuminates one facet of an issue, sending to dark oblivion others." He characterized the strong version of distributed cognition as the view that "while individuals' cognition are not to be dismissed, cognition in general should be reexamined and conceived as principally distributed"; this view was attributed to some of the contributors to his book. By contrast, he and other contributors put forward a less radical view that "'solo' and distributed cognition are still distinguished from each other and are taken to be in an interdependent dynamic interaction". Specifically, Salomon argued that "distributed cognition interact with those elements one traditionally attributes to the mind of the individual: mentally represented knowledge and skill".

The strong version of distributed cognition, as characterized by Salomon, seems seriously unbalanced. Consider Poincare's famous description of a moment of insight while engaged in a completely unrelated activity: "the idea came to me, apparently with nothing whatever in my previous thoughts having prepared me for it, that the transformations which I had used to define Fuchsian functions were identical with those of non-Euclidean geometry." I find it difficult to see how this could be classified as a distributed cognition (or a situated cognition, come to that) or how it could be analyzed without taking into account mental activity within Poincaré's individual mind over an extended period. Likewise, in accounting for the development of mathematical cognition in a child, an analysis of a series of participations in social situations needs to be complemented by some account of the coherent development and restructuring of that individual's knowledge and conceptualizations over extended periods of time.

An emphasis on the importance of social factors rather than individual intellectual achievements is also to be found among some current philosophers of mathematics. Representative of this view is the statement by Tymoczko that "any serious attempt to understand the evolution of mathematics should begin by locating the practicing mathematician in a sociohistorical context." Although agreeing with this statement in a review of the book that Tymoczko edited, Wells argued that the account is incomplete if it does not also consider the psychology of individual mathematicians and asserted that the history of mathematics makes it clear that psychological and social factors interact. Again, the need for complementary perspectives seems clear.

Formal Education Versus Everyday Learning

Elshout commented that "Educational philosophy seems to be locked into a pendular motion, in some periods favoring formal schooling as its ideal, then swinging to the position that the best of learning is to be found in everyday life."

Several lines of research have contributed to this swing (which, perhaps, it should be pointed out is located in certain academic circles, and rarely in educational systems). Within experimental psychology, a wide range of findings effectively demolished naive normative theories of rational thinking. Among these findings, those from the extensive literature generated by Wason's "selection task" may be taken to be prototypical. Empirical investigations showed that in many areas people's thinking, decision making, and so on simply do not conform with formal normative models. A different broad group of studies has been concerned with the reasoning processes of various cultures and subcultures, such as occupational groups, and of children engaged in authentic activities involving mathematics.

How relevant are these studies to education in general, and mathematics education in particular? One suggestion has been that education should be modeled on the forms of learning that take place in apprenticeship. A case may be made that certain aspects of apprenticeship learning could be adapted with advantage to classroom teaching, but the idea that apprenticeship is appropriate as the sole model for mathematics education is untenable. Typically, apprenticeship leads to reproduction and maintenance of the status quo, which is incompatible with any progressive philosophy of education. For example, Greenfield. in a study of weaving among Mayan people in Mexico, observed that the apprenticeship learning common in 1970 resulted in a limited and unchanging repertoire of patterns. In contrast, 20 years later, as a consequence of economic and social changes, a more independent exploratory type of learning resulted in a wide variety of figurative and geometric patterns. Perhaps we should bear in mind Levi warning: "Beware of analogies: for millennia they corrupted medicine, and it may be their fault that today's pedagogical systems are so numerous, and after three thousand years of argument we still don't actually know which is best. "Mathematics (and science) transcend everyday cognition (and it is just as well that they do for people who like to fly to conferences and type their papers on word processors). Chevallard referred to "the intrinsic cultural discontinuity between mathematical and everyday cultures." Resnick highlighted a number of key differences between (mathematics) learning within and outside of school:

- Learning and performance in school is primarily individual, whereas out of-school activities are much more often carried out in groups.
- School activities are often carried out with limited use of tools. Cognitive activities outside school typically use tools (materials, books, calculators).

- School stresses decontextualized learning, whereas out-of-school activities are situated.
- School stresses general knowledge and skills of wide (potential) applicability, whereas knowledge and skills outside school are situation specific.

Two comments may be made on this list. The first is that, at least in some instructional environments, the differences Resnick refers to are significantly reduced. The second is that education is not, nor is it intended to be, like learning in everyday contexts; if it were, why would it be necessary? (I assume, for the purposes of this discussion, that it is necessary.) The theory of didactic transposition may be invoked here. This theory is based on the observation that knowledge is normally developed originally to be used, not to be taught. Didactic transposition refers to the process of transforming such knowledge so that it becomes teachable.

None of the foregoing should be taken as denying that education, and mathematics education in particular, should be made more relatable to everyday experience, reflecting the grounding of mathematics in the description of aspects of reality and in the solving of practical problems. More specifically, I have argued elsewhere that people in general need to have a discriminating appreciation of the nature of mathematical modeling and of its limitations.

One salient theme of the critique of formal knowledge has been a questioning of the effectiveness of decontextualized knowledge as transferable across situations. This debate is particularly important for mathematics, because, as argued in Greer and Harel the detection and exploitation of structural similarities underlying super- ficially different situations is one of the most powerful strategies used by mathematicians. (This is illustrated by the earlier quotation from Poincare—who once defined mathematics as "the art of giving the same name to different things.") More generally, Hatano suggests that gaining expertise may be a process of desituating knowledge, so that problem-solving competence becomes less context bound.

Greer and Harel (in press) argued that the considerable body of psychological research on transfer is mostly of limited relevance to mathematics education for several reasons, including the questionable motivation of subjects and the limited time-span typical of such experiments. It is suggested that transfer is only to be expected within a sustained instructional environment in which the analysis of structural relationships is nurtured.

Mathematics as Intellectual Activity

In the previous section, I suggested some issues on which there is a danger of taking one-sided positions; this section continues on that theme. Although recent emphasis on social, cultural, and historical contexts has been entirely appropriate, there has been a tendency to forget that being human, both individually and culturally, also includes being intellectual. I agree with Thompson, therefore, when he declared that "I consider it imperative that the mathematics education community regain the sense that mathematics is a deep and abstract intellectual achievement."

In this regard, I consider it perverse to argue that what I will call "academic mathematics" (the term "Western mathematics" that is sometimes used seems a clear misnomer) has no special status among the multiple forms of ethno-mathematics (the mathematics practiced within identifiable sociocultural groups). Important features of academic mathematics that differentiate it from localized mathematical activities and practices include the length and complexity of its historical development, the multiplicity of cultures that have contributed to that development, the degree of recording and communication and thereby criticism and negotiation of meaning between mathematicians (particularly in modern times), the technological advances that have generated problems stimulating new mathematics, the creation and codification of abstract mathematics, and-perhaps of the greatest significance— the degree of reflection on the nature of mathematics. Chevallard proposed that "At some point in the history of the world, for unknown reasons, people came to take a reflexive — not only conscious — view of what can now be thought of as proto-mathematics.

In reading a recent chapter in a book on language, I was struck by a passage in which it is stated that there was during the 1980s "a boom in those disciplines which study the language-system in a state of formation (child language acquisition, creolistics), or in a state of variability (dialectology, sociolinguistics), or in a state of spontaneous, informal performance (pragmatics, conversation analysis)". The parallel with recent mathematics education research is inviting. Adamson continued by saying that "at the end of the decade, these separate studies are beginning to come together to foster a revitalized historical linguistics which aims to establish the relation between language as a system and language as an activity of speakers."

The claim that it is meaningful and useful to speak of mathematics, like language, as a system is based on the existence of organized knowledge within mathematics, and on identifiable mechanisms for growth within mathematics; these structural aspects of mathematics markedly distinguish it from other cultural constructions (e.g., etiquette). The systemization of mathematics will never achieve completeness; rather, it is partial and forever evolving, as Freudenthal's comments on the Bourbaki codification of mathematics makes plain. Nevertheless, there is inherent organization of knowledge within academic mathematics as structures and structures of structures, and so on.

There have been many attempts to define psychological structures underlying the development of mathematical cognition – most notably Piaget's. Piaget perceived a striking parallel between his structures and those of Bourbaki, which Freudenthal interpreted as Piaget's assimilation of the Bourbaki system to his theory. A more local organizing framework is provided by Vergnaud's concept of conceptual field, which combines mathematical and psychological aspects: "A conceptual field is a set of situations, the mastering of which requires several interconnected concepts. It is at the same time a set of concepts, with different properties, the meaning of which is drawn from this variety of situations".

Freudenthal commented that "in no other field does organising display itself in such purity, impose itself with such force and infiltrate so profoundly as it does in mathematics. Mathematics grows, as it were, by its self organizing momentum."

Some of the mechanisms of growth may be identified. Mathematics is generative; for example, from any set a more complex structure can be derived by analysing its power set (i.e., the set of subsets of the original set). Mathematical concepts characteristically evolve by restructuring so that they apply to broader and broader domains. The driving force of disequilibrium and the restoring of local equilibrium through restructuring can be seen, par excellence, in the development of number concepts (e.g., the lack of closure of the natural numbers under subtraction and division being resolved by extension to directed and rational numbers, respectively). In such processes, symbols and notation are often key facilitators, as is strikingly examplified by the following statement of Laplace quoted by De Morgan:

> *Newton extended to fractional and negative powers the analytical expression which he had found for whole and positive ones. You see in this extension one of the great advantages of algebraic language which expresses truths much more general than those which were at first contemplated, so that by making the extension of which it admits, there arises a multitude of new truths out of formulae which were founded upon very limited suppositions.*

Another characteristic tendency is what Freudenthal termed "anontologisation", by which he meant cutting the bonds with reality.

A further set of mechanisms may be broadly classified as evolutionary. Rav outlined an interesting theory of the interaction between biological and cultural evolution; as he pointed out, "Given its remarkably long history, mathematics has been subjected to a lengthy cultural molding process akin to an environmental selection." Prominent among the evolutionary pressures have been problems – both external, practical problems and internal problems relating to incompleteness, inconsistency, refinement of definition, and so on.

Above all, there is in mathematics an interplay between the grounding in reality, human experience, and cultural creativity, on the one hand, and development of abstract systems on the other. This interplay is beautifully illustrated in Weyl classic discussion of symmetry, which begins with the recognition of symmetry in biological form and cultural artefacts, finds applications in scientific fields, notably crystallography and quantum mechanics, and leads "up the ladder from intuitive concepts to abstract ideas".

The relationship between the historical development of mathematics and the development of mathematical cognition in a student may be considered of interest for many reasons. Piaget and Garcia suggested broad parallels between psychogenesis and the history of science. Indeed, the earlier reference to dis-equilibrium within mathematical structures was intended to invite analogy with the role postulated for it within Piaget's theory of cognitive development. Increasingly, scholars are turning to the historical record for possible indications of the ways in which concepts may develop, the types of cognitive obstacles that may hinder learners, illumination on the relationship of knowledge to problems, and so on. Examples are Kaput analysis of early ideas of calculus, and Carraher appeal to conceptualizations of rational number that can be traced back to the Greeks.

A major area for development in the coming years is likely to be the broadening of the domain beyond its current disproportionate focus on early conceptions; in this regard, the book Advanced Mathematical Thinking edited by Tall is an early milestone. As commented by Thompson in reviewing Tall's book, "If in the distant future an archaeologist were to build an image of mathematics education based on artifacts from the educational research community, she might conclude that, as late as 1990, mathematics had not progressed past proportional reasoning." Thompson argued that it is not just a matter of studying more advanced topics, but of conceiving of long-scale development so that as early as possible, mathematics is taught with a view to its long-term goals. This means building in advanced ideas early, a fine example of which is the work on proof in an elementary school in New Jersey described by Davis .The analysis of mathematics as organized intellectual activity raises questions about the goals of mathematics education. As argued by Davis students—irrespective of whether they are going to study mathematics to an advanced level—should have a appreciation of what mathematics is about and what it is for, and a sense of its value within human cultures. Moreover, for responsible citizenship, it is important to have an understanding of the ways in which mathematics is used to model social as well as physical phenomena, and the limitations of such models.

Continuing Relevance of Cognitive Analysis

In setting the scene for this section of the book, I have tried to sketch the immediate historical background to the present state of ferment within the field, to identify important issues currently being hotly debated, and to provide a framework for the remaining chapters in the section. Many of these issues are dealt with at much greater length in De Corte, Greer and Verschaffel .Improving mathematics education is a massively complex human problem, in the cause of which all relevant forms of knowledge need to be mobilized. In pursuit of the (perhaps unattainable) goal of a comprehensive theory of learning mathematics, multiple contributions are required. As pieces of that jigsaw, essential roles will continue to be played by efforts that:

- Relate to general theories of cognition and cognitive development whose primary focus is on the mental processes of individual minds .
- Analyze the structure of mathematics and the processes of development characteristic of it in relation to the development of mathematical cognition in students.
- Are aimed at understanding intellectual functioning within planned instructional environments.

General Theories of Cognition

In recent years, there has been a strong move toward recognition of the importance of domain-specific learning and thinking. Mathematics, in many ways, has been a prime example. In fact, the process can be taken further by recognizing mathematics as a federation of subdomains, within each of which there are specific forms of argument, specific cognitive obstacles, and so on—the most obvious example of a subdomain with its own characteristics being probability.

Nevertheless, Hatano argues the case for continuing utility of general accounts of aspects of cognition, notably expertise and knowledge representation. As he points out, the conclusions of comparative analysis are of interest whether they point to commonalties or contrasts across domains. General post-Piagetian theories of cognitive development are of considerable relevance to mathematics education, including those that emphasize the grounding of cognition in action, perception, and experience.

Davis argues for the utility of a general theory of mathematical thinking, which he characterizes as based on information processing and using analogies from computer science (although he does not consider computer simulation a necessary tool). However, his approach is much more based on detailed analyses of children's mathematical behavior, and on recourse to multiple sources of metaphors and other explanatory resources, than is typical of mainstream information-processing studies.

Analyses of Mathematical Cognition

There is a vast amount of research on specific areas of mathematics, such as geometrical and spatial reasoning, number concepts and arithmetic, and algebra. Of all the subdomains, probability is a particularly interesting case and deserves attention for many reasons, including its relatively late historical development as a branch of mathematics, the general difficulty of reasoning about probabilistic phenomena, and the continuing profound philosophical problems in its foundations; moreover, probability is arguably the branch of mathematics that most demands an explanation in constructivist terms.

As discussed earlier, a major need is to spread the effort more evenly over the full range of mathematical education, up to the most abstract mathematics. As Fischbein commented, "most of the more complex mathematical concepts are still insufficiently investigated from the psychological point of view." This is not to deny the crucial requirement to understand, and so improve the teaching of, early mathematical developments such as the extension of number concepts beyond the natural numbers to rationals.

Observation and documentation of the construction of knowledge through social interactions in classrooms need to be complemented by detailed studies of the cognitive processes of individuals in relation to specific mathematical topics and by studies of the development of mathematical understanding of individuals over considerable periods of time.

Intellectual Functioning Within Designed Environments

The concept of the environment within which an individual learns has been substantially elaborated beyond the essentially biological conception of Piaget. Certainly, any idea that other people can be considered as just another part of the environment has been rejected. The recent work on situated cognition and distributed cognition may be considered as further elaborations of the role of the immediate physical and social environment, and of the social activities being enacted within that environment.

A further very general aspect is the notion of "designed environments," implying designers who create environments with specific educational goals in mind. There are many examples of detailed studies of the cognitive effects of learning within such environments, including the work of Cobb, Wood and Yackel and projects at Rutgers University described by Davis. Recently Collins called for a "design science of education which must determine how different designs of learning environments contribute to learning, cooperation, and motivation."

A final highly significant aspect is that computer software, as exemplified in the software described by Carraher and Thompson, makes possible the design of environments with features previously impossible to implement. If we accept the basic premise of Piaget that mathematics arises through reflective abstraction on actions performed in the environment, then extensions of cognitive theory are needed to take account of the new types of action that have been made possible, and what Thompson refers to as the "dialectic between intention, action, and expression."

5

KNOWLEDGE ACQUISITION AND ITS IMPLICATIONS FOR ARITHMETIC EDUCATION

We discusses characterizations of knowledge acquisition offered by recent cognitive studies, how these characterizations can be applied to mathematical cognition, and what implications for mathematics education can be derived from them. Such an attempt may no longer be appealing to the mathematics education community, who may contend that:

- General theories of learning or acquisition, of either the behaviorist or cognitivist varieties, have not been as informative to mathematics educators as approaches specifically focused on mathematics.
- So-called general theories of learning are in fact about the acquisition of knowledge regarding aspects of the actual world (e.g., physics, biology, and psychology), and thus not relevant to the acquisition of logic of mathematical knowledge.
- The course and process of development in the domain of mathematics are unique, so that studies in other domains of expertise cannot be instructive.

- What one has to acquire to become an expert or master in mathematics is radically different from other domains, and also the domain of mathematics is expected to embody a different set of innate constraints.

However, most, if not all, mathematics educators would agree that students' mathematical cognition constitutes a theory-like knowledge system, that is, an organized body of knowledge that concerns a specific set of objects or entities and that, like scientific theories, involves coherent explanations. The acquisition of a mathematical knowledge system will share, at least to some extent, features common to all other theory-like knowledge systems, such as naive physics, everyday biology, and a developing theory of mind. Thus, we can expect that characterizations of the acquisition of theory-like knowledge systems advanced by cognitive studies will provide mathematics educators with some clues for better understanding the development of mathematical cognition and trying to enhance mathematics education. Davis argues forcefully that characterizations of the acquisition of knowledge advanced by cognitive studies are relevant to mathematics education; able mediators like him are needed urgently to facilitate communication between cognitive scientists, mathematicians, and teachers.

Even if the acquisition of the mathematical knowledge system is unique and the characterizations offered give few direct suggestions for mathematics education, examining that knowledge system in relation to general features of knowledge acquisition can illuminate its unique aspects, and can thereby provide a more solid basis for designing mathematics education.

Knowledge Acquisition as Characterized by Cognitive Studies

Let me summarize in a short list of five interrelated characterizations what we cognitive researchers know about the long-term acquisition of knowledge by humans. As a whole, the list represents a coherent conception of knowledge acquisition, although it is decidedly short of being a "theory." (Any adequate theory would have to include a process model of knowledge acquisition, from which these characterizations can be generated, and also explanations for the model in terms of human information processing.) In deriving these five characterizations, I have relied primarily on studies in expertise, everyday cognition, and conceptual development, rather than on experimental studies in the laboratory, because the former types of study have usually been concerned with the acquisition of a body of knowledge prevalent in our society, the prototype of which is a theory-like knowledge system, whereas the latter type deals mostly with the learning of fragmentary pieces of knowledge of an artificial nature. I must admit that the selection of these characterizations reflects my personal biases. It is virtually impossible to construct a list of characterizations of knowledge acquisition that would fully satisfy most cognitive researchers. However, I believe a majority of them will agree that each of the characterizations selected is important as well as tenable, although they may want to add some others that they regard as equally or more important. In other words, although conceptions of knowledge acquisition vary considerably among cognitive theorists, many of them concur with at least most of the characterizations listed next.

The first characterization indicates that knowledge is acquired by construction; it is not acquired by transmission alone. Human acquire knowledge richer than the knowledge they are presented with, or even invent knowledge that has never been presented, often as a by-product of their problem solving and/or comprehension activity. This characterization is self-evident when there is no teacher or when the teacher cannot verbalize (or encode in another symbolic form) the target knowledge. However, knowledge must be constructed, at least partially, even when the teacher gives the learner the target knowledge in a verbalized form, or when she carefully monitors the learner so that his behavior can come to approximate the model behavior. Knowledge can be transmitted to some extent, but transmitted knowledge becomes usable in a variety of problem-solving situations only after it has been reconstructed—that is, interpreted, enriched, and connected to the prior knowledge of the learner. Needless to say, this process of reconstruction is not a purely individual enterprise, because, as will be seen, it is constrained socio-culturally.

The second characterization states that knowledge acquisition involves restructuring; that is, not only does the amount of knowledge increase but also one's body of knowledge is reorganized as more and more pieces of knowledge are acquired. Conceptual change in the history of science and in cognitive development is the best known example of the restructuring of knowledge. Knowledge systems before and after restructuring are different in organization; for example, one piece of knowledge may become differentiated, while other separate pieces of knowledge may become amalgamated. Historically, powerful ideas in mathematics, such as group theory, integrated many previously disparate pieces of knowledge. Relationships between pieces of knowledge may also change as restructuring takes place; for example, the same phenomenon may be explained differently, some instances may become prototypical whereas others may become marginal, and so forth.

The third characterization indicates that the process of knowledge acquisition is constrained. The construction and successive revision of knowledge take place under a variety of constraints so that the acquired knowledge is often similar, if not identical, between different individuals. Because of those constraints, which eliminate in advance a large number of logically possible hypotheses and interpretations in human problem solving and knowledge acquisition, people can reach a reasonable choice readily and quickly in most cases. Needless to say, the same constraints may have negative effects, because they make it extremely hard for some correct hypotheses to even come to mind. The construction process is constrained both internally (by innate tendencies and by acquired prior knowledge, i.e., cognitive constraints) and externally (by culture as a set of artifacts including language and notation, and by other persons, i.e., sociocultural constraints).

The fourth indicates that knowledge is usually acquired domain by domain. The entire body of knowledge humans have is divided into a number of domains, that is, more or less self-contained knowledge systems within which problem solving or comprehension usually takes place. Knowledge acquired through problem solving and comprehension activity is, in turn, stored within the domain. To put it differently, the acquisition of knowledge is basically domain specific.

Domain specificity certainly serves for cognitive economy, because it allows one to examine only a portion of one's stored knowledge in problem solving and comprehension, and also in appending and ultimately integrating a new piece of knowledge. What is acquired in a domain may be transferred to another (e.g., through analogy) or generalized to a variety of domains (e.g., by abstracting structural commonalties), but this is rather exceptional. It is hypothesized that there are distinct "disciplines" or universal theory-like knowledge systems, a dozen or so in number, which constitute domains.

The fifth and final characterization specifies that knowledge acquisition is "situated" in contexts. Human activity, through which all knowledge is acquired, occurs in particular contexts, or is coconstituted between a person and contexts, and thus is associated to (or situated in) them. Some contextual features—for example, what goal the activity is directed toward—are inseparable from the acquisition of the target knowledge. The growth of theory-like knowledge systems typically occurs in the context of argumentation and in the course of using conceptual resources productively and enjoyably.

Acquired knowledge is also situated; that is, it reflects how it was acquired and how it has been used. The knowledge humans "possess" in their heads includes not only public and abstract representations of "collective" experiences, such as laws, formulas, and rules described in textbooks, but also representations of experiences that are of a personal, concrete nature. Using the terminology adopted by Thompson, human knowledge involves "imagery" in the widest sense. Many contextual features are irrelevant to the target knowledge in its mature form. Accordingly, gaining expertise may be a process of decontextualizing or "desituating" knowledge. This makes one's problem-solving competence less context bound, and weakens its associations with contextual features—for example, reducing a bias based on particular personal experience.

I next elaborate each of the characterizations in a little more detail. To support them, I refer to empirical findings from studies of expertise, everyday cognition, and conceptual development, as well as our informal daily observations. Although many of the best known findings in these areas are about mathematical cognition, I do not refer at this stage to mathematical examples, because they are discussed in the following section.

Knowledge Is Constructed

Here the constructivist view of the knowledge acquisition is contrasted only with the empiricist (transmissionist) view. The nativist view is not considered as an alternative to the constructivist view, because (a) they are not necessarily incompatible, and (b) a radical nativist position does not seem tenable for (advanced) mathematics.

That knowledge is constructed is a corollary of the "zeitgeist" among contemporary cognitive theorists that human beings are active agents of information processing and action. Humans often explore tasks beyond the demands or requirements of problem solving, and environments that do not permit active exploration are experienced as unpleasant. Humans may create problems to solve rather than solve problems that are imposed. Thus, they often construct knowledge as a by-product of their spontaneous or required problem solving. More specifically, they acquire strategies for avoiding bad consequences and attaining good consequences. Humans also construct knowledge through comprehension activity. They try to find the "meaning" or a plausible interpretation of their observations of facts and effective procedures, and this enterprise sometimes results in the construction of knowledge of a more conceptual nature (e.g., what the target object is like). Procedural bugs and misconceptions are taken as the strongest pieces of evidence for the constructive nature of knowledge acquisition, because it is highly unlikely that students have acquired them by being taught.

That knowledge is acquired by construction does not deny that it can be transmitted to some extent. Most knowledge we have, as D'Andrade put it, has been learned from other people. A recipe for cooking or a manual for assembling a kit is useful because the knowledge described there can be transmitted. When a piece of procedural knowledge is coded in the verbal form that refers to external objects and actions, it can be conveyed more or less "accurately." Even a piece of conceptual knowledge can be transmitted to the extent to which it is adequately coded and the code systems of the sender and receiver are alike. Experts in science, who share a large amount of knowledge and terminology, can exchange quite complicated conceptual knowledge through verbal or symbolic communication.

However, transmission cannot be perfect, because any language or other symbol system is able to describe only part of the target knowledge, involves some ambiguity, and allows somewhat different interpretations. Even in the case of procedural knowledge, a transmitted version may not be applied in the same way as the original. More importantly, active humans almost always try to interpret and enrich what is transmitted—in other words, to supplement it by construction. Even when the target knowledge is transmitted effectively, its acquisition is not a once-and-for-all process. It is gradually incorporated into the existing body of knowledge.

Knowledge Acquisition Involves Restructuring

As one gains expertise in a domain, one's knowledge becomes not only richer but also better organized. In other words, the process of knowledge acquisition involves restructuring as well as enrichment. Conceptual change can be regarded as a form of restructuring, probably the most radical one, in the sense that knowledge systems before and after the conceptual change are incommensurable; that is, some pieces of knowledge in one system cannot properly be translated into the other. However, "restructuring" includes milder and more subtle forms.

Reorganization of the knowledge system takes place at a number of different levels, from individual to societal, and also in various forms. Constituent pieces of knowledge, and/or concepts included, can change; for example, a few pieces of knowledge are amalgamated into a unitary piece. As children learn biology, they combine the data that animals have babies and that plants have seeds to produce the knowledge that living things reproduce. Relationships between pieces of knowledge and/or component concepts, such as which instances are prototypical, can also change. The perceived status of humans changes as students acquire more and more biological knowledge. Humans are regarded as a typical living thing by the less knowledgeable, but they are a very special species for the more knowledgeable. Finally, there can be general, metacognitive changes in the knowledge system, such as those of patterns of inference, modes of explanation, and so forth. For attributing unknown properties to an animate object, young children rely on similarity-based inference, whereas older children and adults use category-based inference.

The Process of Knowledge Acquisition Is Constrained

According to contemporary cognitive theorists, knowledge acquisition can be concisely described as the process of constructing and reorganizing knowledge under a variety of constraints. Here the term constraints refers to conditions or factors that facilitate the process of acquisition as well as restrict its possible range. Cognitive theorists differ widely in the importance they assign to each of the constraints. For example, whereas investigators of expertise emphasize prior knowledge in the target domain, those who focus on conceptual development take innate constraints to be more critical. Nevertheless, most of these theorists would agree that the construction process is constrained both internally (by cognitive constraints) and externally (by sociocultural constraints).

Innate or Early Cognitive Constraints: Recent cognitive studies have shown that preschool children are more competent than used to be hypothesized. In other words, preschool children, due to innate and early cognitive constraints, possess some knowledge and can learn quickly in several specific areas. The existence of innate or early cognitive constraints is best known in language acquisition, but we can see good examples of early acquisition due to such constraints in a few other areas as well, including the domains of physics, psychology and biology, particularly that concerning the human body. In this last domain, young children recognize the mind—body distinction at early ages and thus they do not rely on intentional causality for biological phenomena inside the human body. For example, children of ages 4 and 5 years recognized that the activities of their bodily organs are relatively independent of their intention. In addition, a great majority of these children clearly understood that weight change is caused by food intake rather than intention or desire. This early distinction of mind and body may be facilitated by their innate tendency to establish certain causal connections between external events and human physical reactions.

Prior Knowledge as Cognitive Constraints: Recent cognitive studies have reported that young children show more advanced modes of reasoning in any domain where they have much experience, in other words, where they possess substantial knowledge and can use it. Domain-specific knowledge can help problem solvers aptly represent a given problem so that they can readily handle it. Domain-specific knowledge has also been shown to enhance the acquisition of new pieces of knowledge within the domain.

Chi, Hutchinson, and Robin found that children of 4-7 years of age who know a good deal about dinosaurs have hierarchically structured knowledge about them, and, using that knowledge, they can make deductive inferences that Piaget's theory assumed only older children would make. For example, "dinosaur expert" children assigned unobservable attributes to novel dinosaurs, using category-based inference (e.g., "He's prretty dangerous.. 'Cause he's a meateater").

Shared Artifacts as Cultural Constraints: By cultural constraints we mean artifacts that are shared by a majority of people of the community or a subgroup, including physical facilities and tools, social institutions and organizations, documented pieces of knowledge, common sense and beliefs, and more. Because these constraints virtually eliminate a great number of possible hypotheses and interpretations in advance, people can usually be expected to find what they should do quite easily in everyday situations. Moreover, they can acquire needed knowledge and skill rather quickly.

Cultural constraints are basically external to individuals. However, as they engage in practice by relying on the constraints, people tend to internalize them as knowledge in their mind. Much of our acquired knowledge is cultural in origin, and as such involves the internalization of cultural constraints. As people gain expertise in a given domain, they acquire not only knowledge and skill needed for solving problems in the domain, but also metacognitive beliefs that might be called values and evaluative criteria, which are shared by those regarded as experts in the domain.

Social Constraints: Interactions with Seniors and Peers: The term social constraints includes behavior of other people, interactions with them, and social contexts created by them. Most of what we do and acquire in everyday situations is affected by other people. It may be an empiricist idea that we copy knowledge directly from others, but that our learning is constrained by other people is acceptable even for a constructivist.

As aptly pointed out by Vygotsky, a child can do more under adult guidance or in collaboration with a more capable peer than he or she can do alone. Initially a child deals with a problem by taking partial charge of it under adult guidance, then gradually takes on responsibility for the whole, and finally becomes able to solve the problem by himself or herself. In other words, adult guidance helps children reduce their possible alternatives of what to do next and, as a result, enables them to deal with problems with less uncertainty. Although this formulation can more readily be applied to the acquisition of knowledge through apprenticeship or parent—child interaction, classroom learning can also be conceptualized in this fashion. Children learn from their peers, who, though not necessarily more capable, may propose innovative ideas at the critical moment.

Knowledge Acquisition Is Usually Domain Specific

Recent cognitive studies have demonstrated that individual competence varies considerably from domain to domain. In research on conceptual development, Piaget's stage theory, which posited that subjects' competence depended on their logicomathematical structures applicable across domains, has been challenged or even rejected by many current investigators. Investigators in expertise have asserted that the most critical determinant of problem-solving competence is not general intelligence but the relevant domain-specific knowledge and also that one gains expertise or accumulates knowledge only in a domain within which one solves problems repeatedly. Likewise, in research into everyday cognition, it is generally agreed that what is acquired is related directly to (and a function of) activity one engages in and that generalizations from such experience are highly limited. Although a scientific inquiry or an everyday attempt to understand the world may use information from all domains, as claimed by Fodor, it usually takes place within a particular domain. Knowledge produced through such an activity is also incorporated in the relevant domain only. Thus, knowledge is usually acquired separately for each domain, although analogical transfer or generalization of knowledge based on the recognized isomorphism across domains may sometimes occur.

In addition, many cognitive theorists believe that the course and process of development vary from domain to domain. This is because what one has to acquire to become an expert or master can be very different in different domains and each domain is expected to embody a different set of innate constraints. In other words, knowledge is acquired, in part, in a unique fashion in each domain.

The term domain refers to a range of knowledge or behavior that can be explained by a more or less coherent theory. Thus, how domains are divided is in a sense a cultural product. However, how knowledge is divided into domains is determined at least partially on innate bases, too.

Knowledge Acquisition Is Situated in Contexts

Human knowledge acquisition is conceptualized as a process of representing experience with an object, event, or conceptual entity, so that the resultant representation (i.e., knowledge) can readily be used in future problem solving and understanding. Thus, it is situated in contexts in which experience occurs and cannot but be influenced by various features of these contexts. Contextual features of acquisition are not limited to cognitive ones. Knowledge acquisition is more than "purely cognitive," in the sense that it takes place through interaction within social and cultural contexts that are embedded in the larger cultural historical setting. Knowledge acquisition goes hand in hand with participation in a community in which the target knowledge is shared and thus is based on social motivation to become a full member of the community as well as on motivation to understand and/or to be competent.

Acquired knowledge is also situated in the sense that it reflects the history of its acquisition and use, including associations with contexts. Although textbooks for a given domain summarize a body of knowledge as a set of propositions, the knowledge individuals "possess" in their head includes representations of a more personal, concrete nature. For example, knowledge in the form of a rule is often accompanied by some preferred examples, such as those that were used when the rule was first introduced and that the learner was able to solve for the fist time by applying the rule. It may also be flavored by the social context of its acquisition (e.g., how the teacher explained it and other students reacted). Experts' knowledge in a domain is often inseparably associated with beliefs and values that the members of the community of experts of the domain share.

These personal representations are not just useless adjuncts. They serve as clues for retrieving a rule when it is appropriate. Without them, it is almost impossible to retrieve relevant rules promptly. This explains in part why gaining expertise takes so much time.

As humans gain expertise, knowledge underlying their performance becomes decontextualized (or "desituated") in the sense that it is no longer tightly associated with the situation in which it was originally acquired. Qualitatively different progress is made, when people acquire mental models of major objects or entities of the domain, forms of conceptual knowledge that react or change in response to mentally exerted actions and that thus can be used to run mental simulations. When they possess a mental model of the target object, they can understand the meaning of each step of a given procedure in terms of the change it produces in the object. By running the mental model, they can also predict what will occur in unprecedented situations. The problem solving competence of experts is no longer context bound in the same sense as for novices. They are able to achieve goals across contexts, and to solve various novel problems in the domain. However, this does not mean that experts have and use public and abstract rules only. On the contrary, experts seem to rely heavily on their accumulated personal experiences. Experts do not solve the whole problem in their heads, either. Often they have acquired knowledge needed to use external constraints; for example, they are able to "offload" part of the computation involved.

Acquisition of Mathematical Knowledge

The Dual Nature of Mathematical Cognition

Before trying to apply the preceding characterizations of knowledge acquisition to mathematical knowledge, let me point out its dual nature. Although mathematical knowledge is not about the material world as such, it is nevertheless very useful for solving real-world problems accurately and efficiently. This dual nature is reflected in the makeup of the mathematical community. Mathematics is used daily by many people, whereas it is studied professionally by a small number of scholars called mathematicians. However, these two groups constitute a community, because they share, at least to some extent, what is called mathematical knowledge.

For almost all users of mathematical knowledge, it is primarily a set of tools, by which they can solve real-world problems. According to Davis, most people view mathematics as consisting of "employing a few rote procedures"; I would insert "but magically effective" after "rote." More precisely, it consists of procedures for converting real-world problems into mathematical representations and vice versa, and procedures for manipulating these representations to find mathematical solutions. "Just plain folks," including the weight watcher described in Lave, though often not aware that they are doing so, perform mathematical operations to find solutions for their everyday problems (e.g., divide a "pie" into quarters and take three to change the original recipe for four into that for three). Most scientists also use various forms of mathematics in order to describe, predict or even create phenomena.

For most users, either laymen or scientists, acquiring mathematical knowledge is subjectively not different from acquiring other procedures for problem solving. They want to learn, primarily, how to use, and when to use, ready-made procedures. The acquisition of a procedure depends on its usefulness as a tool, in other words, how promptly and accurately it leads to a solution. However, as they use the procedures, they may try to understand, adjust, or elaborate the procedures, that is, they may try, like mathematicians, to do, and not merely use, mathematics.

Mathematicians deal with patterns or structures and their relationships. They may invent new pieces of mathematical knowledge by endlessly applying operations on operations. What mathematicians do with abstract entities is analogous to, and is in fact derived from, human actions on physical objects, but is often driven by the pure pleasure of intellectual exploration. The truth of mathematical knowledge is based not on its empirical confirmation or practical utility, but on its rigorous derivational or proving steps. Its significance is dependent on what kind of a new structure is introduced, how much the nature of the structure is specified, and so on. However, mathematicians may want to apply mathematical knowledge to real-world problems, or to help others who are trying to apply it. Even when they remain "pure mathematicians," they usually will be willing to admit that the mathematics they do is potentially relevant to real-world problems.

Mathematics education programs take into serious consideration this duality. Good programs try to enhance the acquisition of mathematical knowledge through solving practically significant and/or intellectually challenging problems. For example, Gimbayashi, a current distinguished leader of the Association of Mathematics Instruction in Japan, emphasizes both the practical utility of mathematics and understanding of the meaning of mathematical procedures.

Applying the Characterizations to Mathematical Knowledge

How well do the five characterizations described in the first section fit the acquisition of mathematical knowledge? Are any modifications, qualifications, or reservations of the characterizations necessary?

First, can we be sure that mathematical knowledge is acquired by construction, not by transmission alone? Some may wonder if, although mathematical knowledge is a human construction, it can be transmitted once it is constructed (by mathematicians), because of its rigorous, formal nature. Others may wonder if mathematical knowledge as a set of tools can be transmitted, like other kinds of procedural knowledge. I admit that mathematical knowledge expressed in terms of laws or formulas can apparently be transmitted. However, before learners become able to use a given law, they have to understand it, that is, interpret it in relation to their prior knowledge—in other words, reconstruct it in their mind. For example, they have to judge which terms are constants, and which are variables.

That students construct mathematical knowledge by themselves can clearly be seen in procedural bugs and misconceptions they reveal. In other words, procedural bugs and misconceptions are produced because students do not swallow a given rule or algorithm but try to construct something subjectively tenable by induction. It is well known that lower grade children show a variety of buggy algorithms for multi digit subtraction. Whether necessitated by the impasse caused by a missing or erroneous production or more spontaneously induced to reduce mental effort, these procedural bugs are certainly students' inventions. Similarly, misconceptions are invented by learners themselves, through their attempts to make sense of their limited experiences. For example, the often observed misconception that division makes the dividend smaller seems to be a result of repeated experiences of division with a divisor larger than 1, but never (before fractions are introduced) with one smaller than 1.

Thus, the first characterization of knowledge acquisition holds with mathematical knowledge. Mathematical knowledge that can be used in a variety of situations as an intellectual tool is acquired by construction, not by transmission alone. This implies that we might adopt a version of the constructivist position for mathematics instruction, either a radical one or a more realistic one.

Second, does mathematical knowledge acquisition involve restructuring? The history of mathematics as an academic discipline reveals something more than mere incremental processes. When revolutionary ideas were presented, reorganizations of the entire discipline have occurred. Old and new versions of mathematics would not be incommensurable, but more often than not, the new included the old as its part. Likewise, when students learn mathematics, their progress is often discontinuous. When they achieve some key insight, their ways of solving a variety of problems may change, which suggests at least local restructuring.

It is an interesting conjecture that some restructuring is needed in order to proceed to a more advanced version of mathematics, and that many dropouts in mathematics are due to failure to restructure. For example, some students have great difficulty in understanding multiplicative structures including fractions, ratio, proportion, and so forth, probably because they stick to mathematics based on additive composition. Another impressive shift in the development of mathematics is that from empirical to logical orientation. Although younger students judge a mathematical procedure to be invalid solely based on the fact that it does not predict the reality, older ones may refer to inconsistency or contradiction with known mathematical facts as the basis for its rejection. The former orientation is similar to the "empiric" orientation found among the Kpelle in Liberia by Scribner.

Thus, although we may not observe conceptual changes therein, it is obvious that the development of mathematical cognition involves restructuring. Mathematics educators should not expect students to show a monotonic increment of mathematical knowledge. Moreover, students' initial understanding of a mathematical concept could be considerably different from its mature, if not final, form.

Third, that the process of mathematical knowledge acquisition is constrained is evident. However, the constraints that play a more critical role in the acquisition of mathematics may be different from those for other domains. For early and universal competence in mathematics, such as counting and protoquantitative reasoning schema, innate or early cognitive constraints seem to be critical. For example, as suggested by Gelman and Gallistel, five principles underlying counting, which even children 3 and 4 years of age understand, help them acquire a general procedure of counting from a small number of observations, by restricting the range of possible interpretations. More advanced mathematical knowledge can easily be acquired only when students are helped by prior knowledge in mathematics. This implies that a teacher should pay close attention to what students know before formal instruction. Here students' prior world knowledge that can constrain the range of possible operations and answers, as well as their understanding of mathematical entities, such as how to formulate a given problem mathematically, is important for mathematical knowledge acquisition.

The acquisition of mathematical knowledge is also constrained by sociocultural contexts. The most salient example here is information provided by teachers and textbooks, including terminology, notation, and graphical resources in mathematics. Thanks to those constraints that work in human mathematical problem solving and knowledge acquisition, both in external and internalized forms, a large number of possible hypotheses and interpretations are excluded in advance, so that people can reach a reasonable choice readily and quickly in most cases.

It should be noted that by emphasizing cultural constraints in the acquisition of knowledge, current cognitive theorists are at a distance from the radical or "romantic" constructivist position, although they do not favor didactic teaching, either. These theorists claim that human capabilities are inherited not only in the form of innate constraints (or in a genetic form) but also as artifacts. The competence of learners in any domain varies with how well they incorporate or appropriate the artifacts. For example, even a talented student cannot solve problems without mastering the mathematical notation and graphical representation as well as acquiring basic mathematical knowledge like axioms in advance.

Fourth, it should be emphasized that mathematical knowledge is unique because of its domain-general character. It is true that mathematics as a discipline constitutes a separate domain. A talented mathematician may be very poor at other domains of knowledge, such as the interpersonal. Expertise in mathematics not only is relatively independent from that in other domains, but also may have distinctively different features. However, mathematics as an intellectual tool can be applied to a large number of domains, though when thus applied it is not content-free.

Carey has already suggested that knowledge about measurement (or quantification in general) may produce a somewhat domain-general difference between young children and adults. Piaget repeatedly claimed that logicomathematical knowledge could be applied across domains, creating a uniform stage in problem solving within individuals. Although post-Piagetians tend to doubt this claim, they too will admit that logicomathematical knowledge can form "a domain across domains." Mathematics is powerful as an intellectual tool mainly because it enables us, through formalization, to detect structural commonalties in apparently very different domains, and thus to apply general problem-solving algorithms to them more or less consciously.

Finally, that mathematical knowledge acquisition is situated in contexts seems tenable. As described earlier, it is obvious that the mathematical knowledge novices have is closely tied to the context of its acquisition, such as how a new mathematical concept is introduced. Even when two or more students know a mathematical formula in common, how it is represented may vary among them. Rumelhart proposed that how fractions are taught influences students' understanding of fractions, as reflected in differential patterns of performance. More specifically, when fractions are introduced by using the pie analogy, students can learn pretty easily how to add and subtract them, but multiplication or division involving fractions is much harder. In contrast, when fractions are introduced as a form of division, learning to multiply or divide them is easier than addition or subtraction.

How fractions are introduced is critical, as claimed by Rumelhart, for fifth and sixth graders, but its effect will be much attenuated for high scholars. Speaking generally, mathematical knowledge that experts (experienced users with mathematical understanding as well as mathematicians) possess is no longer associated tightly with the situation in which it was originally acquired. This is partly because experts' knowledge reflects the long history of its use as well as its original acquisition—that is, it has been used in varied situations. Their knowledge may be "desituated" in the sense of being useful even outside of the situations experienced, because experts can adapt known procedures or even invent new ones based on their understanding of a set of conceptual entities. Thus, how a new mathematical concept is introduced in instruction is critical, but even more important is to try to develop students' conceptual understanding, unless the goal of instruction is to teach routine procedures that are useful only for limited problems.

Cognitive Conception of Knowledge Acquisition for Mathematics Education

What practical implications for mathematics education can be derived from the characterizations of knowledge acquisition applied to mathematical knowledge? I briefly discuss this question in this final section.

Students' Active Participation: This stems directly from the first item on the list, that mathematical knowledge is acquired by construction. It is important, but is not very distinctive: Educational methods recommended by the current cognitive conception may vary, from those that have many features in common with previous constructivists' (e.g., Piaget's) to those emphasizing students' meaningfully incorporating mathematical ideas as given by a teacher. Constructivism generally emphasizes that students construct knowledge by themselves, not by swallowing ready-made knowledge from the outside. Thus, those methods that merely require students to practice given algorithms or those that do not allow students to explore various possible ideas are considered to be less effective.

However, what is taken as critical in this characterization is students' understanding, that is, how they interpret a given mathematical idea in relation to their prior knowledge. Therefore, current cognitive theorists, like Piagetians, encourage students' active participation, but unlike Piagetians, do not necessarily expect students to invent mathematical knowledge by themselves. Instead, they expect students to examine a given process or product of mathematical inference against that of another inference as well as with reality, and to use their prior knowledge as much as possible for making sense of their "observations." Needless to say, the contemporary conception of knowledge acquisition recommends teachers not to impose their ideas nor to present an overwhelmingly large amount of information.

Inducing Successive Reorganizations of Mathematical Knowledge: Because restructuring seems necessary for mathematical cognition to advance, mathematics educators should try to facilitate its occurrence. They should allow students to take time to reflect and reorganize, neither expecting nor desiring them to show a monotonic mathematical development.

As our knowledge about specific features of restructuring in the development of mathematical cognition increases, such as from what knowledge state to what state students tend to shift, we can better design mathematics education programs as well as better predict their progress. This will allow us to make more sensible decisions about teaching, for example, where teachers might slow down and spend much time, and conversely, where they might speed up to save time. Students may need a large amount of time for initial understanding when new entities, like "variables," are presented, and for reorganization when new mathematical structures, such as multiplicative ones, are introduced.

Use of Students' Prior Knowledge as a Constraint: The cognitive conception of knowledge acquisition, especially the idea of constraints, suggests a number of instructional strategies to facilitate the process of students' mathematical knowledge construction, although it does not assume that students' progress in the domain can be totally under the control of educators. It is recommendable for educators to focus upon constraints over which they have control. They can intervene through social constraints, and they can manipulate a variety of cultural constraints as well. Moreover, although the body of acquired domain-specific knowledge in mathematics is internal and not directly subject to educators' control, modifying it prior to the target lessons is often not too hard. As mentioned earlier, cognitive studies have indicated that acquired rich and well-organized knowledge in a specific domain enables students to process information effectively (acquire new pieces of knowledge as well as reason in advanced modes).

Using Sociocultural Constraints to Facilitate Students' Learning: Mathematics educators should consider how to make maximal use of sociocultural constraints. Unlike Piagetian educators, who at most try to set up a generally stimulating environment, educators inspired by the cognitive conception might involve themselves more actively, by organizing and directing the process of students' construction of mathematical knowledge. For example, they can (a) present various models to enhance students' understanding, (b) use tools for inducing initial success, (c) amplify conceptions generated by students, and (d) ask students to reflect on what they actually do.

Encouraging students to share ideas is also recommended. Even elementary school children can judge the plausibility of ideas proposed by their peers, and learn a lot by discriminatingly incorporating them. Here too an educator plays a critical role, first by setting up situations where a group of students are able to engage in their collective inquiry, and second by taking the role of a "more capable peer" in their attempts at knowledge acquisition. For instance, she can give an example that will stimulate the students' thinking or help them clarify ideas they have put forward.

Teaching Mathematics in Relation to a Domain of Students' Interest: That the acquisition of mathematical knowledge may not be domain specific has an important implication for mathematics instruction. It does not exclude the possibility of teaching pure mathematics within its domain or teaching mathematical procedures to solve problems only in a specific content domain, but a wiser alternative seems to teach how to solve problems in relation to a variety of realworld problems in domains other than mathematics, by mathematically representing and transforming them, and then to develop mathematical knowledge itself, through reflection and abstraction, so that it can readily be generalized to other domains as a set of tools for problem solving. Placing mathematical solution in the context of the real-world problems that interest students highlights its significance. Moreover, looking afresh at the real-world problems through "mathematical eyes" will enhance their understanding of the problems. What Gimbayashi and his associates have attempted is exactly in this direction.

Choosing Proper Contexts for the Acquiring and Desituating of Knowledge: Three implications emerge from the situated nature of the acquisition of mathematical knowledge. First, a teacher should arrange proper contexts for the activity that will lead to the acquisition of the target mathematical knowledge. The activity should not just be preparation for tests, because students tend to acquire knowledge readily applicable only to a limited range of problems, not usable productively and enjoyably, through such an activity. Second, because mathematical knowledge that novices have is closely tied to the context of its acquisition, a teacher must be very careful in organizing instruction, especially how a new mathematical concept or skill is introduced. Third, he or she must organize a sequence of instruction so that students can experience varied contexts for using the concept or skill, and come to acquire mathematical knowledge that is useful even outside of the experienced situations. In other words, mathematics education should aim at helping students become adaptive experts, that is, experts who can adapt known procedures or even invent new ones based on their understanding of a set of conceptual entities.

Some Suggested Principles for Mathematics Education: Let me propose several guidelines for designing lessons in mathematics by summarizing the preceding discussions. They can be taken as embodying the cognitive conception of the mathematical knowledge acquisition mentioned above. They are admittedly very tentative, and also must be enriched by mathematics educators' intuition. However, I hope they are stimulating and suggestive, if not of immediate practical use.

1. Pose interesting problems. If possible, encourage students to pose problems of their own. The problem should induce a

variety of ideas from students, and also motivate them to understand presented relevant ideas, especially those about mathematical representations and their manipulations. Davis argues that students should tackle novel problems that no one has told them how to solve, leading to the invention of mathematics. In other words, the problem should arouse epistemic curiosity or motivation for understanding, and lead to the construction of significant mathematical ideas.

2. Place a problem in pragmatic or familiar contexts, unless students are mature enough for pursuing a purely mathematical problem. This strategy, by situating the problem within students' domain of interest, motivates them to explore various ideas intensively. It also makes them recognize the power of mathematics in solving practical problems.
3. Encourage students to bring in their prior skills and ideas. Students are more competent than one might realize and may well know quite a lot even before any systematic instruction is given.

We can compare their competence by respecting their ideas.

1. They will try hard to construct knowledge themselves only when they have confidence.
2. Suggest that students use tools that enable them to do easily what they want to. Tools here include such things as a calculator and also mathematical symbols and graphics.
3. Use peer interactions for motivating students as well as for constraining the process of their knowledge construction. Students may solve collectively a problem that individually they are unable to solve.
4. Intervene in peer interaction whenever appropriate, as long as it does not endanger students' spontaneous construction of knowledge.
5. Give ample opportunities to reflect after successful performance so that students can acquire mathematics in more or less disembodied forms. I fully concur with the proposal made by Davis that students should reflect at length on what they did after they have invented solutions. Time pressure often makes it impossible for students to pursue the meaning

of mathematical formulations and transformations involved in problem solving.

6. Metacognitive beliefs enhancing mathematical cognition should be established through solving and reflecting on the series of interesting mathematical problems. Although it is very important for students to develop good taste and evaluative criteria of their own for judging whether it is an interesting problem, whether it is an acceptable solution, what kinds of problems might be handled mathematically, and so on, these should not be imposed on students through the teacher's authority.
7. Put problems in order so that students' solutions and justifications can gradually be refined into formal, mathematical ones, and so that they can fully participate in the culture of experts in the domain of mathematics.
8. It may be necessary to require students to do some exercise that will enhance the consolidation of important component skills of mathematical problem solving. The exercise should be engaging to students. Avoid as much as possible relying on mechanical drills, which may weaken students' search for sense making.

6

ALGEBRA

Introduction

- Investigate some historical foundations of algebra
- Explore careers that assume an algebraic background of employees
- Develop a manipulative approach to multiplying algebraic expressions
- Use manipulatives to factor algebraic products
- Determine some drill and practice procedures that will stimulate student interest
- Investigate a multitude of technological applications within the algebra curriculum
- See how the power of technology can be used to place a broader segment of the algebra curriculum within the grasp of more students

The first records dealing with adding or subtracting the same magnitude on both sides of an equation are found in the Arabic writings of Al-Khowarizmi about 830 A.D. This is an important work on which subsequent algebraic developments were based. The word *algorithm* is derived from the name of this ancient mathematician. Algorithm originally meant "the art of calculating."

In England mathematicians were called calculators. Now algorithm means calculating by any method following a given set of rules. Just as the definition of algorithm evolved, so does the concept of algebra continue to evolve. Originally, algebra in Al-Khowarizmi's time contained no mathematical or numerical symbols. Its rules were proclaimed "as if they were divine revelations, which the reader was to accept and follow as a true believer". Ironically, today's mathematics student who does not fully absorb the concept being taught may feel there is a leap of faith involved in some algebraic calculations. There was a void created in the history of mathematics when the Greeks dropped algebraic proofs in favor of geometric language due to the Pythagoreans' inability to deal with irrational numbers. Algebraic reasoning was resurrected by Al-Khowarizmi, which eventually led to the proof of the existence of irrational numbers, allowing mathematicians to once again embrace algebraic reasoning and carry on from the point where the Greeks had abandoned it.

Leonardo da Pisa introduced algebra to Italy about 1200 A.D., and Robert Recorde introduced it to England in a 1557 A.D. publication. Algebraic methods and notations have been improved and revised. Unlike arithmetic, where 3 + 4 = 7 (written that way for bases 8 and larger), algebraic notations like $x + y = z$ take on different meanings in different contexts. Thus, the subject of algebra provides challenges for some individuals because of their difficulty in dealing with the abstractions associated with unknowns.

The major contribution of Diophantus of Alexandria was the syncopation of algebra. He used symbols as shorthand for often-used quantities and operations, that is,

K for cubed

? for squared

? for subtraction

Ù for equals sign

M for units

Descartes contributed to the development of algebraic symbolization. He used symbolic notation to express algebraic calculations. He also used letters at the beginning of the alphabet (a, b, c) to denote known quantities (Does this sound familiar from your high-school days?) and letters from the end of the alphabet (x, y, z), particularly x, to indicate unknown quantities. He used numbers to indicate different powers of a quantity. We write $4x^3 - 6x^2 = 2x + 3$. Diophantus would have written K^T4 $*^T6$ * 2M3. Descartes would have written it $4xxx - 6xx + 2x + 3$.

Some disagree about the timing and ability of students to adapt to comprehend the varying levels of abstractions. The philosophy of organizations such as NCTM in stating that *all* students can learn mathematics is not accepted by everyone. Individuals with skills limited to computational ability offer little to society mathematically. Technology can do the arithmetic. Society needs thinkers to employ technology. Still, discussion continues relating to what should be learned in mathematics and how it should be taught. In many algebra classrooms, students are not permitted to use technology until fact and operational mastery is evident. If a student cannot exhibit the skill of multiplying decimals at some satisfactory level, that student is prohibited from advancing algebraically until that computational ability can be mastered. How much better it would be to use a calculator and see what can be accomplished mathematically. There is a difference between arithmetic and mathematics, isn't there?

Traditionalists say, and many parents agree, something like, "The mathematics I learned and the way I learned it was good enough for me, so it is good enough for my child." Unfortunately, that statement is far from true. Yet the resistance to curricular and conceptual change is formidable. Today's world is much more mathematical than yesterday's, in that productivity in today's world requires greater mathematical abilities than did yesterday's. Even most common percents, ratios, and discounts are done with calculators instead of by hand. Tomorrow's world will be even more mathematical than today's. As technological advancements continue, some segments of mathematics will decrease in importance whereas others will grow. This can be seen in the continuing decrease of emphasis on computational skills involving large numbers because of the ready availability and low cost of calculators.

How do we rationalize the emphasis on factoring to determine the roots of an equation when it is so much faster to do the problem with a graphing calculator? Solutions can be derived in different manners. The results will be approximations, but the tolerance for error determines what is acceptable and what is not. Any approximate solution could be substituted into the original equation and simplified. If unacceptable, alterations can be made in the solution approximation and the substitution process repeated. This procedure of adjusting the approximation provides an opportunity for additional learning. For example, suppose an approximation for one of the solutions for a third-degree equation is 2.5, and substitution shows it is not acceptable. The exercise now becomes one of knowing how to adjust 2.5 to get a better approximation. Is it 2.51 or 2.49? The decision is not a major hurdle.

Although some skills receive less emphasis, others attract greater attention because of the growth of technology. The use of technology in the mathematics classroom is essential for today's students to learn the necessary mathematics for tomorrow. The development of the NCTM Professional Standards for Teaching Mathematics was based on the following assumptions for Grades 5-8:

- In Grades 5 and 6, a four-function calculator will be available, at all times, for each student.
- In Grades 7 and 8, a scientific calculator will be available at all times to each student.
- Every classroom will have at least one computer available at all times for demonstrations and student use. Additional computers should be available for individual, small-group, and whole-class use.

Some of the NCTM Standards that recommend the study of algebra for Grades 9-12 include:

- Computer graphing to develop conceptual understanding
- Computer-based methods such as successive approximations and graphing utilities for solving equations and inequalities

At the same time, NCTM recommends a decreased emphasis on algebraic topics such as:

- Use of factoring to solve equations
- Operations with rational expressions
- Paper-and-pencil graphing by plotting points

NCTM encourages the integration of problem-solving techniques throughout the curriculum. One facet of problem solving focuses on the ability to interpret responses. This is an outgrowth of complaints from industry about the inability of employees to interpret answers. An algebraic application of this position could be built around the assumption that a decision needs to be made about pay procedures in a company. Should they offer positions that are commission only, or should they provide a base salary supplemented by a commission? Basic algebra provides the answer, but often individuals struggle with the solution. Time is money, and if an employee wrestles too long with this dilemma, there is a negative impact on the productivity of the company.

Need of Learning of Algebra

Most of today's mathematics education world presents the position that algebra should be learned by *all* students if they are to be functional contributors to the world of the future. This is based on suppositions like:

- The need for the development of a logical thought process
- The expected increase in the use of technology
- The need for employees to interpret professional literature

Motivating a student to learn algebra is a challenge. There are avenues of pursuit that will help relieve this predicament. One remedy could be the chart from *"When are we ever gonna have to use this?"*. Topics are grouped by the subject areas of basic math/pre-algebra, first-year algebra, geometry, second-year algebra/ trigonometry, and other topics (calculus, calculator use, computer use, problem solving, mathematical modeling, and so on) First-year algebra topics listed are using formulas, linear equations, linear inequalities, operations w/polynomials, factoring polynomials, rational expressions, coordinate graphing, linear systems, radicals, quadratic equations, and algebraic representation. Over one hundred career options are listed on the chart. Career choices include all the mathematically obvious ones like engineer and scientist, but they also list trades like carpenter, electrician, mechanic, painter, and plumber. The medical professions are represented with categories like dentist, dietitian, doctor, nurse, physical therapist, veterinarian, and x-ray technician. Airline pilots, TV camera operator, museum curator, farmer, fire fighter, golf pro, real estate agent, and waiter/ waitress are also listed. As students ask for rationalizations about the need to learn algebraic concepts, the careers listed should convince them of the universal advantages of having a command of the subject.

One vision for including algebra in the curriculum of all students is the broad range of careers and subjects that depend on algebraic underpinnings. Another curricular point stems from the idea that so much of the curriculum prior to algebraic exposure is repetitious. About 75% of the time in a seventh-grade mathematics text is spent reviewing. "... not much new material is introduced in seventh or eighth grade, so the mathematics experience is boring and counterproductive." Indications are that a preponderance of new information is encompassed at the end of the book in sections frequently not covered. By introducing only small amounts of new material in courses preceding algebra, students are essentially lulled to sleep. Then when the student enters algebra, where so much of the information is new, difficulties are encountered.

First-year Algebra

What constitutes first-year algebra? Are Algebra 1, first-year algebra, beginning algebra, introductory algebra, and pre-algebra all the same course? Will students entering an Algebra II course from each of these courses be adequately prepared for the expectations? Often the text drives the curriculum, which is a large portion of the dilemma. Challenging pre-algebra texts are similar to easy first-year algebra books. The quandary becomes more involved because different teachers, schools, districts, and states specify different topics to be included in the first-year algebra course. Some (teachers, texts, schools, districts, states) cover quadratics, some do not. Some focus on word problems, some do not. Some word problems show applications, some do not. Some include applications, some do not. Some teach for understanding, some do not. Some stress skills, some do not. And so on. A text-driven curriculum allows for the omission of many algebraic concepts. If quadratics are not introduced in the text, then this topic is often neglected in the curriculum. What should be taught in the first-year algebra course? Who should determine the concepts for a first-year algebra course?

The dilemma of what to include in first year algebra is also encountered in second-year algebra. In addition, the second-year algebra curriculum is impacted by what is accomplished in the first year. Many school districts define an algebra course as the material covered in a year, usually consisting of 180 days, thereby implying that approximately 150 hours have been spent on algebra instruction (assuming 50-minute periods). In reality, teachers often hope for 120 hours of instruction, if they are lucky, because of time taken out of periods for announcements, getting settled, shortened days for assemblies, pep rallies, visits from guests, days off and, of course, time for tests and quizzes. Extend the discussion by having more than one first-year algebra teacher doing the course. Second-year algebra teachers are faced with students who have had different teachers who emphasized a variety of first-year algebra concepts in a varied number of days. The one commonality these students have is credit in first-year algebra, even though the likelihood is great that there are extensive differences in what completion of that course means. Usiskin presented the following as a jumping off point for his discussion on what should or should not be included in a first-year algebra course. Standard First-Year Algebra Content:

- Operations with positive and negative numbers; evaluation of expressions
- Solving of linear equations, linear inequalities, and proportions
- Age, digit, $d = rt$, work and mixture word problems
- Operations with polynomials and powers
- Factoring of trinomials, monomial factoring, special factors
- Simplification and operations with rational expressions
- Graphs and properties of graphs of lines
- Linear systems with two equations in two variables
- Simplification and operations with square roots
- Solving quadratic equations (by factoring and completing the square)

He then argued in favor of four alterations to the standard first-year algebra content to make a realistic first-year algebra course:

1. Use applications rather than contrived word problems.
2. Delete factoring trinomials (keep monomial factoring and special factored forms).
3. Delete rational expressions requiring factoring.
4. Use the quadratic formula to solve quadratic expressions.

The Ohio Department of Education published a content outline defining an average first-year algebra class. It did not include optional topics or ideas that could be used for enrichment, assuming rather that different texts, teachers, schools, districts, or states would include things deemed appropriate for the needs of their students. The Ohio list is shown in Fig. 10.5. Other lists would give comparable results. Points of emphasis, or de-emphasis, become the option of the local authority (the teacher). However, it must be realized that those decisions have a dramatic impact on the first-year algebra learning of the students. This has a bearing on the offerings of the second-year algebra program, as was mentioned earlier.

First-year algebra is new for students. Prior to this point in their mathematical development, generalizations played a relatively minor role in the scheme of mathematics. Now, generalizations and processes occupy center stage in their mathematical learning. Variables are introduced formally, and notions from their arithmetic background are extended to the set of real numbers. Language becomes more formalized, and symbolic manipulation and its associated skills begin to be central themes of each student's mathematical existence. Unification and blending of topics and subjects begins to occur. Problem solving occupies a more central location, and expectations about systematic reasoning increase.

I. Algebraic Expressions
   A. Variables and expressions
   B. Evaluating expressions
   C. Writing expressions
   D. Absolute value
II. Real Number System
   A. Computations

   B. Properties and structure
   C. Finite and infinite systems

III. Linear Equations and Inequalities
   A. Language of sets
   B. Number line and Cartesian plane
   C. Open sentences in one variable
   D. Open sentences in two variables
   E. Problem solving

IV. Polynomials
   A. Addition, subtraction
   B. Exponents, multiplication
   C. Factoring
   D. Division

V. Rational Expressions
   A. Ratio and proportion
   B. Simplifying, computing
   C. Fractional equations and inequalities
   D. Direct and indirect variation
   E. Problem solving

VI. Relations, Functions, and Graphs
   A. Relations and functions
   B. Graphs

VII. Systems of Linear Equations and Inequalities
   A. Equations in two variables
   B. Inequalities in two variables
   C. Problem solving

VIII. Exponents and Radicals
   A. Radical exponents
   B. Radicals

IX. Quadratic Equations
   A. Equations in one variable

First-year algebra begins to apply pressure to the mathematical framework of the student. For many, this is the initial exposure to mathematics beyond memorization, or a cookie-cutter type curriculum. The course is a transition from the specifics of arithmetic into a confusing world where things are allowed to change. How these changes occur influences the final outcome. Before, they were told that division by zero was undefined. Now they are expected to be able to extend that to the realization that if a denominator of a fraction is "X + 3.2," then X cannot be n3.2 because that would yield zero for the term. Such maneuvers are not easy for all students to see immediately.

A significant part of the first-year algebra work is highly dependent on the arithmetic processes covered earlier in the curricular development of the students. For the sake of this discussion, we assume individuals in a first-year algebra course have been exposed to finding a difference like $53^2 - 24^2$. We further assume that there was some discussion about solving this problem by taking (53 + 24)(53 - 24). Algebraically, there is a desire to extend this work to the generalization $a^2 - b^2 = (a + b)(a - b)$. Because the difference of two squares is so common in algebra, students have been encouraged to memorize this as one of the special factored forms, often with no relation to problems like 532 - 242 or any concrete explanation about why the solution is as it is.

Certainly 532 - 242 could be presented to the students in the $a^2 - b^2 = (a + b)(a - b)$ form by lecture. On the other hand, if a clue is taken from the work of constructivists like Piaget, the presentation can be done concretely first. The thinking is that the physical manipulation establishes a stronger basis for understanding the process. At the same time, concrete manipulations can assist students in developing the capability to create mental images of the operation being performed. You should do this activity as you read these instructions. Perform each step before reading on.

Variable

Logicians spend lots of time carefully defining open variables, closed variables, and so forth. Many mathematicians prefer to think of variable as a name for a number. Because they are not sure what the number is, they call it x. It is generally accepted that the concept of a variable is difficult for beginning algebra students to comprehend. They may have been exposed to the idea of a variable in a multitude of settings prior to coming to algebra class. They may or may not be aware of the times when they used a variable. Concretely, the situation could have evolved from combining a set of two trucks with a set of three dolls to yield a set containing five elements. As the scenes from their past changed to the semi-concrete stage developmentally, the objects gave way to pictures of the objects to represent the two trucks and three dolls.

That move involved a variable of sorts in that the pictures represented the actual trucks or dolls. Still later, as the students progressed to the semiabstract stage of their development, the pictures of trucks could have been depicted by a "T" and the dolls with a "D." This abstraction begins to show a more common algebraic use of a variable, again probably without any comment to that effect. Eventually, beginning in the early grades, they dealt with equations like $2 + 3 = \cdot$. Most probably they were not aware of the idea that the · represented a variable, and yet it did. It stood for an answer they were looking for. Later, as students are exposed to word problems and formulas, variables appear in natural settings. For example, when they find the area of a rectangle, they use the formula $A = /w$, and it is accepted that "A" stands for "area," "/" represents the length of the rectangle, and "*w*" is the width. As they do word problems and translate them into equations to be solved, words give way to letters that represent the words and the concept of variable appears again. These informal exposures to variables give way to more formal approaches in the beginnings of algebra. Students like to make the correlation of a variable to a meaningful concept like A = Area and / = length. Why do we use "*x*" as the missing variable in most text book equations more so than "*n*," which could stand for number, or "*m*" for missing number? Recall Descartes and "*x*"; perhaps we are simply creatures of tradition when it comes to symbolic notation.

A very easy way to discuss a variable is through the use of a name. For example, my name is Douglas Kent. All my life my father and grandfather called me Mike. Others addressed me as Doug, although at times at home if I was out of line, it was Douglas. If I was way out of line, it was Douglas Kent and then I knew I was in serious trouble. Different names were used for the same person in different settings. Students probably have experienced similar situations, and that example helps them begin to have a feeling about variables.

Extend the name idea to include an example involving more than one student from the class having the same first name. They are familiar with this situation and realize the need for more explanation to be able to identify the appropriate individual. This is a situation showing a variable in the form of a name and that variable represents a set of individuals.

Often variable is defined for students. *The Standard College Dictionary* defines variable as *Math.* a. A quantity susceptible of fluctuating in value or magnitude under different conditions. b. A symbol representing one of a group of objects". Microsoft's *Encarta* states "Equation usually involves one or more unknown quantities, called variables or indeterminants". Typical mathematics textbook definitions are:

> "A variable *is a symbol used to represent one or more numbers".*

> "A variable *is any symbol, like* h, x, *or* ·, *that may be replaced by numbers". "Letters or symbols like m,* ·, *and O used to take the place of numerals are called* numerical variables, *or simply* variables".

Note that the dates for the definitions given go from 1955 to 1994 and there is little difference in the wording. Unless you have a feel for the concept, the definitions add little to clarify the situation. It is almost like saying, "A rose is a rose is a rose." If you know what a rose is, you understand. If you do not, the definition does little to enlighten you.

Once a variable is defined, typically the texts go into how to write variables and how to operate with them. One significant technological issue is raised at this point. Most textbooks define five times a number *N* to be either 5·N where the "dot" is elevated, (5)(*N*), 5(*N*), or 5*N*. Then the texts almost universally abandon all forms except for 5*N*, which uses implicit multiplication. "Everyone knows that the multiplication symbol is there" expresses the common mentality on this issue. Students become accustomed to writing 5N. The question is whether the student understands this notation to represent the product of "5" and "*N*." When technology is used, many software versions require insertion of the multiplication symbol. Thus, at least part of the world of technology is significantly different from the written text world. Is that difference acceptable? If the difference is accepted, how is it explained to the students? Because we are now well into the technological age, we need to be prepared to explain to students why mathematical notation is not universal.

The multiplication symbol is an excellent place to introduce this topic. The * operator is a common computer symbol for mathematics. We could not use a period because of its many other uses in computer languages. Many students might ask, "What about the symbol ×?" Computer languages are forced to recognized × as the English letter.

Once the definition of variable is established, the work usually focuses on substituting some number for that variable and evaluating the expression. Extended exposure includes other variables that are added, subtracted, multiplied, and divided, but no exponents are used with the variables. Students are asked to convert word phrases into algebraic expressions using variables with problems like:

A number decreased by 4.

Some number M *is 5 greater than 13.*

A value V *is tripled, then added to 86.7.*

In the curricular continuum, exponents are generally one of the next places variables are encountered. In a setting like x^n, x is defined as the base and n is the exponent that "shows how many times x is used as a factor." One question that should be asked eventually about the definition is, "What if the exponent is 0.5? How do we write x as a factor 0.5 times?" Consider that exponents are a short-hand notation for expressing the same factor. That is, a^3 is really $(a)(a)(a)$, which is now expressed in expanded form. This can lead into scientific notation and the use of exponent rules to deal with very large or very small numbers.

Disregarding the question about how an exponent should be defined, the students are asked to evaluate expressions involving exponents. From there they move to the laws of exponents, which leads to another exposure to variables as factors.

Multiplying A Monomial and A Polynomial

After instruction on the laws of exponents, most first-year algebra texts introduce the product of a monomial and a polynomial. **It is** assumed that previous exposure has included collecting like terms. Frequently, there is some review and extension of the distributive property of multiplication over addition on the set of real numbers. Significant amounts of time are spent dealing with situations containing negative factors. The distributive property becomes an essential ingredient in the understanding of future explanations involving the product of two polynomials. Most of the time, the multiplication is expressed horizontally in forms like $5(2m^3 + 6m^2 - 7m - 8)$. The monomial eventually includes variables and exponents, and the polynomial may involve more than one variable. However, there are some advantages to showing the product in vertical format as well.

The idea of vertical multiplication is particularly advantageous if the students have had prior experience with expanded or partial product forms of multiplication. This can often be related back to concrete stages of multiplication learning with base 10 blocks. Base 10 block multiplication would show the product 3(21) as three sets of two longs (L) and a unit (U) block. Examples of the basic base 10 blocks are shown in Fig. 6.14 . The pieces would be rearranged to show six Ls and three Us for a total of 63. Expanded notation would involve the distributive property of multiplication over addition on the set of counting numbers by showing 3(20 + 1) = 60 + 3. That would be written in partial product format as:

21 x3

3 from 3 times 1

60 from 3 times 20.

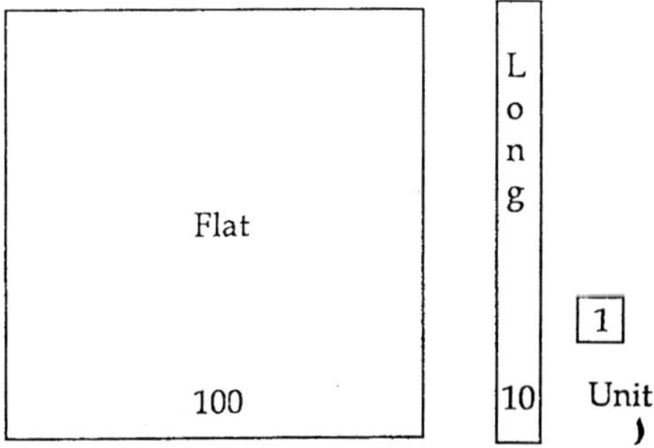

Fig. 6.1. Created with Geometer's Sketchpad

The 20 is significant in showing how place value is determined. The vertical writing is important in establishing format, because the partial products can be collapsed into the standard algorithm. It is meaningful to relate the current work to prior efforts as students are guided to a deeper level of understanding. Both formats are vital to helping students conceptualize different models of multiplication commonly used in algebra.

A set of manipulatives can be created that is similar to the base 10 blocks. These manipulatives are available commercially, but they can be made easily. Refer to the big square as X^2, the rectangle will be named X, and the little square will be a unit or 1. We are going to build some rectangles with these pieces. There are a few ground rules. It may appear that a number of units are the same length as an X if they are placed edge to edge in a straight line segment like square bricks in a wall. (In the commercial sets the units will not add up to an X or Y. They just don't fit that way. The creators made sure of that!) It is not permitted to make trades in such an instance. Trades such as this were permitted with base 10 blocks, and ten ones could be traded for one ten or ten tens would be traded for one hundred. The reason these trades cannot be done with the algebra manipulatives is that X is a variable or unknown. If six units are traded for an X when the value of the X is really nine, errors would be produced. Thus, exchanges are not permitted between pieces in the set.

The set of algebra manipulatives can be used to express products in a manner very similar to that used with the base 10 blocks. $3(2X + 1)$ would be shown as three sets of two Xs being added to a 1, giving a grand total of six Xs and three 1s. The students would then interpret this product with a final expression of $6X + 3$. Note the similarities between this and 63 expressed as $6(10^1) + 3(10^0)$ or $6(10) + 3$. The product needs careful association with the manipulatives to assist the students in creating a mental image of the product. As with young children in their early development of the concept of multiplication, care must be take to not rush too quickly to the abstraction. Assure that appropriate intermediate steps are provided to assist the students in visualizing the overall operation. The students will want to shed the manipulatives as quickly as possible, which is fine, as *long* as they have had some time to understand the impact of the operation. The degree of difficulty of the problems can be expanded with manipulatives, but these examples can quickly become cumbersome.

Multiplication of a constant times a variable expression like $3(X^2 - 5X + 8)$ is easy to show. The size of the constant factor can make the setting overly complex because of the number of pieces needed to show the product. However, it is important to realize that even the large, cumbersome products can be shown – they just take time to create. The ideal is to work with small products, which are easy to show, and have the students understand what is happening. Then abandon the manipulatives as quickly as possible with the perception that they can be used if needed. Establishing a solid foundation with the small, simple problems is crucial to the students' ability to handle more complex issues. Discarding the manipulatives too quickly is akin to just telling the students the process. That method is not effective. Ultimately, if the manipulatives are not permitted to run their full course, it is better to not use them at all. Lecture on! Your students will not be as capable as they could be, but at least they will not have developed a negative attitude toward the use of the manipulative. Partial use of any teaching tool and then "telling the secret," for whatever reason, is more damaging than no use at all.

Exponents greater than squares can be shown with the manipulatives. Creation of the tools becomes cumbersome. X^3 can be built with a normal three-dimensional approach to building a cube that is X units on an edge. These are represented in many of the commercial sets. Beyond that, representations become difficult. This amplifies the need to establish a solid foundation with the X, X^2, and perhaps the X^3. The hope is that the underpinnings will be sufficient for the students to visualize the processes necessary to complete the assigned tasks.

Similarly, multiplication by variables is possible in a limited format. For example, multiplying $(X + 2)$ by X can be shown by building the appropriate pieces (X^2 and $2X$ in this case). However, the explanations necessary to build the appropriate manipulative results can become artificial. At that point, questions about the advantages of a model-replacing lecture, when that model requires extensive lecture to explain, need to be raised. Again, the hope is that appropriate formative background can be established with settings easy to represent. Then, once the conceptualizations are established, the manipulatives will be abandoned in favor of abstractions. Still, the possibility exists of returning to the concrete if necessary.

Product of Two Binomials

Most authorities agree on the value of having students understand the operations to be performed at some level beyond mechanical. Regrettably, there are some text series that still stress doing the process to get the answer, while overlooking a multitude of opportunities to connect the operation with previously covered topics and establishing groundwork for future study. Prior to working with the product of two binomials, students cover the products of two monomials and the product of a monomial and polynomials. FOIL (First, Outer, Inner, and Last) is a mnemonic used by many teachers to instruct students on how to find the product of two binomials. Let $(A + B)$ and $(C + D)$ be the two binomials to be multiplied.

Multiplying the *First* terms of each binomial gives AC.

Multiplying the *Outer* terms of each binomial gives AD.

Multiplying the *Inner* terms of each binomial gives BC.

Multiplying the *Last* terms of each binomial gives BD.

Although FOIL accomplishes the task of having students be able to find products of two binomials, little opportunity for understanding the process is evident. Use of the distributive property of multiplication over addition, even here, would give one rule that works for all polynomials. The major tragedy is that many students who learn to FOIL with limited understanding then proceed to apply this special case to polynomials, not just binomials.

If the idea of the distributive property of multiplication over addition on the set of real numbers was developed during exposures to the products of monomials with polynomials, then that idea can be extended to the product of two polynomials. Manipulatives can be used, but again, the complexities of being able to physically represent some products concretely arise; however, developmental work can be established. Furthermore, if the students grasped the abstractions involved when finding the product of a monomial and a polynomial, it is possible that they will not need additional concrete exposure at this point. If they do, careful selection of problems can provide limited concrete exposure that should lift students over the obstacles they are experiencing.

Consider the product of two binomials $(X + 3)(2X + 4)$. It should be noted that all the signs are positive in this example. Negatives need to be considered, but, because of the potential difficulties involved in multiplication of signed values, it is advisable to avoid them in initial explanations. Once the students begin to understand the situation, complexities like those involved with multiplying by negative values can be inserted. If the distributive property of multiplication over addition on the real numbers was used earlier, then the problem can be expressed as $X(2X + 4)$ and $+ 3(2X + 4)$ or $(X + 3)(2X)$ and $(X + 3)(4)$. Note that $+ 3(2X + 4)$ is purposely used here with the intent of showing continuity and laying groundwork for negative factors. Initially it is important to maintain order and use the commutative property of multiplication on the set of real numbers to change things if desired. Once this becomes a student's reflex behavior, the formality can be de-emphasized. When the problem $(X + 3)(2X + 4)$ is converted to $X(2X + 4)$ and $+ 3(2X + 4)$ or $(X + 3)(2X)$ and $(X + 3)(4)$, reference can be made to prior work and the results compiled accordingly. If this relation is clearly made, then factoring of trinomials becomes an easier concept to grasp. The concrete exposures can be inserted as necessary. However, the students should see the similarities and proceed, because a thorough understanding at this point will only increase conceptual development later. The distributive property approach to the product of two binomials explains why FOIL works and provides a vehicle to be used when dealing with the products of polynomials with more than two terms.

Topics to Help Visualize Factoring

The algebra student will have been exposed to factoring in previous classes. There is a good possibility that they will have forgotten, and the following lesson can help them overcome that memory lapse. At the same time, the lesson can be used to establish a basis for visualization of factoring. Any time factoring is done, essentially the area of a rectangle is given and the task is to determine the dimensions. This can be established as a part of the introductory review. In the sample teacher questions that follow, it is assumed that the teacher would display appropriate enthusiasm and excitement as the described discussion develops. Furthermore, it is assumed that questions would be altered to meet the needs of a class and to probe for the desired responses. The major message is that phrasing the question is important to enhance student understanding. The following shows where the prior exposure occurred and how to build on that information to deal with an algebraic setting.

Question: When multiplying, what names are given to the numbers?

Probable response: Numbers.

Better question: When multiplying, what are numbers called?

Probable response: Factors and product.

Question: Where is multiplication used in geometry?

Probable response: Finding area. Each time two numbers are multiplied, you are finding the area of a rectangle. When dividing, you are given the area of a rectangle and one dimension.

Question: What, then, is the task in division?

Student: To find the other dimension of the rectangle.

Teacher: What are other names for the length, width, and area?

Student: Factor, factor, and product.

Teacher: So if you have a product, what does it represent?

Student: The area of some rectangle.

Teacher: What else can you determine if you have the product or area of a rectangle?

Student: Its dimensions.

Teacher: Those ideas of dimensions and areas are used in algebra, too. We used that idea when we found the product of two binomials. Each factor was a dimension and the product was the "area" of a rectangle.

Teacher: You each have a set of manipulatives. If I had an X^2, two Xs and a unit, can I build a rectangle?

Student: I can build a square, but all squares are rectangles.

Note: At this point more examples would be given and the homework assignment should have the students using given sets of pieces to build rectangles. At this stage of their development, no mention is made of the rectangle's dimensions and all examples will result in a rectangle. For example, make a rectangle from two X^2s, three Xs and two units; two X^2s, five Xs and three 1s; and so on. Each time, the student is to sketch the solution using representations of the manipulatives.

The next lesson would begin by discussing the figures formed out of the given pictures, with students showing their sketches.

Teacher: Look at the picture made from two X2s, five Xs and three ones. What shape is the figure?

Student: Rectangle.

Teacher: What is the area of the rectangle?

Student: 2X2 + 5X + 3

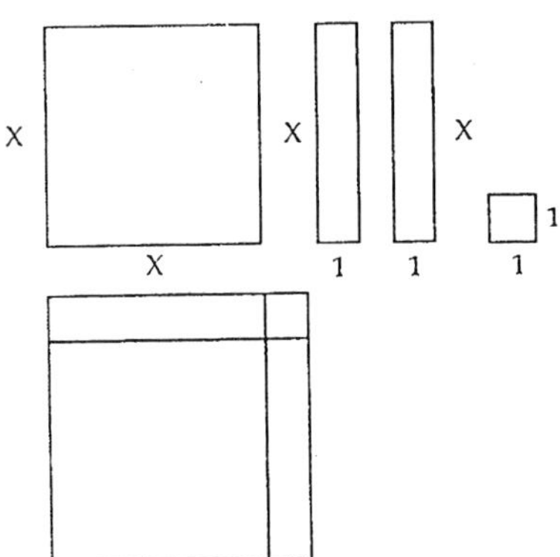

Fig. 6.2. Created with Geometer's Sketchpad

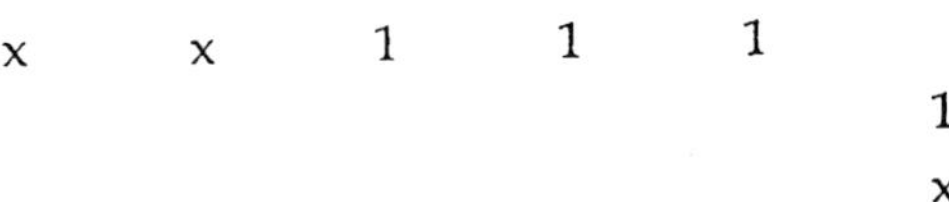

Fig. 6.3. Created with Geometer's Sketchpad

Teacher: How did you determine 2X2 + 5X + 3 is the area?

Teacher: What are the dimensions of the rectangle?

Student: $2X + 3$ long and $X + 1$ high.

Note: Replicate as necessary. Emphasize the idea that the area is derived by looking at the dimensions of the rectangle. Those dimensions become the factors of the product.

Teacher: Think back to your basic multiplication. Is there more than one set of dimensions for the area of a rectangle?

Student: Maybe. For prime numbers the answer is no, but for composite numbers the answer is yes. For example, if the area is 12, the dimensions could be 1 by 12, 2 by 6, or 3 by 4.

Teacher: So a product might have more than one set of factors?

Student: Yes.

Teacher: Do you suppose that would be true with the algebraic expressions we have been dealing with?

At this point the students would be assigned the task of determining if different sets of manipulatives could be arranged in more than one way, indicating whether or not there is more than one set of factors for a given product. The ensuing discussion would focus on the process and the algebraic name of factoring. The preceding vignette shows a series of questions, answers, and activities that can be constructed to assist students in creating mental images of the tasks they are asked to perform. One student who was very resistant to using the manipulatives because they were "baby stuff" responded at the end of this string of lessons, "Oh, I get it! Every time I factor something, I get a picture of the rectangle in my head and look for the dimensions. That's easy!" That reaction is exactly what is desired. From then on, factoring should take on a different meaning for the student.

Reconsider Usiskin's discussion about deleting instruction time involved in teaching students subtle differences in factoring trinomials. Even though many agree with Usiskin, the hard fact remains that most texts, tests, and curricula still adhere to the practice of extensive coverage of trinomial factoring. Generally, the description begins with a review of the process involved in finding the product of two binomials. This review provides connection to prior learning, refreshes basics, and establishes a beginning point for factoring.

Drill in First-year Algebra

There is a need for some drill. The question becomes how much. The number of different answers to this question can be astounding. Some will insist on lists of problems to assure mastery of even the smallest nuances. Others will say that as long as the student "really understands" the concept, there is little need for drill, because the students have mastered the process. Many adopt the middle-of-the road approach. One important factor is for you to arrive at your own conclusions about how much drill and practice is necessary. If you establish your position based on what someone else has said, the position presented in this text, the number of problems available in your textbook series, or what you had to do when you took first-year algebra, you are not doing what you need to do. You should listen to the authorities you come in contact with, read articles from the professional literature, discuss ideas with your peers and colleagues, and then reflect. Based on such exposures, you establish your position which, by the way, should be open to change as influenced by your experiences. Do not forget, students will influence you and your decisions also.

Drill and practice can be made more enjoyable than it often is. Many number tricks have an algebraic base. For example, do the following problem and record the amount of time it takes you to get the answer.

$$\frac{1234567890}{(1234567891)^2-(1234567890)(1234567892)}$$

If you did this by performing the operations, even with technology, there is a quicker way. Algebraically, the problem is

$$\frac{X}{(X+1)^2-(X)(X+2)}$$

Simplifying the denominator gives X2 + 2X+ 1 - (X2 + 2X) = X2 + 2X + 1 - X2 - 2X, which is 1. The solution is the numerator of the original problem, 1234567890. Certainly, there is nothing wrong with doing the problem via the arithmetic route. However, as students become accustomed to thinking algebraically, the potential increases that they will get used to using their newfound skills and knowledge as they approach different environments. Students can easily be convinced of the need to "think" algebra when confronted with problems like the one used here and other "Pick a number" tricks.

Drill can also be developed in the game format. A commercially available game, Winning Touch, provides a setting for practicing arithmetic facts. Winning Touch can be altered to entice algebraic practice. Make two game boards that are the same size and shape: One will be left blank and the other will be cut apart to form the playing pieces. The game board is rectangular, made up of a series of unit squares. For this example the operation will be multiplication, but that could be changed. The top row and left column show the factors for each row and column. In the game, the products are placed on the respective cells of the game board. The factors (top row and left column) are discarded. The playing pieces are placed face down on the table. Each participant draws the same number of pieces (five, for example, so that not all the pieces are taken). The first person to correctly place all pieces under the rules of the game is the winner.

The first player puts a piece on its correct square of the board. No new piece is drawn to replace that one. The object of the game is to play all the pieces. Moving clockwise around the board, the next individual must place a piece so it touches an occupied square on one of its horizontal or vertical edges. Inability to place a piece results in a loss of turn, drawing an additional piece to play, or continuing to draw pieces until a play can be made. The disadvantage of drawing additional pieces quickly becomes apparent. The decision to allow diagonal touches becomes yours.

Technology affords a multitude of opportunities for drill and practice. There is software available that essentially turns the computer into a glorified copy machine. In this mode, problem after problem is given to the student to work. For all practical purposes, the computer becomes an extension of the textbook in that a long list of problems is given to the student to practice. This appears to be a gross misuse of the power of the computer, and yet it is a popular mode because many students are enamored with the use of a computer. The computer becomes an avenue in which the student wants to practice algebra skills.

Technology In First-year Algebra

There are ways in which technology can be used for practice. A caution about technology first: Students must become aware of the fact that technology is only as good as the person using it. That is, an answer should not be accepted just because it was derived using technology. Estimation skills and reasonableness of the response are an integral part of the setting. Certainly, a graphing calculator or software could be available that would afford any student the opportunity to determine if an idea for the sketch of a graph is correct. However, it is possible that errors used to arrive at an answer can be carded into the technology. For example, suppose the task is to graph all values greater than 2x + 3. Typically the student is taught to graph the equation and then select a point to determine the region to fill. If the student does this problem on a graphing calculator, with most pieces of software, that same selection process could be used and thus the same region filled. If the student understands and uses the process correctly, all is well. If somehow the student fills the wrong side of the equation, all is not well. A skill that students should possess is estimation of values. Technology affords the opportunity to check the accuracy of those estimates. The use of a calculator to reinforce the concepts of exponents is an example. Does 32 = 23? Students can test their hypothesis easily without the aid of a calculator, but does $8^9 = 9^8$? Are 9 factors of 8 equivalent to 8 factors of 9? The assistance of a calculator can help students develop a conceptual understanding of exponents quickly and easily.

Solving two equations in two unknowns is a typical activity found in first-year algebra courses. Most of the time, the first approach is graphing solutions, followed by substitution, addition/ subtraction, and multiplication/division. Many text series devote an entire chapter, or at least several sections, to the treatment of these concepts, which means several days of instruction. Technology offers an alternative.

The graphing window can be enlarged or zoomed-in on to inspect the point of intersection more closely. For the sake of this discussion it is assumed that the two equations have a unique solution. It is further assumed that there is a projection device available for teacher demonstrations, a lab of computers with appropriate software for student use during the class, and that the students are familiar with the software so they can use it as an investigation/learning tool. For this discussion, assume the students did not have access to graphing calculators and, thus, equations were either graphed with the software or, for homework, with paper and pencil.

The following is a description of a few lessons dealing with solving two equations in two unknowns. The first demonstration dealt with graphing two equations and determining the point of intersection by zooming, tracing, and inspection using software. For homework the students were to graph pairs of equations and determine the coordinates of the point of intersection. Their results were to be sketched on paper for the next class.

One frequent question about using software to teach mathematics is whether or not the material being covered transfers to paper/pencil tasks because they are still the dominant mode used in testing settings. The answer is a resounding "yes." In the class following the homework of sketching graphs of intersecting linear equations, the students were presented with the graphs of two intersecting lines ($y = x + 3$ and $y = {}^{-}x + 7$) on the viewing screen and asked to determine the point of intersection. By inspection, they determined that the common point had coordinates (2, 5). The class was ready to proceed to the next topic.

The software permitted storage and recall of equations. The first equation, $y = x + 3$, had been stored in compartment A and $y = {}^{-}x + 7$ was placed in B. Investigating the impact of operating on the stored equations led to a discovery. We looked at A + B, which gave "$y = x + 3 + y = {}^{-}x + 7$." Simplifying gave "$y + y = x + 3 - x + 7$," leading to the observation that all the ys were on the left and all the xs and constants were on the right. Another simplification resulted in "$2y = 10$" and one student said that because that was one equation in one unknown, the y value would be 5. As this statement was being made, several students vocalized that this was the same as the y value obtained when graphing that pair of equations. A summary of what had transpired followed, and the class went to the computer lab to work with a group of equations (all coefficients of variables were positive or negative one) that had been stored. Their task was to experiment and arrive at some conclusions. They could add or subtract the stored equations, dealing with two at a time. The ensuing discussion focused on realizations like:

- Adding two equations where the respective signs of the variables were the same resulted in one equation in two unknowns.
- Subtracting two equations where the respective signs of the variables were the same resulted in a nonsense situation like $0 = 6$.
- When the signs of the respective variables were opposite and the equations were added, something like $0 = 6$ appeared.
- If the signs of the respective variables were opposite and the two equations were subtracted, one equation in two unknowns appeared.
- If one of the variables had the same sign and the other had opposite signs, either addition or subtraction would yield an equation in one unknown, which could then be solved.

Once the solution was determined, it could then be substituted into one of the original equations, and that situation solved for the value of the other unknown. After a short discussion of their perceptions, the class appeared to have a solid grasp of the general impact of adding and subtracting equations. At this point the students were asked how they would deal with a situation like "$y = x + 3$" and "$2y = 3x + 4$." Comments were quick and incisive, particularly considering that they had just done addition and subtraction. The basic statements made by the class were:

- It won't do any good to add or subtract them because you will get one equation in two unknowns.
- If we had $2y$ we could subtract.
- That means we have to multiply that one equation.
- Yes, but don't forget to multiply both sides.
- Then we can subtract one equation from the other and get one equation in one unknown.
- Maybe we should multiply by a negative 2 because we make fewer sign mistakes when adding as opposed to subtracting.

At this point, the class was sent back to stored equations on the computers. These equations had integral coefficients. In a short time the class defined most of the rules for multiplication, division, and substitution as a means for solving two equations in two unknowns.

All of the activities described since the review of solving two equations in two unknowns were completed in less than an hour. The students were able to transfer their computer work to paper-and-pencil assignments and complete them satisfactorily. Their retention was good. They were able to apply the knowledge throughout the rest of the class. Most important, what often takes several weeks to accomplish in a typical classroom setting that does not use technology as a teaching/learning tool was completed in a few hours, and the students' attitude about solving two equations was positive.

In the preceding discussion about solving two equations in two unknowns, technology was used as a discovery tool. There is ample opportunity for students to discover basic concepts with technology. Consider learning about the impact of changing the coefficient of x in a linear equation written in slope intercept form. Traditionally, the teacher leads a discussion that guides students to the appropriate conclusions. During the course of that discussion, different equations will be sketched with varying degrees of precision. That same lesson delivered with technology can be much more dynamic, assuming the teacher is working with a projected image of a linear equation. For the sake of this discussion, it is assumed that the class is familiar with the use of technology by the teacher. Thus, it is safe to assume they will ask what happens if the 2 in $y = 2x + 3$ is changed to 4. Then, what happens if the 4 in $y = 4x + 3$ is changed to $^{-}5$. And so forth. It does not take long for the students to conclude that as the coefficient of x increases, the line gets steeper. They have just described the concept of slope and the definition could now easily be formalized. Certainly, this could be done without technology, but the speed, precision, spontaneity, and flexibility would be lacking.

It is possible that some student would want to change the constant. Careful discussion on the part of the teacher can lead to a delay of that idea until the slope exchange is completed. Eventually both the slope and the constant would be changed, but at that point the students should be adept at predicting the impact on the graph of the equation as either is altered. The advantage of technology is that it assists the students in creating mental images of what is happening. This, in turn, strengthens their understandings and provides stronger foundations for future work. Equally significant is that the students become willing to ask "What if" questions, something that will be invaluable in helping the student become self-motivated lifelong learners.

The Casio CFX-9850G has the ability to do dynamic graphing. An equation like $y = Ax + B$ can be used where B remains constant and the value of A, which is the slope, can change across some defined range at some interval. When in operation, the calculator will display a collection of lines, one of which is highlighted. The calculator will automatically step to the next line and equation, or it can be done manually. A few examples using this technology will benefit students as they attempt to understand the concept of slope.

An inequality such as $y * 2x + 3$ is typically graphed by shading the region below the graph of the linear equation $y = 2x + 3$, showing all values that satisfy the inequality. If more than one inequality is graphed on the same axis system, different shading routines are used for each, and the common solution area is shown as a combination of the different shadings. This is difficult to do with technology, because there is no way to show the different colors on top of each other. However there is an easy and useful way around the dilemma. When graphing, color/shade the side that does not satisfy the inequality. When doing more than one inequality on the same axis system, the background screen color will show the region that satisfies all graphed inequalities. A natural extension and application of this idea is found in linear programming. By coloring the region that does not satisfy the inequalities, the resulting polygon of solutions will surround a region in the background color. We are moving into a more technological teaching world. We need to be able to deal with the graphing of inequalities. This linear programming discussion points out the need for an alteration of the curriculum as it is currently delivered—rather than texts and teachers emphasizing the shading of the regions that do satisfy an inequality, the accent should be on coloring non-solution areas. This is merely another impact of technology on the secondary mathematics curriculum.

One advantage to integrating the mathematics curriculum with other subject areas is that students have the opportunity to see the information they are learning used in a different setting. It is possible that one of the subjects selected will be an area of interest for them, so the process might have a positive impact on their mathematics attitude. One excellent opportunity to integrate mathematics and science is through the use of probes that can be used to gather data. The following activities describe one possible use of the probes.

Using the distance sensor, a series of activities can be used to build the concept of the slope of a line. Students often deal in a world of absolutes. That is, they are confident they can stand perfectly still. Have a student stand in front of the distance probe assigned with the task of standing "perfectly" still for a few seconds while their distance from the probe is measured. As the experiment is conducted, a horizontal (or so it seems) line appears on the screen. Magnification of the graph shows that it is not a horizontal line but may vary by as much as 5 centimeters . The students are amazed about this but soon come to realize that they do make small movements, their clothing will move because of breezes in the room, they will make slight reflexive body movements because of heartbeat or breathing, and so forth. After this discussion, the screen is re-scaled so the small variations are not evident.

Next, a student is asked to walk at a constant rate away from the probe. It usually takes a few tries before a relatively straight line is established. This line will be used as a reference as another student is asked to walk, making a line parallel to the one on the screen. Even though they may not be able to formally express it, most middle-school students know the meaning of parallel. As this is attempted, comments from the kibitzers in the class will encourage the walker to go faster or slower. The comments begin the understanding of slope. The term slope will probably not be used, but comparative statements like one line is steeper than the other will be common. This is the beginning, and the class can be guided to a formal definition of slope from here. This discussion can be extended to the difference between parallel lines. Proper calibration of the software can have the lines intersecting the y-axis at different points and yet the lines will be parallel. Prior to this activity, the students learned about the slope intercept form of the line. Here, or at any point in the discussion, the mathematical characteristics could be discussed in the detail necessary to accomplish the objectives of the lesson.

One extension of the line walking activity can stimulate some interesting and informative conversation and learning. A line is established, and a student is assigned the task of walking a line perpendicular to it. Before long the class will determine that the student needs to walk toward the probe if the initial line was established by walking away from the probe. In most instances the same walking rate will not work. Once a line that appears perpendicular is walked, the equations of the two can be investigated. Repetition of the experiment a few times should lead to equation pairs that have slopes that are close to being multiplicative inverses of each other and their signs will be opposite. Out of that, the class can determine the definition of slopes of perpendicular lines. At this point, they need to revisit standing still in front of the probe. After a horizontal line is established, ask if it is possible to walk a vertical line. Attempts at acting this out in front of the probe can become quite lively. Students will jump, duck, move their hands as fast as they can, group together and move quickly, place several books in front of the probe, each held by a different student, move the books quickly out of range, and so on. These attempts will not result in a vertical line. However, the students are honing in on the idea that they must move instantaneously if they are to walk a vertical line. Soon they will conclude that it is impossible for them to be transported from one location in front of the probe to another without some change in time. Thus, it becomes impossible to walk a line perpendicular to horizontal, and the concept of an undefined slope for a vertical line is established.

Applications of Algebra

Research shows that activities can have a positive impact on the attitudes of students. Questions like "When will I ever use this?" are common. A likely translation of questions such as that is, "Where can I find an application of this concept in my world today?" It is imperative that the world be viewed from the perspective of a secondary student at this point, not from the perspective of an adult trying to convince the student to accept what is being given. There are situations that show algebra basics being used in the real world, as demonstrated by the following dialogue between a student and a tutor, which lead to an activity called *"Speed Trap"*.

Student: Why do I need to put in steps when solving something like $2x = 6$? Everybody knows the answer is 3.

Teacher: True, but you are learning a process. What if you had something like 14.5267y = 53. 79825? You wouldn't know the answer to that one. You learn the process in 2x = 6 so you can solve things like this.

Student: OK, but where would you get something like that?

Teacher: Let's talk about law enforcement officers catching speeders. Modern technology allows a car to be timed as it travels a known distance. If the cargoes through the distance too fast, the driver is exceeding the posted speed limit and, more than likely, that driver is going to have an opportunity to meet a representative of a police unit. We will go to a local road and establish a speed trap like to see the equations that are generated.

A variety of other things will need to be done to complete this activity. They include: Measure a reasonable distance, marking the beginning and end to establish the speed trap (100 yards provides enough time lapse to decrease the impact of many time measurement errors) Calculate the minimum legal time to cover the trap distance. Establish the car part used to indicate entrance and exit of the trap (the front bumper does fine).Determine how entrance and exit will be signaled to the timer (raising and lowering hands will work).Station an individual at each end of the speed trap so the timer can see both of them. Clock cars going through the trap. Knowledge of speeders will be immediately evident from the recorded time. At this point, the students need to determine how much over the legal speed the car was traveling. In order to answer this question, the students need to compute the speed using the known time and distance. They are now solving equations that they will not reflexively know the answer to. In the process, they have also seen an application of the concept being discussed in class.

Algebra in Patterning Situations

Gauss' discovery of a fast way to find the sum of consecutive counting numbers was discussed. The description shows how Gauss used a pattern to arrive at a solution and, ultimately, that pattern was extended to express a generalization. Most generalizations are going to require algebraic skills and notations in their final expressions. One such example involves the idea of being paid a penny on the first day, two cents on the second, and each subsequent day finds the pay to be double that of the preceding day. Typically, the discussion focuses on how much money is earned on any given day, and that is often generalized because of the pattern.

Day	*Pay for day*	*TOTAL pay*
1	1	1
2	2	3
3	4	7
4	8	15
5	16	31
N	2^{N-1}	$2^{N}-1$

However, another generalization can be derived from the problem. If the pay was doubled for each of 30 days, starting with a penny on the first day, the pay for the 30th day would be $5,638,709.12 and the total payment for all 30 days would be $10,737,418.23. Without the assistance of patterning and algebraic skills, the solution to the question would be difficult to obtain (but not impossible). The idea of patterning and some basic algebra, coupled with the power of technology, puts a problem such as this within the reach of a wide selection of students. Number theory relies on patterns that frequently can be generalized, calling in the use of algebra. These equations offer a plethora of pattern and algebraic opportunities. The students need to have had experience investigating such information and to have learned the power of being able to generalize. There is a need to have an attitude of inquisitiveness about how and why numbers react to give patterns. This attitude comes essentially from exposure, and it largely becomes the responsibility of the teacher to ensure that activities or questions such as these are inserted into the curriculum as often as possible. In this instance several observations are possible. The first equation uses the first three counting numbers. The second equation uses the next five counting numbers, the next seven, and so on. Each equation begins with a perfect square, which makes sense if the students have been exposed to the task of finding the sum of consecutive odd counting numbers beginning with 1. ($1 + 3 = 4$; $4 + 5 = 9$[where $4 = 1 + 3$]; $9 + 7 = 16$ [where $9 = 4 + 5$ and $4 = 1 + 3$]; and so on.) Even beginners to patterning will soon notice that the first addend in each equation is a perfect square, algebraically expressed as N2 where N represents the row number. A little prompting should lead to the conclusion that there are N addends on the left of the equal sign and N - 1 to the right. Given that information, a student should be able to describe any row.

The Role of Algebra In Proof

Most nongeometric proofs rely heavily on algebraic skills. The concept has roots in beginning patterns, perhaps as simple as getting the next counting number. Young children often get to the next counting number in their exposures by adding one more object to a set of elements that comprise the number they just learned. That is, once a child masters "fourness" (four objects can be recognized in any configuration), five is presented. Often the presentation involves showing a set of five things, which is discussed and manipulated until "fiveness" becomes a part of the world of that child. The concept builds on the idea of one more than the last, and even though it is not expressed algebraically, the foundations are there. We would say that is just "X + 1" where X represents the last number the child mastered.

As students progress through their learning exposures in mathematics, the complexities of the settings increase and the concept of proof begins to evolve. Young children see a set of three objects and a set of two objects placed together to form a set of five objects. They take the same sets of two and three and get five. The reversal of cardinalities is significant because eventually the setting is summarized into problem pairs of 2 + 3 = ? and 3 + 2 = ?. At this point, the child gets an initial exposure to the commutative property of addition on the set of counting numbers. Eventually that becomes generalized to the commutative property of addition on some given set like the real numbers expressed as A + B = B + A. These formative abstractions are important proof building blocks.

Once the abstractions are started, more formalized expressions of proof become possible. The ability to represent things in algebraic terms is helpful at this stage of development. For example, students might conclude that the pattern will generate a list of perfect squares, which could be generalized algebraically, leading to the need for algebraic capabilities. This then becomes the beginnings of proof.

At the appropriate level, the information can be expressed by the statement "The sum of the first *N* consecutive odd counting numbers is N^2." One nice advantage to this pattern is that it can be shown concretely.

$1 = 1$

$1 + 3 = 4$

$1 + 3 + 5 = 9$

$1 + 3 + 5 + 7 = 16$

Etc.

Pairing this generalization with that from the discussion about Gauss' generalization of the sum of the first *N* consecutive counting numbers to be leads to a wonderful opportunity for a generalization that turns out to be false. We have:

N^2 = the sum of the first *N* consecutive odd counting numbers

It would seem reasonable that would yield the sum of the first *N* consecutive even counting numbers. Assuming that and simplifying, which is negative and cannot possibly represent the sum of the first *N* even counting numbers. Many algebra texts contain a "proof" that 2 = 1. It is presented here to show you another example of the need to convince students to pay close attention to each step and detail in a proof.

Let A = B	A and B are any real numbers
$A^2 = AB$	Multiply bothsides of equation by same value
$A^2 - B^2 = AB - B^2$	Subtract same value from both sides of equation
	Divide both sides by the same value
A + B = B	Result after division
B + B = B	Substituting A for because A = B
B = B	Addition
2 = 1	Dividing both sides by same value

This result contradicts what is known to be true and yet students often take a long time to recognize that because A = B, they cannot perform the step involving dividing by A - B.

Number tricks offer a wonderful opportunity to lead students into the world of algebraic proof. Suppose 9 and 5 are two of the three digits in a three-digit number. You are to find a third digit so that an addition equation can be formed where both addends and the sum are permutations of the same three-digit number comprised of 9, 5, and the third digit you find. This problem could be solved using guess-and-check routines, which some teachers use to generate the need for proof expressed at an abstract level. However, an algebraic approach shows some advantages. Let N be the third digit used to make the three-digit numbers to solve this problem. The six possible combinations that can occur are $95N$, $9N5$, $59N$, $5N9$, $N95$, and $N59$. Neither of the numbers with 9 in the hundreds place can be an addend because that would force regrouping so the sum would be a four digit number. Assume that the sum must begin with 9. Assume one of the addends begins with 5. $9N5 - 59N$ is one possibility for the other addend. Expanding gives

$$900 + 10N + 5 - (500 + 90 + N)$$
$$=100N + 50 + 9$$
$$400 + 9N - 85 = 100N + 50 + 9$$
$$91N = 256$$
$$N = 2.813 \text{ (not digit)}$$

Another possibility would be

$$95N - N59 = N95$$
$$900 + 50 + N - (100N + 50 + 9)$$
$$= 100N + 90 + 5$$
$$950 - 99N - 59 = 100N + 90 + 5$$
$$796 = 199N$$
$$4 = N$$

Is this solution unique? This seems to be a reasonable question that the power of algebra can be used to answer. Another example of the power of algebra in answering why something works (or proving it) can be shown by investigating a different algorithm for multiplication when the ones digits of the two factors sum to 10 and all other digits of the two factors are duplicated (143×147 or 52×58). Find the product of the ones digits. That product becomes the ones and tens digit in the answer. In 52 × 58 it would be 16 because of 2 × 8. Call all of the digits to the left of the ones digit Z. Note that in each example the value to the left of the ones digit is the same. Multiplying Z and Z + 1 will provide the rest of the answer. In 143 × 147, that would become 14 × 15. This product is placed to the left of the product of the ones digits. To show why this works, let 10A + B be the first factor and 10A + (10 - B) be the second.

$$(10A + B)(10A + (10 - B)) = 100A^2 + 100A - 10AB + 10AB + B(10 - B)$$
$$= 100(A^2 + A) + B(10 - B)$$

The number of opportunities to employ algebra as an investigation tool in proof is ample enough that, with a little energy on your part, each student can be shown the power of this branch of mathematics.

Word Problems in Algebra

Word problems are an integral part of mathematics in general and first-year algebra in particular. Students need to deal with word problems as they begin working with real-world applications of the concepts they are studying in mathematics. The word problems they encounter need to be from their perspective, not from that of an adult. The word problems should appeal to a student, and it is not always sufficient to assume that the text problems will hold sufficient attraction for the students. In fact, in many instances, the text problems hold little appeal for students. One research study analyzed word problems, looking in particular at the context used for the problem along with the mathematical model used, if any. The conclusion was that algebra text problems provide little value as far as convincing students of the usefulness of mathematics. These conclusions were very similar to a study done in 1924. It seems ironic that word problems changed little over 45 years with both studies showing little appeal to students. How can we justify continuing in the same mode?

Frequently textbook word problems are grouped by problem type. That is, a section in a book will deal with rate, percent, mixture, or age problems. In the respective sections, the problem type is considered almost exclusively. Generally they apply some newly studied principle. It is common for a section of mixture problems to follow exposure to a study of percents in first-year algebra. The mixture problems will deal with applications from the real word of chemistry and industry where solutions of a mixture are given and the desire is to change the content of one ingredient. Often a procedure is established for the student to follow as the problem is worked. These procedures are beneficial to completing the assigned task of doing a mixture problem, but are they damaging in that the student is almost programmed to follow a routine. The reinforcement comes because the assigned problems are built around teaching the student the routine with, perhaps, some subtle alterations. Procedures and organization such as this lead to some difficulties for some students. Essentially, they become specialists in a given problem type for the time it is being studied. After the test is given, another problem type may be discussed and developed. After a few days of dealing with the second problem type, the first is forgotten. Thus, the way we approach word problems can handicap students as they attempt to apply their mathematical skills in real-world settings.

7

GEOMETRY

Introduction

- Theory of how students learn geometry
- Geometry history in our mathematics curriculum
- Geometry located throughout the preK-12 curriculum
- Specific topics from the geometry curriculum
- Attract students' attention with unusual measurement

It is not enough for a child to have mathematical knowledge. They must have Mathematical Power *to succeed.* Mathematical power *is the ability to feel* comfortable *in using mathematical knowledge to solve problems, to use mathematics in the real world, and to be willing to "try" and not feel afraid to fail. It is programs like Geometers Sketchpad that help students transcend the gulf between mathematical knowledge and power.*

Programs like this also give "teacher power." Teacher power *is the ability for the teacher to provide opportunities for students to learn regardless of the student's stage of learning, the number of computers in the room, or teaching style. Adaptable to your teaching style, Geometer's Sketchpad can be used in a geometry lesson presented as teacher or student-centered, individually or as a group, or as a lecture or lab. Geometry can even be presented in an algebraic or axiomatic orientation. This latitude provides you, the teacher, the power to help students learn.*

Where have we come in the past few years as far as the teaching of geometry? Consider teaching about the medians of a triangle and the idea that they are all concurrent. Not too many years ago, teachers had only chalkboards, chalk, board compasses, and straightedges to work with. Usually, for the sake of time, figures were drawn freehand on the board and used as the focus of discussion. Often the productions were sufficient, but many times the sketches were inaccurate and statements to the class like, "Well, you know what I mean" were common. Figure 7.1 gives an example of how that statement was used.

In Fig. 7.1 , triangle ABC is constructed with side midpoints F, E, and D. In most instances the triangle itself and two of the three medians (AE and CF in this case) were rather quickly produced without much difficulty. In Fig. 7.1 , AE and CF intersect at J. Often, when the teacher went to draw in median BD, inaccuracies developed when trying to align the three points B, J, and D on a straight segment. Frequently J would not lie on BD and so some maneuver like the one shown here, or a curve in the "median," was drawn to have it pass through J. It was at that point that the infamous "Well, you know what I mean" was uttered. Surely most students knew "what was meant," but some did not and yet said nothing. It cannot be assumed that all students understand what is going on in the class. Is it reasonable to wonder whether "Well, you know what I mean" had a negative impact on the understanding of geometry?

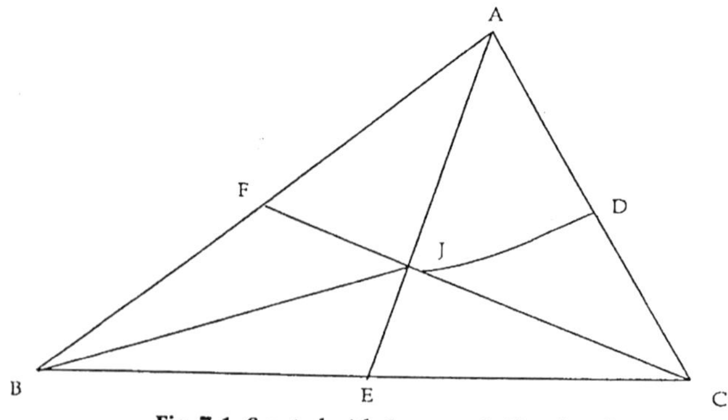

Fig. 7.1. Created with Geometer's Sketchpad

The dilemma could be resolved by taking care to construct the figure. Even then, however, minor details like chalk thickness could alter results enough that a little "fudging" might be necessary in order to have all three medians concurrent. Perhaps the "midpoint" determining the third "median" would be moved to accommodate getting all three "medians" passing through the same point. Once again, it was time for the infamous "Well, you know what I mean." And, for the most part, the students did.

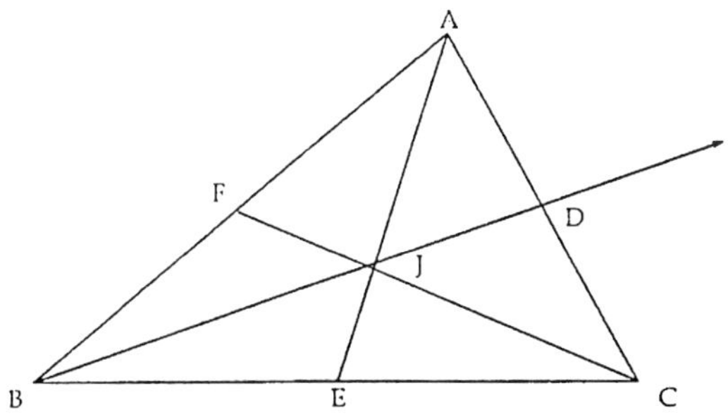

Fig. 7.2. Created with Geometer's Sketchpad

More recently teachers began using the overhead projector. A sketch of the medians of the triangle could be prepared ahead of time and put up for the class when needed. That provided a more accurate figure to work with, but the possibility of problems because of pen width still existed. Usually these discrepancies were not as dramatic as those in Fig. 7.2 , for example. There was a point of difficulty for some students with this method, however. Some students could not absorb all the information being presented by a picture that did not show the construction step by step. For them, seeing the setting constructed helped their understanding. When using overhead transparencies, a method of revealing information in a step-by-step process is to partially cover the transparency with a sheet of paper and expose the material as desired. That method works well with text, but it does not lend itself to constructing the medians of a triangle. That difficulty can be overcome by making a series of transparencies and then building the median figure one transparency at a time. Some people will tape them all together at the edges and then flip up the sheet as needed, which helps with alignment and, in the process, can avoid that "fudging" as shown in Figs. 7.1 and 7.2 . Even at that, the class sees a picture that deals with only one triangle. Many students are not convinced that this will be true for any triangle constructed. Even when we tell them it is so, some doubt. Rather recently, that objection has been removed.

In the late 1980s two innovative products, GeoDraw and Supposers (Sunburst), were introduced. Both of these pieces of software allowed for accurate median situations to be produced. With the advent of projection panels and large screen monitors, a class could observe a better representation of the sketch. These pieces of software permitted moving the triangle and, in the process, the medians stayed concurrent as is shown in Fig. 7.3 .

In the early 1990s Geometer's Sketchpad (Key Curriculum Press) and Cabri were introduced. These represent newer generation software. They combine chalk, board, overhead, and beginning software advances while taking advantage of the growth within the computer and software industries. The triangle median construction is easily done with these, and the figures can be dynamically altered in real time. When the sketch is altered, measurements change accordingly, and things like the ratio of BG:GD remain constant. Using this software shows a dynamic representation of the mathematics being developed. It is not possible to deliver the full impact of this situation in printed text. Seeing is believing. You should do this.

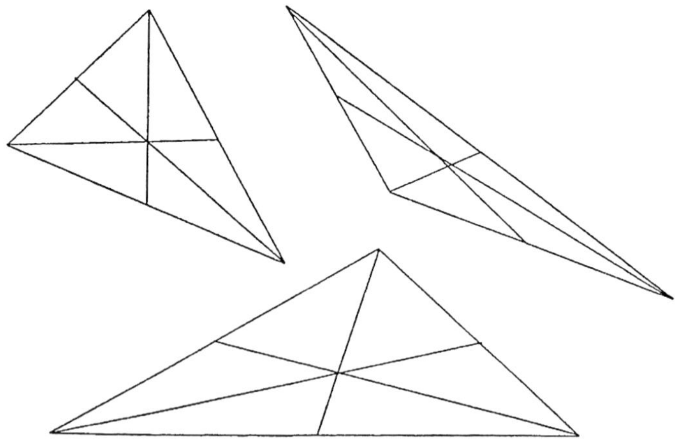

Fig. 7.3. Created with Geometer's Sketchpad

There is one problem with the description that has been presented in this chapter. Even with the technology that is available today, many teachers are still using the board to produce Figs. 7.1 and 7.2 . How can that be justified? Especially in light of positions presented by NCTM, which state that every teacher should have a computer, large viewing capabilities for a class, and appropriate software available for all classes at all times. After all, we do live in the technology age.

Research in Geometry Learning

Diane van Hiele-Geld of and her husband Pierre van Hiele both did doctoral dissertations in 1984 that dealt with students learning geometry. Both dissertations dealt with the van Hiele assessment tool, which consists of five levels: visualization, analysis, informal deduction, formal deduction, and rigor. The van Hieles contended that students can be moved from one category to another via appropriate experiences. Each of the five levels could be defined as follows, going from lowest to highest:

Visualization (level 0) – Students are aware of space. Geometric shapes are recognized holistically by their appearance without paying attention to component parts. Students functioning at this level can recognize geometric shapes and can reproduce them on request. These students recognize squares and rectangles, but do not realize the presence of right angles, opposite sides of the same length, and so forth.

Analysis (level 1): Students begin analysis of geometric concepts. Parts of geometric figures are recognized. Generally, definitions are repeated but not understood. Relations between properties are not explained. Students would be able to conclude that opposite angles of a parallelogram are congruent. They may not believe a figure can belong to more than one general class. For example, they might accept that a square is a quadrilateral, but they might resist the idea that that same square is also a parallelogram or rectangle, or both.

Informal deduction (level 2): Definitions now make sense. Informal arguments about why things are as they appear begin to be formulated. Students know there are relations between properties of a figure—for instance, if opposite sides of a quadrilateral are congruent and parallel, the figure must be a parallelogram. They also become aware of connections between groups of figures, like all squares are rectangles, but not all rectangles are squares. These students know there is a collection of rules and axioms, but they cannot put them together via deductive techniques yet. They can follow formal proofs, but the logic of connections is not fully understood. Changing the order of steps or doing a proof in different ways confuses them. These students are essentially unable to construct an original proof when starting with different material.

Formal deduction (level 3): Students understand the role of axioms, rules, terms, theorems, definitions, and how they are interwoven. The ability to construct, not just memorize, proofs emerges. Doing a proof more than one way is within the sphere of these students. This means they are ready to study geometry as a formal mathematical system. As a part of that study, they will be able to write formal proofs using "if — then" type logic.

Rigor (level 4): Abstractions are comprehended. Students can investigate and compare different geometry. An example would be taxi-cab geometry in which it is assumed a city is organized with all city blocks being unit squares. A cab is limited to driving on streets, assumed to have no width. As the taxi moves from point A to point B the distance covered is 2 units. If the cab could go off the roads, as is done in Euclidean geometry, the distance would be.

$$\sqrt{2}$$

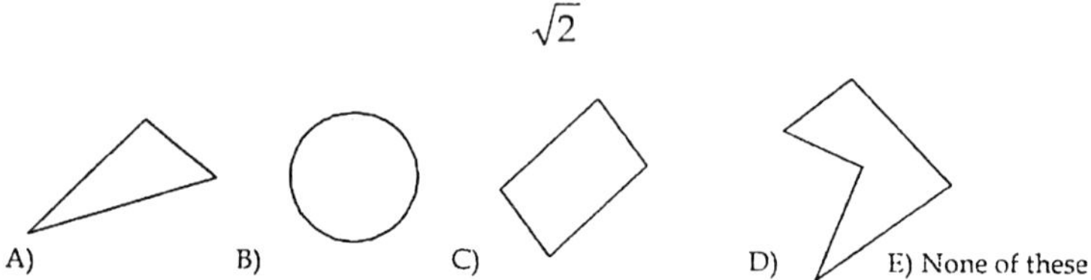

Fig. 7.4. Created with Geometer's Sketchpad

In Euclidean geometry, the locus of all points equidistant from a given point is a circle. In taxi-cab geometry, the locus of all points equidistant from a given point is a "square." If we could put alleys between the streets at the half unit mark, point K would also be 2 units from A (1.5, 0.5). Extending the alley idea one more level, point

L is also 2 units from A (1.75, 0.25). Continuing this process in the same manner will result in a "square" when the points are joined.

Geometry in The Elementary School

Before reading the next paragraph, please do the following. Take out a sheet of paper and draw a rectangle on it. After you have done that, read on. Remember, if you are going to be an effective teacher of mathematics, you need to walk the walk as well as talk the talk.

The amount of geometry covered in the elementary curriculum is considerable. Children come into school having been exposed to a variety of shapes and related geometric concepts. They have a feel for geometry and a formalization process begins for them. Starting at an early age, the formalization begins to create areas of confusion for students, often in a very subtle, frequently unrealized manner. For example, "standard position" of a figure usually means that one side of the figure is drawn parallel to the bottom of the board or page. Consider a rectangle. Most of the rectangles students are exposed to are in standard position. Teachers draw them that way. Books show them that way. In other subjects, as well as in mathematics, pictures and special ideas are often presented in rectangular shaped boxes that are in standard position. The number of students who select option (E) in this example is amazing. Do you have any idea about why they might select (E)?

Before reading on, look at the rectangle you drew earlier. Was it in standard position? Color the rectangle. There is no need for you to get out your crayons, just mark the rectangle in some manner that indicates it is colored. When you colored your rectangle, did you fill the inside? That is not the rectangle! That is the rectangular region. The rectangle is the set of line segments that comprise the border of the figure.

Compare the ratio of the long side length to the short for the rectangle you drew. Frequently the value is close to the golden section, which has a line segment, AB, giving x2 + x - 1 = 0. Solving for x yields 0.6180339. . ., the golden ratio, or golden section.

Some historians assert that the properties of the golden section aided the Pythagoreans in discovering irrational numbers, actually their geometric equivalents – incommensurable lines. It is certain, however, that since antiquity many philosophers, artists, and mathematicians have been intrigued by the golden section, which Renaissance writers called the divine proportion. It is widely accepted that a rectangle with sides in this ratio exhibits a special beauty.

All the preceding information about rectangles is important but needs to be considered for another reason. It is common for the university mathematics faculty member to say to the community college mathematics faculty member (in a much more polite manner and phrasing), "If you had taught them correctly, I would be able to do what I want with them mathematically. However, because they did not learn from you, I have to redo what you covered." In turn, the community college mathematics faculty member says a similar thing to high school teachers of mathematics. The high school teacher makes a similar statement to the middle-school teacher, who in turn puts the blame on the elementary teacher. In such a way, we absolve ourselves of ownership in the problem, placing all guilt at the feet of the elementary teacher. Secondary mathematics education majors would be well advised to take an elementary mathematics methods course. This course would provide insight into the teaching and learning of mathematics at a fundamental level while enhancing understanding of student learning processes. It is our objective for students to learn the subject well. The best way to accomplish that is to teach it well and correctly the first time. Thus, an argument can be made to put the strongest teachers of mathematics in settings where students are learning the basics of the subject. Then much repetition could be deleted and students will have the readiness skills needed to learn the higher level mathematics concepts we want them to.

The reason you were asked to draw and color a rectangle is to emphasize the problem faced in the teaching of mathematics at all levels. You have the advantage of having had several college mathematics courses. Yet you probably drew your rectangle in standard position and colored the interior. In so doing, you indicate a tendency to not be mathematically precise. If we, as teachers of mathematics, are not accurate, how can we expect our students to be?

With that background, consider geometry in the elementary school. Current elementary education majors have a much broader exposure to mathematics than did their predecessors. They often take a mathematics content course and a mathematics methods course designed for the teaching of elementary mathematics as a part of their program. In addition, most colleges are requiring students to take a college algebra or finite mathematics course as a graduation requirement. Many states require at least two and often three mathematics courses for high-school graduation. In the not too distant past, students were permitted to graduate from high school with one mathematics credit, and elementary education majors might not have even been required to take a mathematics methods course. Certainly, this had a negative impact on the mathematical learning of elementary students. With all the changes in our field over the past half century, it is unreasonable to expect elementary teachers with weak mathematical backgrounds to adequately prepare students mathematically to move on to the secondary level.

Even with all the changes in mathematical expectations for elementary education majors, the possibility of exposure to geometry is woefully lacking. Often, individuals intending to major in elementary education at the college level avoid mathematics classes in their secondary careers. Because they are required to generate a given number of credits, they often enroll in mathematics courses that are not as rigorous as those taken by some of their peers. In college, their mathematics course options, if required (college algebra or finite mathematics), generally do little with geometry. In their education courses, assuming both the elementary mathematics content and elementary methods are required, geometry is a topic for discussion. However, it frequently is one of those things that appears late in the course. As such, there is a good chance that it will not be covered as extensively as would be desirable, or perhaps even at all. Thus, the opportunity exists for an elementary education major to be graduated and certified with little geometric exposure other than what they had in elementary school. Then they are asked to teach new geometric concepts they have not been exposed to from a weak, old, background. How reasonable is this?

Yes, geometry is taught in the elementary school. Line segments, rays, lines, angles, shapes, perimeter, and area are integrated throughout the curriculum. Shapes appear in other subjects in the form of boxes to highlight information, pyramids or arrowheads in history, playing fields or areas in physical education, and so forth. Textbooks include a wide variety of exposures for the students. Once again, however, the topic may appear at the end of a year when it may get less than adequate coverage. The standards of a state for any given elementary grade level will list expectations about geometry. However, once again, they may appear late in the year.

Software exists that can be used to help students learn geometry. The beauty of software, particularly a piece that provides tutorials and the opportunity for "free play," is that the student has the opportunity to experiment and stimulate curiosity. Thankfully, producers like Key Curriculum Press and Texas Instruments are creating collections of ideas and applications appropriate for elementary students. This certainly should help, but only if the materials get into the hands of the students. That cycles back to the need for vertical communication so the elementary teachers have some idea of the expectations held for basic student knowledge of geometry by middle-school teachers mathematics series. List the major geometry topics covered, the grade level at which they are presented, and the number of times the students are exposed to each concept throughout the elementary curriculum.

Geometry Taught in The Middle School

Of course geometry is taught in the middle school. But what is taught and where or when? Geometry is scattered throughout the middle-school curriculum. There is no specific course, and as the trend moves toward integrated topics, even if the course exists, it would be destined to become blended into a set of topics covered over the middle-school years. Certainly, the topics broached in the elementary grades are revisited. Why? If the concepts were taught well, understood by the students, and so on, why would they be repeated in the middle school? One reason sometimes put forward is that we have always done it that way. That is not a good reason. If the students know the topic being covered, why go over it again? That only serves to stimulate their dislike of mathematics in general, and geometry in particular. At the same time, if the students do not know the necessary information, it is imperative that they be properly introduced to the topics. A delicate balance, isn't it? How do you learn what to do? For the most part, you need to be aware of your students, their needs, where they have been, and prior exposures. That coupled with the experience you will gain as you teach will provide you with guidance in your decision making.

So, what can be done in the middle school geometry class? Any topics introduced in the elementary curriculum can be extended in the middle school. Triangles, for example, can be revisited, this time looking at the measure of all angles, leading to the discovery that the sum of all interior angles of the triangle is 180°. That can be extended two ways. Investigations could focus on exterior angles and the sum of exterior angles of a triangle or extensions such as discussed in the discovery chapter can be investigated. The beauty of this is that geometry is blended with algebra, discovery, and generalization. The important thing is that you must be willing to investigate geometry. Too many times, teachers make the decision to bypass geometry because of the lack to time in the school year. The thought is that the students can live without geometry this year because they will get it next year! When does this stop? Geometry should not be an unfamiliar topic in the 10th grade.

Intuitive backgrounds can be established for a variety of topics. It shows a standard set of steps for showing that a parallelogram can be transformed to a rectangle, leading to the conclusion that the area of a parallelogram is base times height. This should, at the same time, establish a connection between two shapes and how to find area, and raise a question. Because the new figure looks like a rectangle, why don't we use length and width as elements of the formula for the area of a parallelogram? Or, reverse the wording and use base times height for the area of the rectangle? It may appear as no big concern for us because we know, but students now have two more vocabulary words to learn and are identifying the same thing by two different names, each of which is to be used in a given setting (length with rectangle and base with parallelogram). Does that make sense? Does it really matter? Could we be more consistent in our discussion with students?

$$\frac{(b_1 + b_2)}{2}(h)$$

This formula can be written in a variety of formats and, depending on the algebraic skills of the students, confusion can exist as teachers attempt to shift from one form of the formula to another. For this discussion, use the form shown here and state it as the average of the bases, times the height. Using that, look at finding the area for a rectangle, parallelogram, square, trapezoid, triangle, and circle. Even though the figures are not in standard position, you can see that the area for each of them can be found by taking the average of the bases times the height.

The rectangle and parallelogram transformations are relatively straightforward. For square, the area is usually given as $A = s^2$. Using that idea and the trapezoid formula of the average of the bases, the area of a square becomes:

$$\frac{(Side + Side)}{2}(Side) = \frac{2(Side)}{2}(Side) = (Side)^2 = S^2$$

The triangle seems a little confusing at first, but the lower base is the side to which the altitude is drawn. The upper base is the vertex, which is the top of the altitude, and has a length of zero. So for the triangle area, using the average of the bases,

$$A = \frac{(base + zero)}{2}(height) = \frac{base}{2}(height)$$

The circle area approached through this "one formula fits all" approach seems strange initially, and it does require some editorial liberty to discuss. We normally think of bases as being straight line segments. For this discussion, the base is a curved line segment, the length of which is one-fourth of the circumference of the circle. That is, for this example, arc AB = arc CD = 0.5*r. The diameter, or height in this case, will be 2r. Using the average of the bases formula, You might be saying, "Why didn't someone show me this before?" "Why don't we teach this method in the schools?" Those are legitimate questions that can be partially answered, but not totally. The easy part of the answer involves preparation to get to the level where a student understands the average of the bases formula.

Given that, it would be difficult for students to understand applying that formula to a variety of shapes. In addition, before applying the formula, areas of rectangles and parallelograms, at least, have to be considered. Once those are done, some would question the reasonableness of returning to them to give a different formula.

The hard part of the question about why we do not teach this "one formula fits all" approach in the schools is not so readily answered. It seems that this approach would be a wonderful extension for those students who have mastered the formulas for area of the shapes mentioned. However, this average of the bases formula is rather obscure in the literature and, in so being, is not well-known to secondary teachers of mathematics.

Most secondary mathematics education majors are aware that the middle school provides the setting for presenting a multitude of topics at an intuitive level that can be investigated in greater depth and more formally later in the secondary curriculum. Joining the midpoints of the sides of a triangle to form four smaller triangles, all of which are congruent and similar to the initial triangle. Here, triangles ADF, FEB, DCE, and EFD are congruent and similar to triangle ABC. Software now available will measure the area of each of the triangles, as well as slopes and lengths of sides. These tools provide students with the opportunity to investigate and develop insight into relations that exist in triangles. For example, they could conclude that the area of triangle ADF is 0.25 times the area of triangle ABC, that segments AB and DE are parallel, and that the length of segment BC is twice that of segment DF. All of these intuitive feelings would spring from simple investigations and discoveries using the technology now available. Later, in a formal geometry class where such things are proven, the groundwork laid via the technology should establish valuable background information, and perhaps even a realization for the need for a more formal authentication of the intuitive feelings. Perhaps the Side-Side- Side congruence theorem would be used to establish that the four smaller triangles are, in fact, congruent.

Another interesting extension involving the initial triangle ABC in the preceding paragraph can be developed. Segment DE was formed by joining the midpoints of sides AC and BC, respectively. Rather than doing that, establish D on AC somewhere. Construct a line parallel to AB through D and create E as the intersection of the new line and side BC. Measure the length of segments AC and CD and the area of triangles CDE and CAB. Establish a ratio between the long and short length and the large and small area. When the length ratio is 2:1, the area ratio will be 4: 1. When the length ratio is 3:1, the area ratio will be 9:1. Before long, the students should be able to generalize the pattern. At the same time, some students will become aware of the differences between linear changes and those of areas. The informal setting leads to an extension that could provide stimulation and a desire for formalization for some students.

Extending the idea of similar triangles that stimulated the last two ideas, it is important that students not only gain a feel for the existence of such things, but also that they see uses of them. In either an informal or formal geometry course, use of similar triangles to measure heights is common, but typically they occur in the form of pictures in the text. There are some activities that can be used to stimulate development and see applications at the same time. One of the most intriguing ways of measuring heights of inaccessible objects involves the use of a mirror, a marble and linear measuring device. For the sake of simplicity, assume the ground is horizontal and that the flagpole is perpendicular to the ground. The marble is used to assure that the mirror lies in the plane of the ground. If the marble rolls off one edge of the mirror, objects would be used to level the mirror before any measurements are made. An individual is positioned so that the top of the flagpole can be seen in the mirror. That mirror spot is marked mentally or physically and measurements are taken. Assuming the ground is level from the point on the mirror to a point below the person's eye (AC), the height of the person's eye above the ground (AB), and the distance from the point on the mirror to a point below the top of the object being used are measured (CD). Precision can be impacted by the angle of the mirror and measurement accuracy, but the similar triangles are observed and used to find the missing height. Triangle ABC is similar to triangle CED. Knowing that the ratio AB:AC is the same as CD:CE and being able to measure AB, AC, and CD permits calculation of DE.

The height of that same triangle can be measured using a statia tube, which is a long cylinder with two parallel strings a known distance from where the eye would be placed at one end of the tube. The strings are a known distance apart. The top of the pole is aligned with the top string, and the bottom of the pole with the bottom string. Segments BG and AF represent the strings, which are assumed to be 1 centimeter apart. The distance from the eyeball, C, to the plane determined by BG and AF is assumed to be 1 meter. Because the ratio of length to height of strings is 100:1, when the top and bottom of the pole can be seen, the viewer will be 100 times the height of the pole away from the base of the pole. Only the distance from the viewer to the base of the pole needs to be measured.

What will happen as the locus of a point or line is investigated. For example, given two points, what is the locus of all points equidistant from them? Given points A and B, segment CD as the radius of the circles centered at A and B, and E and F as the points that are equidistant from A and B. Tracing the locus of E and F quickly reveals that the desired result is the perpendicular bisector of segment AB. Students could be asked to develop the construction and conjecture the results before doing the actual trace. One difficulty with this approach is that the students will know the power of the software, and there is a temptation to use it to answer the question without giving the question much thought. It is your responsibility to sell the students on the advantages of thinking about a situation where the answer can be quickly derived so the patterns and habits necessary for resolving more complex issues can be established. Part of your sales presentation should include the need to more formally prove the things being established. The proof may come later in a formal geometry class, and it may even be in the classic two-column format. The students who possesses this intuitive "feel" for what the situation encompasses should be better equipped to deal with establishing an advanced-level proof.

The trace function of software permits an early approach to the topic of locus. At the same time, it can raise the curiosity level of students enough that they will investigate traces of a variety of things. It shows a triangle that was constructed and shown to a group of seventh graders. Each vertex was located on a circle of random radius length. After construction, each vertex was animated around its respective circle. An animation button was created and then the circles and their centers were hidden. As motion was started, the students were to determine how the construction was created. On doing that, they were to create a similar situation to show the idea had been mastered. They did, and the objective was accomplished. However, one student traced the locus of a side of the triangle as the action was taking place. The idea spread and soon a multitude of traces was taking place. The variety of designs created and the discussion about what could be done were invigorating. Several students created similar designs for other polygons and did traces with them as well. Given the tools, encouragement, and some latitude, students will investigate and discover many things. Perhaps, more important, questions are raised and background is laid for the need for more formal proof, which could be approached at the time, or later, depending on student readiness as well as other factors.

Many middle-school students are fascinated by scale drawings. Often you will see grids drawn on a cartoon character and then a greater scale grid used to produce an enlarged version of the character. That method certainly works, but there is another, perhaps simpler way of accomplishing the objective. Tie a number of rubber bands together by looping one inside the end of another. Fix one end of the string beyond one side of the figure to be enlarged so there is a slight stretching of the string of rubber bands to get the first knot to be over the closest point of the sketch. Place a pencil inside the other end of the rubber band chain. Visually trace the first knot of the rubber band chain along the figure. As this is done, the figure will be enlarged by the pencil at the end of the chain.

Paper folding is a topic of interest. For years, students have been required to construct perpendicular lines using a straightedge and compass. This has historical roots. It is a way to help students see and gain a "feel for" right angles. Another method of accomplishing the task of forming perpendicular line segments is to fold a piece of paper. Open the paper and then refold it so that part of the initial fold lies on top of itself. Opening reveals perpendicular line segments. Repeating the process of folding part of one segment onto the other at a different point on one of the segments will yield parallel line segments. The third segment, perpendicular to the other two, serves as a transversal. A fourth fold could be created to establish an oblique transversal. Doing this folding with waxed paper is advantageous because its translucence permits easier multiple folds. Other classic folding activities involve bisecting an angle and constructing a parabola by folding a point onto a straight line segment. More recently, Patty Paper Geometry has come onto the scene as a distinct topic in the study of geometry.

One additional fascinating paper-folding activity is mentioned here, but there is an abundance of other things that can be accomplished with this medium. An 11-inchlong strip of paper about an inch wide can be used to create what appears to be a regular pentagon. Gently and carefully work the paper until the angles (formed by the top part of a loop and the disappearing end as that loop is doubled back) touch the width of the strip. Gently create each fold, taking care not to finalize the crease until the fold is as close as reasonably possible to aligning with the edge of a hidden section of the strip of paper. The tails should then be folded so they are not visible from the "front" or torn off.

Finally comes the question of how we study informal geometry. In most instances, it is inserted into the middle school curriculum as separate features in the textbook. As the trend to integrate topics grows, the likelihood is that there will be more informal geometry. There is one text on the market carrying the title *Informal Geometry*. This text covers most of a formal geometry course, except rather than proving theorems, they are basically given as fact and the students work exercises using the theorems given. At first glance this may not seem like a good thing to do. However, if the students gain insight and an intuitive feel for what the theorems project, that background can be used later when there is a need for more formal coverage of the topic.

Geometry in Algebra

Peter Hilton stated that if you have algebra without geometry you have answers to questions nobody would ask, and if you have geometry without algebra you have questions you can't answer. If Hilton's statement is accepted, the separation of geometry and algebra is, perhaps, more tragic than one might think. If the two topics were treated together as needed, the curriculum would change. The amount of integration would increase. This flies in the face of tradition. Dare we do that?

Consider the example where a circle is centered at the point (2, 3) and has a radius of 4. One form of the equation of this circle would be $x^2 - 4x + y^2 - 6y - 3 = 0$. Graphing that circle and the line $y = {}^{-}x + 10.8$ yields a situation in which the circle and line appear to be tangent, as shown in Figs. 7.19 and 7.20. Typically, we tell students to solve the situation by substituting ${}^{-}x + 10.8$ for y in the equation $x^2 - 4x + y^2 - 6y - 3 = 0$. On doing that, the result is $2x2 - 19.6x + 48.84 = 0$. Solving for x using software yields a message that there is no solution over the real numbers. With either solution, a large number of students do not comprehend the fact that the circle and line do not touch. To them, the answers are strange conglomerations of numbers that cannot be interpreted. However, zooming in on part of the graph reveals that the two figure do not touch. In this case, geometry answers an algebraic question.

Hero's (Hero of Alexandria, first century A.D.) formula for the area of a triangle where $s = 0.5(a + b + c)$ can provide some interesting application abilities. Many students are of the opinion that the only way to find the area of a triangle is to have the base and height. However, Hero's formula provides a method for finding the area of any triangle for which the lengths of the three sides are known. Suppose you are considering the purchase of a plot of ground that is 20 yards by 45 yards by 75 yards. The real estate agent is convinced the purchase price is very reasonable and is pushing for the sale. The property has not been surveyed, but that can be done once the nonrefundable deposit is submitted by you. Using Hero's formula,

$$
\begin{aligned}
s &= 0.5(20 + 45 + 75) \\
&= 0.5(140) \\
&= 70
\end{aligned}
$$

Something is wrong. Algebra provided an answer to a geometry problem. There is not a triangle.

Order of Covering Topics

As in most areas of the curriculum, geometry textbooks are similar. Certainly, each publisher has differences, but examination reveals a long list of items that are comparable. This has to be, because of our system of establishing objectives that need to be met as a guide to completing a given course. Topics may be treated differently and some emphasized more than others, but still, the likenesses are detectable. As is the case in most subjects, the geometry textbook often dictates the order in which topics are presented. That may or may not be ideal.

Two books deserve special mention here. The first, *Geometry: A Guided Inquiry*, is available as a study, investigation, and learning tool. Activities are interspersed throughout the text and provide formative background preparing the student for more formal proofs.

The thinking is that the intuitive feeling the student gathers from the investigations and activities will stimulate a higher level of understanding. Furthermore, as questions are raised during these research moments, students will begin to want to establish why things are true. In this way, the concept of and need for proof begins to emerge naturally.

The second book is *Discovering Geometry, An Inductive Approach.* Definitions are developed by providing examples of what something is and is not. Then the student is asked to define the item. The major part of the text has students doing a variety of activities and applications of geometry and there appears, at times to be limited connection with either each other or with the ideas normally covered in a formal high school geometry course. However, the last part of the text asks the students to produce proofs. At this point, a wondrous thing happens — the students have a wide variety of intuitive feels for what needs to be done in the proof. It is at this point that the realization begins to surface that these inspirations are a result of the groundwork laid in the beginning parts of the text. Amazingly, a wide variety of proofs is covered quickly and, most importantly, the attitude about them is generally quite positive.

One final note on the order of teaching geometric topics. Howard Eves stated that it seems reasonable to let the history of mathematics be our guide as to the order in which topics are introduced. His thinking is that the development is following a natural order generated by need and expansion of known items. Following Eves' line of thought, many of the developmental topics can be motivated in the grade-school or middle-school environment. Then, as the curriculum becomes increasingly integrated, more extensive coverage can be offered as the students are developmentally ready. Until that time, we will need to rely on the formative work being done in more traditional time frames, but we can still look to the history of mathematics as a guide for order.

Formal Geometry

Is there a need for the formal high-school geometry course? Absolutely. The format of the course may have changed and there might be less emphasis on proof than there was in previous years. However, the value of the course must not be overlooked. Some question the wisdom of changing the course from one of doing proofs essentially every day all year long. Others see that change as a breath of fresh air, citing that students did not like proofs, the course turns many students off from mathematics and, developmentally, students are not ready for the rigor demanded in the course. Recall the comments made earlier in this chapter about the work of the Van Hieles and the idea that the current geometry courses might be being watered down so our students can tolerate them. Still others question the current course in which the formal proof work is frequently done in the first part of the course and the less formal coverage of topics such as area, volumes, and applications are reserved for the second part of the course, citing again the developmental level of the students. Their position is that because the proofs of geometry require so much intricate thought, it would be better to do the less formal topics first and the proof section of the course last. That makes sense to many and seems to align itself with the thinking in Serra's text mentioned earlier.

Regardless of the philosophic position adopted, there is a place for the formal geometry class in the curriculum. Intuition is to be developed prior to the course and then a more formal approach used in the course itself. For example, Fig. 7.24 shows an informal development that can be extended. The sketch and measurements taken indicate that the interior quadrilateral EFGH is a parallelogram. The student should realize that from looking at the figure and the fact that opposite sides are congruent and parallel. Experience has shown that the step to producing a proof is relatively simple if the students realize that each part of the original quadrilateral ABCD can be a triangle. When it is known that the midpoints of two sides of a triangle are joined by a segment that is half the length of, and parallel to, the third side, the establishment of a more formal proof that EFGH is a parallelogram is easier. Similar cases can be made for many theorems that would be covered in a formal geometry course. Consider the theorem, "Tangent segments from a point outside a circle are congruent." Using dynamic software, two tangents can easily be created by constructing lines perpendicular to two radii. If the two tangent lines do not meet on the screen, one of the radii, or both, can be rotated so a convenient figure is available. The intersection of the two tangent lines can be constructed and then the lines hidden. Segments can be constructed between the radii ends and the common point just constructed. The lengths of those segments can be measured, indicating congruence. It shows the initial construction and that moving the figure will still provide congruent measurements, with both values changing as the figure is altered. These sketches create an intuitive feel for the theorem and is true in all cases. The more formal proof will follow more easily when the student is aware of what the results should be, based on prior experiences and observation, as opposed to reading about it as the theorem is stated.

Where Does Geometry Stop?

Geometry study and learning do not stop. Geometry is a dynamic, ever-changing subject. Transformations. Tessellations. Vectors. Coordinate. Taxi-cab. Lobachevskian. Spherical. *Flatland. One, Two, Three . . . Infinity. Donald Duck in Mathmagic Land.* Measurement. Projection. Etc.

Tessellations that can be entertaining and thought-provoking. The Dutch graphic artist Maurits Corneille Escher has been one agent in the popularizing of tessellations. "His work has become increasingly popular because of its unique combination of humor, logic, and meticulous precision with visual trickery". A square tessellates the plane, meaning that a set of squares of a given size can be arranged to cover the plane leaving no gaps. Escher and many others modify a shape like the square to present more interesting creations. It shows how a square can be modified to make a different shape. The example given here is not particularly interesting, but the procedure is demonstrated.

The honeycomb is a practical application of the tessellation of the plane. It is important to show students applications as well as connections within geometry. For example, doing a proof in Euclidean, then coordinate, and finally vector geometry can show the power of going beyond standard Euclidean geometry. The study of geometry does not stop. We live in a geometric world. As we view surroundings, new questions are raised and the need for varied geometric understandings continues.

8

CALCULUS

Introduction

The sad truth is that calculus is not a realization of the secondary school preparation and an exciting beginning to future mathematical study. Instead, calculus continues to serve as an exit from the study of mathematics and related subject areas for many students.

> *Much of the difficulty had to do with the delivery system: classes that were too large, senior faculty who had largely deserted the course, and teaching assistants whose time and interest were focused on their own graduate work. Other difficulties came from well intentioned efforts to pack into the course all the topics demanded by the increasing number of disciplines requiring calculus of their students. It was acknowledged, however, that if the course had indeed become a blur for students, it just might be because those choosing the topics to be presented and the methods for presenting them had not kept their goals in focus.*
>
> *It was to these latter concerns that we responded in designing our project. We agreed that there ought to be an opportunity for students to discover instead of always being told. We agreed that the availability of calculators and computers not only called for exercises that would not be rendered trivial by such technology,*

> *but would in fact direct attention more to ideas than to techniques. It seemed to us that there should be explanations of applications of calculus that were self-contained, and both accessible and relevant to students. We were persuaded that calculus students should, like students in any other college course, have some assignments that called for library work, some pondering, some imagination, and above all, a clearly reasoned and written conclusion. Finally, we came to believe that there should be available to students some collateral readings that would set calculus in an intellectual context.*

The preceding quotes were selected for two reasons. They do describe the current thinking of many individuals involved with the teaching of calculus in secondary, community college, college, and university environments. More important, those statements summarize the approach we have taken throughout this text. Technology is an integral part of our world and should be incorporated into our learning and teaching. Students cannot continue to be passive but must become actively involved in their learning. We cannot expect students to sit and listen as we tell them what they need to know. These individuals have to be convinced of the need to reflect on the mathematical world in which they are being nurtured. They have to see the value of pondering questions, applying their creative skills to topics, and determining where these subjects appear in the real world. Knowing or being aware of such things is wonderful, but it also carries with it the responsibility of being able to tell others what is known, learned, discovered, or created. Thus, the need for communication skills, both written and oral, is present not only in calculus, but throughout the mathematics curriculum.

The Mathematical Association of America (MAA) Resources for Calculus Collection, source of the earlier quotes in this chapter, was developed through a consortium of liberal arts colleges. One of the underlying premises to this work relates to the preparation of secondary teachers of mathematics. The writers developed the Calculus Collection from the vantage point that most secondary teachers seek the opportunity to teach calculus, much like graduate faculty members crave the opportunity to teach an advanced course in their area of specialization.

The MAA Calculus Collection is not the only work in this arena. The UC Davis Calculus Revitalization Project provides a similar description for the teaching of calculus.

> *We hope to be enthusiastically teaching a Calculus sequence that builds students' understanding of the theory and application of the subject while incorporating the use of technology in a thoughtful way. In our Revitalized Calculus Sequence, there is enough time for instructors to share their excitement about mathematics and to pursue digressions into such things as aspects of the field that are interesting to them, historical insights, alternative interpretations, different representations, or sharing personal insights.*

The UC Davis and MAA works are indicative of some of the movements going on today in calculus. They are accompanied by work from groups across the country at locations like Harvard, the University of Michigan, and Duke. Mathematics departments were surveyed in the spring of 1994 by the MAA. Of the 1,048 schools responding, 22% reported major reform efforts taking place and another 46% indicated they were involved in moderate revision attempts. The data gathered from the survey indicate that about 150,000 students (about 32%) taking calculus during the spring, 1994, semester were in reform based classes.

A major result of the study was that what was being taught in the calculus class has not changed much, but how it is taught has. A basic theme of the reform movement has been that students should have a stronger conceptual understanding of the subject. This comprehension is to be developed through interpretations based on numerical, graphic, algebraic, and modeling work. The reported changes include open-ended use of technology, writing, applications, cooperative groups, and projects.

The results of the new efforts are positive. Retention and passing rates are going up. Major reform themes like changes in the mode of instruction and use of technology are appearing in courses that precede and follow calculus. Enrollment in post-calculus courses appears to be increasing. Positive images of the study of mathematics are being generated by the extensive use of technology.

Some concerns have been generated by the reform calculus movement. Faculty concerns have focused on time for preparation, assessing student projects, meeting with students, and dealing with technology. At the same time, the invested time results in faculty growth and professionalism. Faculty discussions have focused on teaching and learning how to teach as well as mathematics. These exchanges are resulting in an increase in research about how students learn mathematics. These beginnings are generating calls for more investigations into traditional and reform calculus teaching and learning. The appearance is that conversion to reform calculus is inevitable.

Much of the outline and basic ideas contained in this chapter are attributable to Dr. Joby Milo Anthony, associate professor of mathematics at the University of Central Florida. It is taken from personal discussions as well as a set of tapes he developed to accompany a calculus class.

What We Teach

Calculus is broken into three basic components: derivatives, integrals, and infinite series. The application of limits is a significant part of the study of calculus. Many times the idea of limits becomes obscure as the emphasis shifts to specific ideas or formulas. That is one reason why the study of limits is so important as foundation information.

Calculus grew out of Descartes and Fermat's work with analytic geometry. They were the first to solve algebraic equations using geometry. They also developed geometric proofs involving algebra. This foundation spread to England and Germany where Newton and Leibniz, working separately yet almost simultaneously, developed most of the calculus we know today. By 1672, Leibniz had invented a calculating machine that added, subtracted, multiplied, and divided. Leibniz produced what we know as the fundamental theorem of calculus and many other theorems of calculus. He published his work in 1677, 11 years after Newton had developed many of his unpublished works on the subject. Newton often published information long after he had composed it. Who created calculus? Both of them. Leibniz was famous for logic. He created the elongated "S" that is our integral sign as a means of expressing the sum of a lot of related values.

Newton is credited with revealing secrets of motion and gravity. While contemplating motion, Newton created what we now think of as differential calculus. In his initial work, he visualized a curve as being generated by a moving point. He called those points *Fluents,* meaning "changing quantities." Newton looked at rates of change that we call *derivatives*. He was looking for a way to determine the equation of a line tangent to a point on a graph.

Technology

Calculus, as a subject area, has not changed much in the past 200 years. The way we can teach calculus has changed recently. We are no longer bound to boards or overheads to graph a function. Calculators, CD-ROMs, and software give us the power to visualize calculus graphically and to solve formulas symbolically. Casio, Hewlett Packard, Sharp, and Texas Instruments all offer graphing calculators, many of which can take derivatives and do integration. The TI-92 incorporates a symbolic manipulator/function plotter and is capable of extensive and complex computations, much like that of many pieces of computer software. Tutorials are now available for all phases of calculus, several on CD-ROM (some of which are interactive). These technological devices can be used as stand-alone material or in conjunction with a specific textbook. There are several software programs that have become a viable tool to solve the most complex calculus problems and much more. Where does all this technology leave the teaching of a calculus class? If we teach with the use of technology, do we alter our assessment methods of the students' knowledge differently? How much do we teach, where does the technology fit in, and how much do we let students learn by discovery? Can we maintain situations at a level where all students have equal access to appropriate technology? If a student is not capable of acquiring the necessary technology for calculus, is that student eliminated from the opportunity to take the class? How much time will be needed to address the use of technology so students go beyond the basics and are able to use it as a learning tool? How much technological background should we expect from students? These are not easy questions to answer. Students must have an understanding of prerequisite concepts and theory as they begin the study of calculus. Will the benefits gained by using technology outweigh time that must be spent to help students become functional with it? Graduates will be expected to be able to use technological approaches in many college courses and, ultimately, in the workplace. It becomes our responsibility to demand technological capabilities of them.

Technology, although a wonderful asset, does have its limitations. Many computations incorporate rounding automatically. Topics like fixing decimal points in a calculator, rounding, approximations, impact of range changes on graphs, and others have been discussed throughout this text. As you approach the study of calculus, it is important that your students be aware of the difference between two items being equal and two items being approximately equal. If they are of the opinion that a technologically based answer is exact, they might have some difficulties in calculus.

Calculus is a study of motion. There is a need for students to learn to visualize ideas as they investigate. We talk about the derivative being the slope of the tangent (if it exists) to a curve. The formulas for evaluating derivatives are really formulas for evaluating the limit without looking at the limit. In the process of developing the idea, we pick a second point close to the first on the curve. A secant line is drawn between the points. Then the second point is slowly moved toward the first. As that point moves, a new secant is created. As the distance between the two points decreases, or approaches the limit, the secant line becomes the tangent line. We can describe this to a class and even model it by drawing a curve, selecting two points, and then using a straightedge to show the new point and the secant it creates. Eventually the straightedge is representing the tangent. This process could also be modeled by paper folding, much as is done to show the parabola as the locus of points equidistant from a point and a line.

Technology can be used to create an animation of the secant line getting closer to the tangent line. Point P would move along the curve. As it moves, it can be seen to be getting closer and closer to the tangent line. You might elect to let the point animate bidirectionally to show how the motion of the point influences whether the secant line approaches or goes away from the tangent line. The important thing to remember is that the power of technology permits the viewing of this motion. The impact is much more powerful than anything you can do by hand, with transparencies, and so forth, and you can change the setup as necessary to meet the needs of your class.

Derivative

The slope of the tangent line was gleaned from the limit of the slope of the secant line. The slope of the tangent line is important in its own right. Many times it has more significance. If we focus on the slope of the tangent line itself, the calculus language for that idea calls it the derivative. The derivative of a function at a point in its domain is geometrically the slope of tangent line at that point. It is the limit of as h goes to zero.

$$\frac{f(x+h)-f(x)}{h}$$

Think in terms of an object moving in a straight line. We can graph its motion by identifying the horizontal axis as time measured from some fixed reference time. The vertical axis would be described as the distance related to some fixed reference. Motion then becomes a function where the time and direction are understood to have the defined meaning. The slope of secant through two points on that graph will have physical meaning because it becomes the average velocity. The slope of the tangent line is not an average velocity; it is an instantaneous velocity. If you are driving in a straight line and look at the speedometer, that number is an approximation of the instantaneous velocity. It is like finding the derivative of a distance function. Realize that the derivative is an instantaneous rate of change. It represents the instantaneous rate at which the vertical variable is changing in relation to the horizontal one. If the horizontal is time and the vertical is distance, you have instantaneous velocity. If you have time as the horizontal variable and a chemical as the vertical one, and the graph represents unused chemicals, the derivative or instantaneous reading is the rate of change of chemical to time.

The question now becomes, what is this limit? There is a need for some algebra skills at this point. This can be another potential danger spot for some students who are algebraically not as strong as they should be. This can be dealt with through technology, but it also raises a question. In terms of readiness for the study of calculus, is there a minimal algebra skill level, or should we let technology resolve the dilemma? You need to proceed carefully to assure none of them gets lost, even though the algebra here is relatively simple for a student with adequate readiness. Finding the LCD in the numerator gives

$$\lim_{h\to 0} \frac{1-\sqrt{1+h}}{h\sqrt{1+h}}$$

At this point, a procedure similar to that used earlier with limits could be used, but that is slow. It is more convenient to develop a set of formulas. Again, calculus is essentially a set of formulas that describes what happens as limits are taken. Fortunately, most of the functions we deal with have nice formulas for evaluating limits and for finding the rule for the derivative. The task now becomes one of determining a formula for Algebraic intuition here may not be overly obvious to some students.

Rolle's Theorem

Every mathematical theorem is a statement that if one thing is true, then something else is true. It is often difficult for students to determine what part of the statement is the hypothesis and what part is the conclusion. They want to accept it all and continue. Mathematics tries to establish the truth of a relation between the hypothesis and conclusion, not the hypothesis or the conclusion. In Rolle's theorem, the hypothesis deals with a continuous function over some closed interval $[a, b]$. In the open interval (a, b), there is a derivative at each point; $f(a) = 0$ and $f(b) = 0$. This is the hypothesis for Rolle's theorem. The conclusion of Rolle's theorem says there must be at least one horizontal tangent line somewhere in the open interval. Another way of saying this would be, "If we have a function whose graph crosses the x-axis at a and b respectively, and if the function is continuous on $[a, b]$ and differentiable on (a, b), then there is some number c between a and b such that $f(c) = 0$." The differences between the two statements of the theorem are slight, but it is important that you be able to express things in more than one way. If a student does not seem to grasp one statement, the alternative expression might provide the necessary clarification. The preceding statement of Rolle's theorem is shown geometrically in Fig. 8.8. Tangent segments are used to represent the tangent lines at each of points c_1, c_2, and c_3. The theorem does not stipulate how many points exist where the derivative is zero; it only says there is at least one. It provides another opportunity to demonstrate dynamically that there are horizontal lines at points c_1, c_2, and c_3.

Mean Value Theorem for Derivatives

The Mean Value Theorem for Derivatives is a generalization of Rolle's Theorem, or Rolle's Theorem is a special case of the Mean Value Theorem for Derivatives. The hypothesis for the Mean Value Theorem for Derivatives is almost the same as that for Rolle's Theorem. The Mean Value Theorem for Derivatives does not require that the function has values of zero at its endpoints.

The mean value theorem for derivatives would be expected to say something about derivatives between *a* and *b*. We look at the segment joining endpoints $(a, f(a))$ and $(b, f(b))$. The mean value theorem for derivatives says that somewhere there has to be a tangent line parallel to the secant line joining those endpoints. If you have a function that is continuous on the closed interval $[a, b]$ and differentiable on (a, b), there has to be a tangent line that is parallel to the secant line. That means the slope of the tangent line at some point equals the slope of the secant line. Figure 14.10 is a geometric interpretation of this discussion of the mean value theorem for derivatives.

As before, there is a desire to describe the geometric information in Fig. 8.10 analytically. The rise is expressed by $f(b) - f(a)$, and $b - a$ is the run. If the secant is parallel to the tangent line at some point *c*, the slope of the tangent line at *c* is $f'(c)$.

$$f'(c) = \frac{f(b) - f(a)}{b - a}$$

Often the equation is rewritten by multiplying both sides by b - a, giving $(b - a)f'(c) = f(b) - f(a)$. We know this point c exists by the mean value theorem for derivatives, but we do no not know where. The mean value theorem for derivatives does not guarantee this will hold; it will hold only if we have certain kinds of functions.

One of the difficult things for students to grasp is the possibility that hypotheses of the theorem are not true. If they are not true, anything can happen. Students need to realize this. The hypothesis is false and so is the conclusion. This thinking requires careful explanation to students.

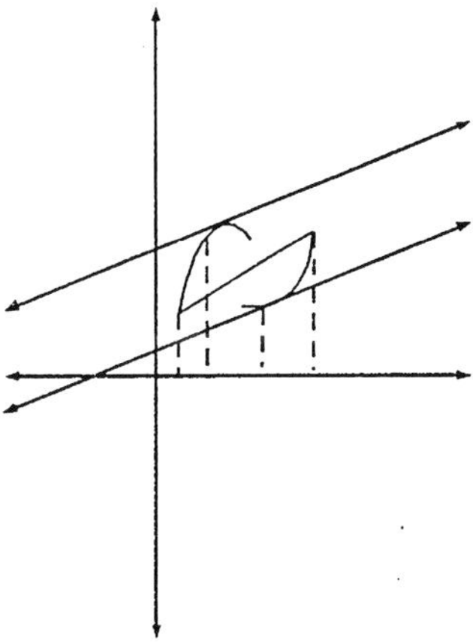

Area Under Curves

Riemann was shy and his health was not good. He had an unquenchable thirst for knowledge, earning a doctorate in mathematics at the age of 24. Gauss was his advisor. Gauss was not easily impressed, but Riemann managed to do it. Riemann studied geometry, functions of complex variables, and areas under a curve. He used the Greeks' exhaustive method of using several thin rectangles to approach the area under curves. Today we call that process *Riemann sums.*

As the discussion shifts to area, we consider a particular kind of area where there is a nonnegative function over some interval on the x-axis. We can approximate the area by using a rectangle. We can get a better approximation to the area by subdividing the interval on the x-axis and even closer with the axis. When subdividing, the width of the rectangle is controlled; eventually that width approaches a limit of zero. The height of each rectangle is the value of the function over the subinterval at the respective point. There are other ways to find the area under a curve, but this one is easy to see, potentially giving it special appeal to you as a teacher of mathematics. It is crucial that the students have a visual image of the issues you discuss. The limiting value of the approximations is the area we are seeking.

Any time an idea is encountered for the first time, it is beneficial to work through a specific example. The process amplifies understanding. Consider finding the area under the curve x^2 between 0 and 1. The approximation procedure would be to subdivide the interval between 0 and 1 in half; 0 to 1/2 and 1/2 to 1. Each subinterval has width 1/2. The left one has a height of 0, so its area is 0. The right subinterval has a height of $(1/2)^2$ and a base width of 1/2. A1, which is the first approximation of the area is (1/2) (0) + $(1/2)(1/2)^2$, as shown in Fig. 8.17 . This approximation is not too good. Factor out $(1/2)^3$ and write A1 as $(1/2)^3(1)^2$ This may appear to be a strange way to write this product, but it is convenient in the long run. We are going to be looking for a pattern and 1/8 is not serviceable for that objective. This may be difficult for some students to perceive. They have been "trained" to write fractions like this as 1/8, not $(1/2)^3$.

A few more approximations will make the decision more obvious for most students. Figure 8.18 shows the base subdivided into thirds, getting the approximation closer. It subdivides the base into fourths, getting the approximate area even closer to what it actually is. At this point we have

$$A1 = (1/2)(0) + (1/2)(1/2)^2 = (1/2^3)(1^2)$$

$$A2 = (1/3)(0) + (1/3)(1/3)^2 + (1/3)(2/3)^2 = (1/3^2)(1^2 + 2^2)$$

$$A3 = (1/4)(0) + (1/4)(1/4)^2 + (1/4)(2/4)^2 + (1/4)(3/4)^2 = (1/4^3)(1^2 + 2^2 + 3^2)$$

This area is not an approximation. It is an area. This is difficult for many students to comprehend. Earlier in the text we discussed the difficulty students have accepting the idea that the repeating decimal 0.999... equals 1. The emotions and quandary students feel are similar in these two situations. The area from Riemann sums is difficult to carry out at times. Pattems are often obscure, and even when they are determined it may be difficult to calculate the limit. Remember, calculation of area is an evaluation of a limit. Formulas are just a more efficient way of doing this.

Every time an area is calculated, in actuality, a limit is being evaluated.

Conclusion

Calculus is a powerful tool. Many people in secondary mathematics departments crave the opportunity to teach calculus. The assumption is that this is where the best and most interested students are and, in most cases, that is true. A hard fact of life is that unless new teachers are extremely fortunate, the likelihood is great that instead of calculus they will be teaching general mathematics. There are bright students who, for whatever reason, elect to avoid advanced mathematics classes. Whatever level class you have, teach them well. The foundations for learning are provided in each mathematics class that precedes it. Remember, the best way to teach something is to teach it right the first time. Teaching it right means students learn it, understand it, and have a positive attitude about learning more mathematics.

9

LEARNING ABOUT FRACTIONS

View from Mathematics

In mathematics a fraction is a number of the form a/b (where a, b are integers and b is not zero) with a set of well-defined and well-known operations and properties, such as commutativity and association of addition and multiplication, identity operations, and so on.

For the present purposes this conception of fractions is relevant but misleading. Fractions are indeed numbers. However part of the concept of fraction is non-numerical. A narrow mathematical conception disregards the role physical quantity plays in the meaning of the concept and consequently obscures the psychological origins of fractions, for there is little doubt that number concepts, including rational number concepts, are developed through acting and reflecting upon physical quantities. The view that "a fraction is simply a number" may make sense in discussions among mathematicians but it is pedagogically naive as well as historically and psychologically inaccurate.

The View from Classrooms

Traditional approaches to fractions in mathematics education do not suffer from this fault but raise another set of issues. In relying upon concrete materials such as pizzas and cakes in the teaching of fractions, mathematics educators implicitly recognize, wisely so, that children develop number concepts on the basis of their knowledge of the physical world. (This does not mean that the concept of fraction is "abstracted" from objects in the classical empiricist view of abstraction of knowledge as a direct transcription or "reading off" of reality). Just as integer addition and subtraction are introduced through operations on discrete objects, fractions are introduced through the actions of breaking up wholes into sets of units of equal magnitude. Many students and some teachers seem to think that a fraction is a part of a whole and the fractional numeral is its "name." The idea that a fraction is material substance is, of course, incorrect. If we adopt such a view we must be willing to conclude that any person, regardless of age, who works with parts of wholes is working with fractions. No mathematical concept can be reduced to a physical embodiment. A fraction entails relations, and relations are not palpable, physical objects. In mathematics education we have no alternative but to steer away from the extreme views that "fractions are simply numbers" and "fractions are simply material substance." In doing so we cannot simply disregard number and quantity. Learning about fractions entails becoming aware of special relations between numbers and quantities and learning to express these relations in diverse ways. In this regard, it is instructive to reflect on how students are taught to identify fractions. Students are shown a set of elements, some of which are shaded, marked, or selected. They are told to count the marked units and to use the obtained cardinal number as the numerator; likewise, they are instructed to count the total number of (marked plus unmarked) elements and use the total as the denominator of the fraction. Fractions are thus tied to the activities of counting and matching. Later students are given rules for carrying out the multiplication, division, addition, and subtraction of fractions. The rules for multiplication and division are taught as computational recipes. Few students understand, for example, why one inverts a fractional divisor before multiplying. It is hoped that students will later make sense of these operations for themselves. Most of them never do. These and other shortcomings of traditional instruction regarding fractions can be subsumed under several categories:

1. Part-whole fixation. Students are taught to associate fractions with parts of wholes. This impedes transfer to other cases and makes improper fractions seem mysterious (how can the part be greater than the whole?).
2. Cardinal sin. Counting and matching tasks mislead students to focus on cardinal number while ignoring the ratio meaning of fractions.
3. Missing links. The links of fractions to integer multiplication and division are missing or misleading. Furthermore, fractions are treated as unrelated to ratio, proportion, functions, and other concepts.
4. No challenge. Authentic problems and puzzles are absent in instruction, and "exercises" given to students are merely computational tasks.

These shortcomings constitute a challenge for any alternative approach to teaching about fractions.

The Present View

Over the last two decades, much discussion has been brewing regarding the learning and teaching of fractions. These works have attempted to render a rich account of fractions and rational numbers and to provide a theoretical and empirical footing that will guide curriculum development and teaching. The field still lacks a coherent account of how fractions fit into students' mathematical understanding, beginning from early childhood and extending into late adolescence. However, it seems reasonable to suppose that fractions are tightly interwoven with ratio and proportion concepts, as well as multiplication and division. These reference concepts will be closely linked to representations, schemes, ideas, and concepts such as decimal number, percent, relative increase and decrease, slope, the Euclidean algorithm and maximum common divisor, linear equation, constant of proportionality, intensive quantities and rates, functions and operations, and measurement, to mention several. Clarifying these relations is a long-term enterprise for the field of mathematics education. A general theoretical framework is necessary for giving overall direction to these efforts. But a general framework is not enough because we need to work out the issues unique to the learning of ratio and proportion in the domain of mathematics. It is easy to accept the general notion that all of the aforementioned concepts are interrelated. But when we focus on particular relations, there is much to work out. Consider, for example, the relations between the concept of fraction and integer multiplication and division. Learning studies (see the section on the arithmetical basis of fractions) sometimes give the impression that the student's knowledge about integer operations impedes learning about fractions. So, precisely how integers are related to fractions is a problem for many students. It is not sufficient simply to treat them as separate topics. If instruction is to be successful, it must contend with what students already know about whole numbers and their operations. It must provide conditions for students to build on what they already know, where possible. However, it must also provide opportunities for students to reorganize and advance their knowledge, where necessary. This requires that we think about very specific classes of learning situations that may be useful for helping students come to grips with diverse relations and concepts. What sorts of learning activities can be useful in engaging students in reflection about these relations? What sorts of evidence, demonstration, or proof could students draw on to raise their own hypotheses and to derive their own conclusions? Here I raise ideas relevant to such a project. First I discuss two kinds of competencies that must play a major role in the emergence of the concept of fraction. Next I describe a model and some associated learning activities that draw on these competencies and serve to establish links between fractions and diverse related concepts. I hope to make a case for the view that, from the very start, fractions should be treated as "shorthand" for certain functions. Taken seriously, these considerations redefine what a fraction is, assigning to the concept an important role in the transition from arithmetic to algebraic thinking.

How Fractions Mesh With What Students Already Know

In order to situate the concept in the student's long-term development, we must look for the roots of the fraction concept in activities engaged in, and knowledge acquired, long before the student can handle expressions. The concept of fraction will rely on former knowledge as well as embody new ideas; it reflects a continuity as well as a break with the past. Two sources of continuity are discussed, namely, (a) students' implicit knowledge regarding ratio and proportion, and (b) their knowledge regarding the arithmetic of whole numbers. Both sources of knowledge are highly relevant to learning about fractions.

The Perceptual-Judgmental Basis of Fractions in Ratios of Quantity: A proportion is an equivalence of ratios. A typical example is3:4 = 6:8 (1)Because the colon expresses the operation of division, we may alternatively write3 ÷ 4 = 6 ÷ 8 (2)or even¾ = 6/8 (3)This means that a proportion can be expressed as an equivalence of fractions. Two points need mentioning:

1. Equations 1, 2, and 3 are by no means equivalent to students. (This exemplifies a widespread phenomenon, that two expressions that are "obviously equivalent" to mathematicians are not seen as the same by students.) For example, Kerslake found that most 11- to 15-year-old students do not think that 3 ÷ 4 expresses the fraction ¾. By extension, they would not accept the equivalence of Equations 2 and 3.
2. All situations involving ratio and proportion are potentially relevant to the concept of fraction. We must therefore look toward how students reason about ratio and proportion in order to understand how the concept of fraction fits into their prior knowledge.

The psychological literature is replete with evidence suggesting that ratio and proportion concepts develop slowly throughout childhood and that children come to understand proportions only during adolescence. For example, Bruner and Kenney found that 5-year-olds use the terms "full" and "empty" correctly to describe glasses totally full or empty, but they take the "fuller glass" to mean the glass with more water or a higher water level. Only over several years do they shift towards the interpretation that "fuller glass" means having more water relative to its capacity. The Piagetian school has long argued that the concept of proportional reasoning is a characteristic of formal operational thought. Indeed, much empirical evidence can be found to support this view. But there is now convincing developmental evidence that the concepts of ratio and proportion begin to develop far earlier than normally supposed. In order to understand this we must distinguish the sort of ratio mentioned in the preceding equations from another sort of ratio.

A ratio of numbers or numerical ratio entails a comparison of two numbers (which could be rational or real numbers as well as integers). It corresponds to expressions such as 2:3, 2 ÷ 3, or B. A ratio of quantities concerns a comparison of two quantities. For example, if A refers to the length of one object and B refers to the length of a second object, then A:B and A/B express the relative magnitude of the two lengths. In general, I use the term quantity to refer to a scalar quantity, namely, a property or quality that varies in intensity, magnitude, or duration, susceptible to ordering along a single dimension or continuum. I prefer to reserve the term measure to refer to the description of a quantity according to a certain number of units of measure. As quantities become expressed as multiples of other quantities, a ratio of quantities can be treated as a ratio of measures (e.g., 2A:3A or 5A:7B); in this sense a formerly unmeasured quantity (e.g., A) becomes a unit of measure according to which other quantities are measured.

In a psychological investigation of ratio and proportion, Spinillo and Bryant asked 5- to 7-year-old children to compare a model figure, part of which was blue and the rest of which was white, to two other figures, one of which had the same ratio of blue to white. The child was told that each of the figures was a photograph of an object made from little blue and little white blocks. The child's task was to decide which of the two remaining figures had the same ratio of blue to white blocks as the model.

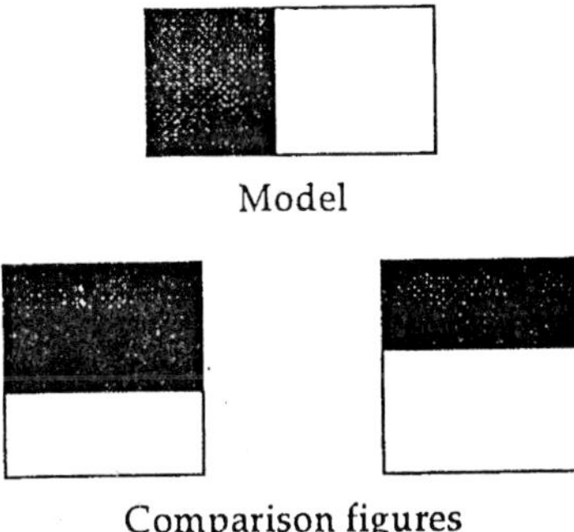

Comparison figures

Fig. 9.1

The task is to decide which comparison figure has the ratio of blue to white as the model figure. Because the individual blocks used to construct the figures could not be discerned, and hence could not be counted, the child had to rely upon non-numerical information for solving the task. Considering that the total size of the figures varied across trials independently from the ratio of blue to white, responses based on the absolute size of the figures could be separate from those based on proportions. Furthermore, because in some conditions the configurations of blue to white was rearranged, the child could not solve the problem by mentally "rescaling" one of the figures in order to make it look like the model figure. In order for the child to solve the tasks successfully, she would have to use the ratio of colored regions. The results showed that children as young as 6 years of age were responding at better than chance levels. The children distinguished three types of first-order comparisons between parts A and B of one figure: A > B, A < B, and A = B. Furthermore, they successfully made second-order comparisons equivalent to the following:

If A < B *and* C > D *then* A:B ? C:D

If A > B *and* C = D *then* A:B ? C:D

If A < B *and* C = D *then* A:B ? C:D

The above comparisons can be regarded as special cases of ratios. The comparison A = B, for example, corresponds to the equation A:B = 1. The inequality C > D corresponds to the case C:D > 1.

The young children were not successful in comparing a pair of inequalities in the same direction. For example, if they were shown figures corresponding to the conditions A < B and C < D, they were not able to decide, at better than chance levels, whether or not A:B = C:D.

In doing so, they recognized that ratio and proportion bear directly on the concept of fraction (one half). It should be emphasized, however, that the children had no understanding of notation regarding fractions.

Lovett and Singer found similar results in a series of studies using a completely different methodology. There was also evidence, in their studies, that by kindergarten children were beginning to order ratios correctly within logical categories; that is, they were beginning to differentiate among ratios on the "same side of one-half."

The foregoing results suggest that children begin to develop a rudimentary understanding of ratios of quantity long before they reach adolescence and well before they can understand numerical ratios such as 2:3. The concept of ratio emerges in the context of perceptual judgments, and initially bears no relation to calculation skills and knowledge of arithmetic.

The Arithmetical Basis of Fractions

On the basis of their experience with integers, students tend to associate multiplication with increase, and division with reduction in amounts. The operation of multiplying by n is related to the physical action of taking n instances of something. Division is related to the action of taking a part of something.

In tasks where subjects are asked to select the appropriate operation to model a word problem, many students—even at secondary and university levels-select the incorrect arithmetical operation when the operator corresponds to a proper fraction. For example, given the task of determining how much one pays for ¾ kg of meat if 1 kg costs $2, many will say that the answer will be given by dividing 2 by ¾. By contrast, it makes virtually no difference whether the operand measure corresponds to an integer or to a decimal fraction. Bell et al. also reported a second study in which 15year-old students either estimated the size of the answer or indicated which operation was to be selected in order to solve the problem. Dramatic differences occurred in performance under the two conditions. Generally, students estimated the sizes of results with a high degree of accuracy, indicating that they understand from the context the effect that the operation must have upon the operand. They select the wrong operation due to a misconception regarding which operation produces the intended effect. The authors concluded that "the estimate is made directly by a semiqualitative ratio comparison, without explicit identification of the operation".

In the problems of Bell et al., quantities were expressed indirectly through written values. Even so, it seems reasonable to suppose that students are working with internal representations of quantities. The students appear to understand interrelations of the quantities well enough to expect a resultant measure greater or less than that of the operand quantity. For example, if 1 k of meat costs $2 and they wish to purchase $\frac{3}{4}$ kg, they know that they will pay less than $2, but do not understand which arithmetic operations will produce the desired effects. Their representations of quantity do not mesh with their representations of number operations.

Students' difficulties with rational operators do not simply reflect a failure to master the computational procedures (e.g., integer multiplication transfers very easily to decimal multiplication), but have to do with making sense of how numerical operations relate to transformations upon associated quantities. Although students' understanding of integer multiplication and division commonly interferes with the concept of a fraction as an operator, this very understanding must constitute a resource for introducing fractions as operators. We know that student's knowledge about fractions must build upon what they already know about whole numbers. Yet integer knowledge is likely to lead them astray when it comes to understanding a fraction as an operator. How can students make use of what they already know without being misled?

To address these questions we must first look closely at the interplay between number and quantity in certain mathematical tasks.

Fractions as Shorthand for Equations Describing Relations Among Quantities

There is something strange about this figure. The figures and corresponding notation appear correct. The fractions written below are in accordance with textbook conventions. But why is one-half of a whole less than two-fourths of a whole? How can one-half be equal to one fifth? Does this mean that $\frac{1}{2}$ = M?

If A refers to the region occupied by one square, B to two squares, C to three squares, D to four squares, and E to five squares, we can state the relations more explicitly through an equation:

$A = \frac{1}{2}B$

The other cases can be expressed in a similar fashion:

B = XC

$B = 2/4\ D = \frac{1}{2}D$

A = XE

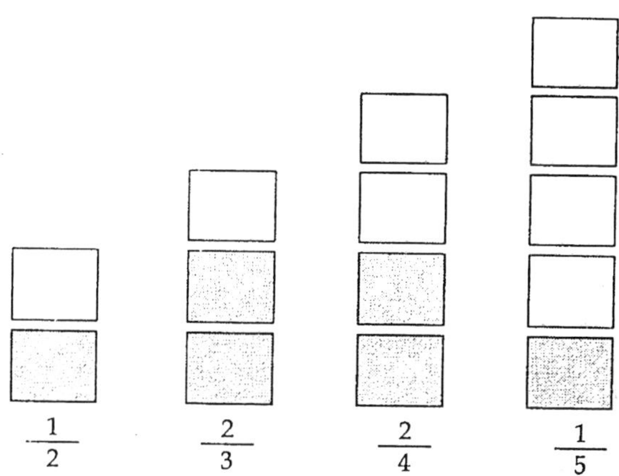

Fig. 9.2. Illustration of the need to consider units when comparing fractions

Consider once again the question "How can one-half be equal to one-fifth?" We now have a clearer means of representing the relations, namely ½B = XE, which corresponds to the sentence "one-half of B equals one-fifth of E." This has clear advantages over the potentially confusing ½ = M.

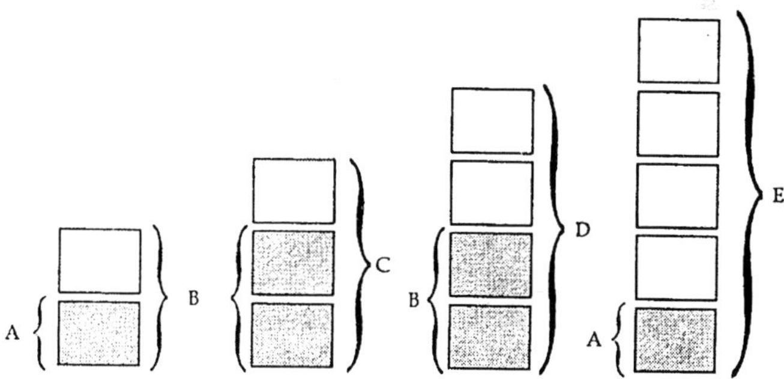

Fig. 9.3. Comparison of fractions, taking account of units

When working with a physical model of fractions, a fractional numeral such as ½ is actually shorthand for a more complete description such as A = ½B, or Y = ½x, where the parameter, ½, is a constant of proportionality. Fractional numerals are shorthand for functions involving ratio and proportion. (It may look as if each letter designates only a single quantity rather than a variable quantity, so that we are not talking about relations between variables.

However, even if the notation is initially used to describe relations between particular quantities, it opens the way for talking later about relations between variables and hence functions.) Each "longhand" algebraic statement expresses a special sort of proportional equivalence of a ratio of quantities to a ratio of numbers. For example the expression, A = ½B expresses the proportion, A:B = 1:2. Algebra thus provides a means for expressing the interrelations of number and quantity.

It is commonly held that algebra instruction should begin in early adolescence after students have studied fractions. Some would argue that algebra should be postponed until students had mastered arithmetic. I am distinguishing here between arithmetic and algebra according to the psychological criterion of whether there is extensive manipulation of variables in problem solving. According to this reasoning, one works with unknowns in arithmetic, but variables are not symbolically manipulated to a great extent. But studies conducted in the former Soviet Union have provided compelling evidence that students in early grades at school can meaningfully use algebra provided they are oriented in how to represent physical quantities through letters. In short, there are good reasons for placing fractions, ratios, and proportions in an algebraic context at a much earlier point. When letters are used to refer to physical magnitudes, as we suggest here, the longhand, algebraic description is clearer than the shorthand version. Algebraic notation potentially may help establish clear links between fractions, ratios, proportions, functions, and other concepts that appear otherwise unrelated in traditional instruction on fractions.

Didactic Suggestions

The analysis to this point suggests two potential resources students can draw on when learning about fractions. Students bring with them perceptual judgmental skills regarding ratios of quantities. And they have considerable experience with integer arithmetic. Now let us consider some ideas regarding the teaching of fractions that could make use of this knowledge.

Eudoxus' Conception of Proportion

Euclidean mathematics offers itself as a useful point of departure because the Greeks of antiquity had not yet invented fractions, but they were able to handle ratios and proportions through integer operations on quantities. This case may provide insights for instruction regarding fractions, because students acquire intuitive knowledge regarding ratio and proportion before they become familiar with fractions.

Mathematicians of ancient Greece adopted a "constructive" approach to problem solving—for them, a problem was solved when the solution was demonstrated geometrically. Such proofs rely upon actions on physical quantities rather than the manipulation of formal symbols. Number was conceptualized in terms of line segments. This confusion between number and quantity enables properties of numbers to be explored through operations on line segments; in the process, line segments are imbued with arithmetical meaning.

The definition of proportion attributed to Eudoxus, found in Book V of Euclid Elements, has been translated as follows:

> *Magnitudes are said to be in the same ratio, the first to the second and the third to the fourth, when, if any equimultiples whatever of the second and fourth, the former equimultiples alike exceed, are alike equal to, or alike fall short of, the latter equimultiples respectively taken in corresponding order.*

In modern notation, this is tantamount to asserting that:

Given the line segments A, B, C, D, A:B = C:D is true if and only if, for any positive integers m and n, one of the three following conditions holds:

$mA > nB$ *and* $mC > nD$

$mA = nB$ *and* $mC = nD$

$mA < nB$ *and* $mC < nD$

A:B OR C:D if there exist positive integers m and n such that any of the following conditions holds:

$mA > nB$ *and* $mC < nD$

$mA < nB$ *and* $mC > nD$

$mA = nB$ *and* $mC < nD$

$mA = nB$ *and* $mC > nD$

$mA > nB$ *and* $mC = nD$

$mA < nB$ *and* $mC = nD$

The goal is to decide whether A:B = C:D.

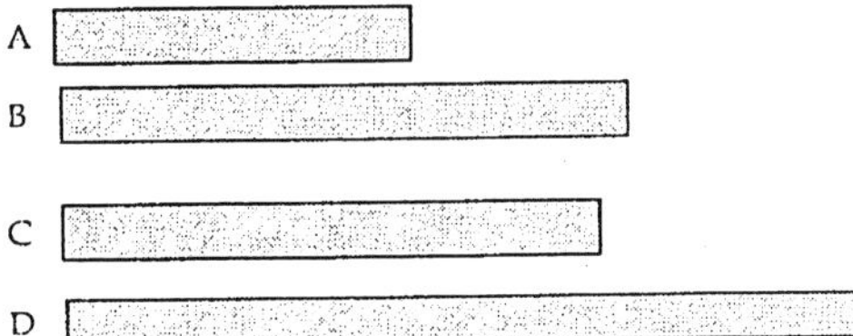

Fig. 9.4. Embodiment in a task of the Eudoxean conception of fractions

Figure 9.5 shows the result of multiplying the first segment of each ratio by 3 and the second segment by 2. Think about it for a moment. What can be concluded from the results shown in Fig. 9.5 ? Is *A:B* equivalent to *C:D*?

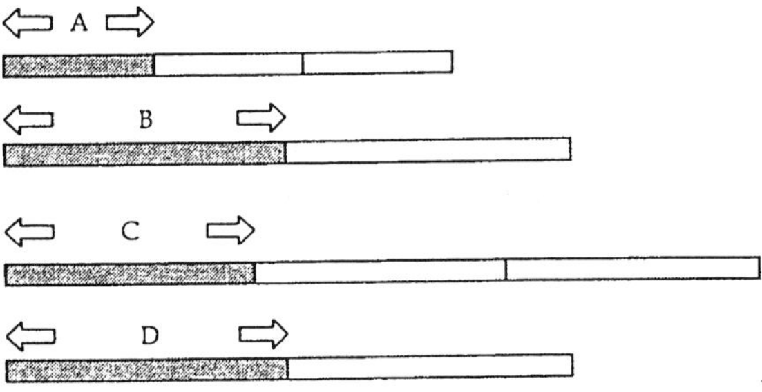

Fig. 9.5. Exploration of whether *A:B* = *C:D* through multiplication of segments

Is the first pair of segments proportional to the second pair?

The result conclusively demonstrates that A:B is not equivalent to C:D (see condition 5). If the ratios had been equivalent, the same effects should have been observed in each case. This did not happen: 3 A's fell short of 2 B's, whereas 3 C's surpassed 2 D's.

What can be inferred?

The Eudoxian definition of proportion provides a test of whether one ratio of segments, A:B, is equivalent to another ratio, C:D, by "multiplying" (n-folding) the antecedents and consequents by m and n, respectively, and comparing the results. The test results are not always conclusive. Two conditions, 1 and 3, do not allow one to conclude that the ratios are proportional, but only that they have not been shown to be non-proportional. Condition 2 alone allows one to conclude that the ratios are proportional. Conditions 4-9 conclusively demonstrate that the ratios are not proportional.

The historical importance of this definition lies in the fact that it allowed Greek mathematicians of antiquity to represent ratios of incommensurable quantities, that is, quantities that have no common measure, such as the ratio of the diagonal to the side of a square. Such ratios were known to exist but were inexpressible as numbers, which for ancient Greeks were restricted to positive integers.

The importance of Eudoxus's definition for the present discussion lies elsewhere. The definition places ratio and proportion squarely in the context of perceptual judgment. This is precisely the context in which children begin to develop the concepts of ratio and proportion, as suggested by studies of psychological development mentioned earlier. The definition specifies actions students can actually carry out on quantities (n-folding). They can then judge for themselves what conditions hold, by visually comparing the lengths of the resultant segments.

It is noteworthy that the Eudoxian approach expressly involves integer operations on physical quantities. As the preceding analysis suggests, this appears to be how children originally understand multiplication and division (before they understand integer operations on integers).

Algebraic Relations in Eudoxian Proportion

Labeling the results of the preceding example can lead to some important insights. The first pair of multiplications shows that $3A < 2B$. The second pair establishes that $3C > 2D$. The results can be rewritten as $A:B < 2:3$ and $C:D > 2:3$, respectively. These results can be joined as $A:B < 2:3 < C:D$. This means that the ratio 2:3 falls between the ratio A:B and the ratio C:D. So we have learned much more from the results than the mere fact that the ratios are not equivalent. We know a ratio that falls between them (and conversely, we can only prove them nonequivalent by finding multipliers that yield such a ratio).

Because only two ratios are necessary to make a proportion, we can eliminate one of the ratios of quantities. The Eudoxian task is now redefined as the problem of discovering what ratio of integers corresponds to a given ratio of quantities. Each time we carry out scalar multiplications on the line segments, we obtain more information regarding the "correct" ratio. By cleverly choosing the multipliers we should be able to move closer and closer to a correct answer.

In Fig. 9.6 , the results of each multiplication are equal in length (we are ignoring for the moment the practical problems of visually deciding whether segments do or do not have the same length). When this occurs the information provided constitutes not an inequality but rather an equation ($5A = 3B$, in the example). In such a case, we can infer the correct or true numerical ratio corresponding to A:B. The ratio of quantities, A:B, corresponds to the numerical ratio, 3:5, or any equivalent ratio such as 6:10 or 1.5:2.5.

In the modified Euxdoxian task, with one ratio of quantities and one ratio of integers, there are three possible conclusions based on three possible outcomes of any trial:

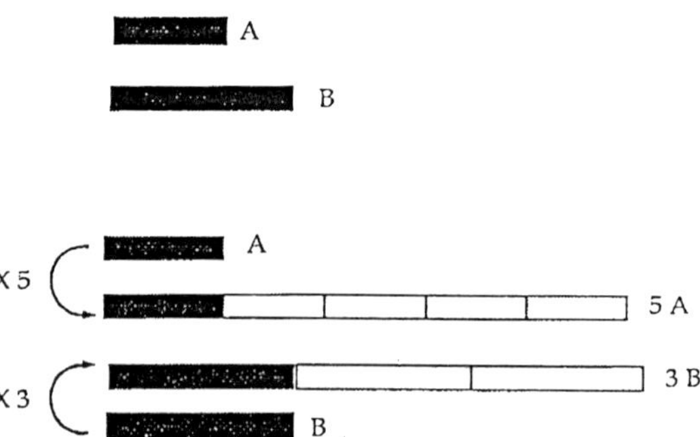

Fig. 9.6. Inference of the ratio A:B through equality of multiplied segments

Problem: What is the ratio A to B? Solution: $5A = 3B$ therefore $A : B = 3 : 5$

$MA = nB$ *implying* $A:B = n:m$

$mA < nB$ *implying* $A:B < n:m$

$mA > nB$ *implying* $A:B > n:m$

Condition 1 is the only one that clearly informs us about the numerical ratio between A and B. The remaining two conditions merely allow one to conclude that the correct ratio is less than or greater than the tested ratio. In Fig. 9.6 condition 1 is satisfied. One can correctly conclude that the proportion A:B = 3:5 is true. It follows that A/B = 3/5 and A = 3/5B. So the modified Euclidean test of proportionality is indeed related to fractions.

But here we must tread with caution. Notation involving fractions only makes sense to those already familiar with it. We cannot presume that students would draw the appropriate conclusion from observing the results in Fig. 9.6 . For that matter, they are not likely to conclude even that A:B = 3:5. The present analysis, directed to mathematics educators, presumes a familiarity with certain ideas and notation. Students are likely to have their own views on how to explain and interpret situations such as that depicted in Fig. 9.6 . In describing the task, they may use concepts entirely different from those of mathematicians or mathematics educators. So what to the experienced mathematics educator looks like a "simple demonstration" may appear to students as a perplexing situation that calls for considerable reflection.

This is not necessarily bad. Overcoming perplexity may be any important part of acquiring new concepts. Besides, students are likely to learn little from tasks they immediately understand. Nevertheless, we should be careful not to appraise tasks simply according to the degree of perplexity they generate in students. Notation does not necessarily become intelligible as students see it again and again. What evidence can students encounter, in the tasks themselves or in ensuing discussions, for making sense of the notation? Where can students borrow meaning from situations they already understand? Where are ruptures or breaks in continuity being introduced?

As a first step in dealing with the problem of making formal notation intelligible, we should note that the present approach is based on the idea that there are important parallels between physical actions and mathematical operations. As we noted earlier, the mathematical operation of multiplying by an integer n is like the physical action of taking some object n times (as reflected in the use of the word "times" to describe multiplication). Division by an integer m is like taking an m th part of some object. These parallels can and should be made explicit to students in order to make sense of hypotheses expressed mathematically.

Mathematical operations can be represented in notation either implicitly or explicitly. Multiplication of the quantity A by 3 can be expressed either as A × 3 or as 3A. Although these expressions are mathematically equivalent, there are important differences between them. The explicit form, A × 3, is more appropriate for highlighting the tie between the mathematical operation (multiplication) and the physical action (n-folding, i.e., taking n of some quantity). It represents, better than the implicit form, 3A, an action that has not yet been undertaken. This can be easily appreciated by simply examining the forms, A × 3 and 3A. "A × 3" conveys the idea of a multiplication that has not yet been carried out; it is likely to represent to students a "problem," an operation to be carried out in the future. On the other hand, "3A" conveys the idea of a measure; it may better represent the result of multiplication rather than the operation itself. Thus we could say that A × 3 yields 3A, but not the converse. The distinction between instances "before" and "after" an operation is technically irrelevant in mathematics but psychologically important.

Discovering Fractions in a Eudoxian Setting

Integer Multiplication and Common Multiples. A hypothesis is a prediction about what will be observed under certain conditions. What is a hypothesis for the modified Eudoxian task? How can it be expressed in notation?

The modified Eudoxian task challenges one to find a numerical ratio that corresponds to a ratio of segments given in visual form. To be more precise, the task entails a search for a "common product" or "common multiple" of two line segments. In natural language, a hypothesis might be represented as follows: " if one multiplies A by 3 and B by 2, then the resulting segments will be the same length."

The same hypothesis can be expressed mathematically by the following equation:

$A \times 3 = B \times 2?$

The hypothesis is tested by carrying out the operations on each side of the equation and observing the results. We saw in the example that A × 3 yields 3A; B × 2 yields 2B. The inequality $3A < 2B$, which describes the fact that the line segment 3A is shorter than the line segment 2B, informs us that the hypothesis is incorrect.

A similar analysis can be made of the correct hypothesis:

$A \times 5 = B \times 3?$

The hypothesis was tested by multiplying segment A by 5, multiplying segment B by 3, and comparing the resultant segments,

5A and 3B. Because 5A was found to have the same length as 3B, the conclusion is that 5A = 3B and, by substitution, A × 5 = B × 3. In other words, the hypothesis has been confirmed by experimental test.

The following steps show how the diverse notation might be linked to the testing of the hypothesis:

A × 5 = B × 3? The hypothesis raised by the student. It can be read as a question: "If I multiply A by 5 and B by 3, will they yield equal results?

A × 5 = 5A The operation is carried out, yielding the first product segment 5A.

B × 3 = 3B The second operation is carried out, yielding segment 3B.

5A = 3B? By substitution, the original hypothesis now becomes: "Is 5A equal to 3B?"

5A = 3B The segments are experimentally found to have the same length; the variation of the original hypothesis is confirmed.

A × 5 = B × 3 Therefore the original hypothesis is confirmed.

Understanding the task requires recognizing how a ratio of numbers can compensate for a ratio of quantities. The numerical ratio should correspond to the reciprocal of the ratio of quantities. Although a correct answer entails numbers, there is no way to solve the task straight away by doing calculations (as there would be if A were broken into 3 units and B into 5 units of the same size). Because the segments have not been broken up into sets of equal units, it is impossible to "count" the length of the segments and perform a calculation on the measured lengths. Some educators would undoubtedly complain that leaving the segments unmeasured in "unfair." They may say: "Shouldn't there be a direct way to compute the answer? No one will solve such a problem on the first try." But this is precisely the point. By leaving the numerical ratio of the segments implicit, the students are forced to reflect upon the relative magnitude of the segments (i.e., the ratio of quantities) in order to discover a solution to the task. No amount of counting, matching, or calculating can by itself produce a correct answer. Instead, students must engage themselves in hypothesis testing until they gain an understanding of how the pair of operators chosen plays a role, together with the physical magnitudes, in producing the results. Integer Division and Unit Fractions. We saw above that a hypothesis such as A × *m* = B × n? addresses the proportion A:B = n: m from the perspective of a common product. Conversely, a hypothesis of the form A ÷ n = B ÷ m? addresses the proportion from the point of view of a common factor or "common measure". This task relies upon the operation of division rather than multiplication. Even more importantly, it introduces notation for fractions both as operators and as measures—the results of operation by fractions. There are two general ways of expressing a hypothesis for the present task in natural language:

- If I divide A by some integer n, and divide B by another integer m, the resulting segments will be equal in length.
- If I take one nth of A and one m th of B, the segments taken will be equal in length.

These sentences correspond respectively to the operations of division by an integer and multiplication by a unit fraction. They happen to be different ways of describing the same relationships.

It is likely that students do not view "× p" as equivalent to "taking one-third" or "dividing by 3." The common measure task may provide a good context for engaging students in discussion about the meaning of such diverse expressions. We need empirical research in order to understand what sense students make of these expressions and how they relate them to actions upon quantities.

A preliminary investigation showed that, when working with concrete materials, some sixth-grade students were inclined to confuse "division by n" with "dividing into n pieces." The division of a bar of chocolate by 3, for example, is understood by some students as cutting it into 3 pieces. Even when the interviewer drew attention to the written operation ÷ 3, some students maintained that the amount of chocolate was the same as it was before the division. Such observations suggest that the belief that "dividing makes smaller" may be called on or not depending on the context.

It would be foolish to maintain that all mathematical expressions are "really" about actions on physical objects. A statement such as ¼A = pB can also be understood as a description of relations. In the present model this can be read as "one-fifth of A is equal to one-third of B." Such an interpretation lacks explicit reference to actions on quantities. It is different from an action interpretation without being incompatible with it. "One-fifth of A" can be legitimately understood as shorthand for the expression "what you get when you divide A by 5." In a sense the action interpretation and relational interpretation complement each other

$$\frac{A}{3} = \frac{B}{5}$$

This

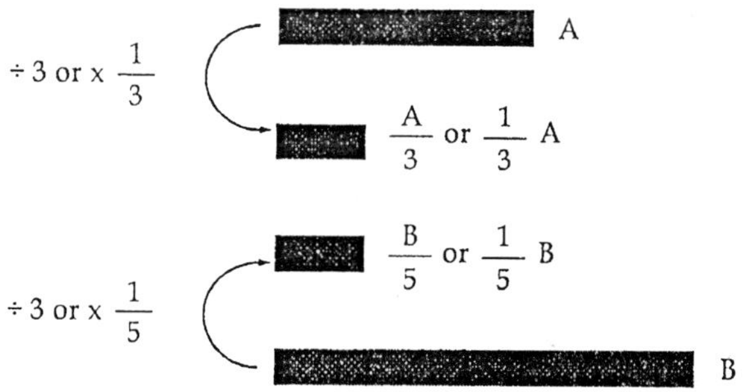

$\div 3$ or x $\frac{1}{3}$ A

$\frac{A}{3}$ or $\frac{1}{3}$ A

$\frac{B}{5}$ or $\frac{1}{5}$ B

$\div 3$ or x $\frac{1}{5}$ B

Fig. 9.7. Inference of the ratio *A:B* through equality of divided segments

These ideas do not exhaust how equations and inequalities can be interpreted. There may be other ways of conceptualizing the expressions within the model at hand, and empirical studies with human subjects may be the best guide to determine this. In a community of professional mathematicians there may be a great amount of diversity in interpreting such expressions. Some, no doubt, will do so without making any reference to physical objects.

A Fraction as the Result of Multiplication and Division. Another way of approaching the relation between quantities is to consider what pair of integer operations would transform one quantity into the other. There are essentially two ways, namely, (a) through addition/subtraction, and (b) through multiplication/division. The latter case provides us with very special conditions for learning about fractions.

If the quantities A and B stand in the numerical ratio n: m then A can be transformed into B by multiplying it by m and dividing the result by n. The hypothesis in this problem can be written in two different ways:

$B = (A \times 5) \div 3?$ *or* $B = A \times R$

A skeptic might be inclined to argue that the latter expression would be meaningless to students who do not already understand what a fractional operator is. There is some truth to this claim. Students certainly cannot be expected to understand at first glance what the expression A × R means. But this is like arguing that parents should not talk to their infant until it has learned what the words mean. The real issue is not whether the learner understands the expressions in the beginning but rather whether, over time, contexts provide support for the learner to come to understand what the expressions mean.

Consider first the effects of the integer operations. It should become clear over a series of trials that the multiplier makes the operand segment "grow," and the larger the multiplier, the greater the growth. The integer divisor makes the operand segment "shrink," and the larger the divisor, the more it induces shrinking. When the multiplier and divisor are equal, they nullify each other. In this case they are inverse operations. The relative size of the multiplier and divisor determines the net effect. This is another way of saying that the ratio of the multiplier to the divisor determines the net outcome. These ideas stand in harmony with students' intuitive beliefs that "multiplying makes bigger" and "dividing makes smaller." Let us now look at the case of multiplication by a fraction.

In multiplication by a fraction, the numerator behaves precisely as an integer multiplier. The denominator behaves exactly as an integer divisor. The numerator and denominator act in opposition, exactly as an integer multiplier and divisor do. When the numerator has the same value as the denominator, the effect of one agent is canceled by the effect of the other. The case corresponds to that of multiplying and dividing by the same integer. Multiplication by a fraction of the form n/n is an identity operation; it is just like multiplying by the number 1. A fraction-operator can be thought of as a succinct way of doing multiplication and division.

Although a fraction can derive considerable meaning from multiplication and division, there are still substantial adjustments to be made in students' thinking. Formerly, multiplication by (natural) numbers always led to increase. Now, in the case of fractions the student must consider the net effect of the numerator and the denominator to predict the direction of the outcome. With practice, students should come to see that proper fractions result in decrease and improper fractions result in increase.

Even greater adjustments in thinking must be made to come to understand the order of fractions. Why does multiplying by 3/5 produce a result less than that of multiplying by 2/3? What fractions will produce results between these values? The multiplication and division of fractions by fractions (e.g., what is 1/3 divided by 2/5?) likewise require considerable adjustment.

Links to Computational Tasks. Let us look now at some ideas about how the preceding three tasks might be related to the sort of ratio and proportion problems typically given in schools. The first thing to note is that one can estimate the fraction of income paid in taxes by examining the relative magnitudes of the two line segments without making any numerical calculations at all. Because the issue here involves the ratio of the segments, the length of each segment, taken alone, must be considered irrelevant.

If multiple instances of the two line segments are available, students can do multiplications—actually, n-folding—"by hand" until they have found a common multiple. This is only part of the solution. Remember, the common multiple produces two integers. However, the problem asks for the fraction or percent of income that goes to taxes.

As students do their n-folding, the context of the problem will naturally be used in describing what they see. Students may note, for example, that the income in 2 months is approximately equal to the taxes paid over 5 months. In another context, mathematically similar results may lead to what appear to be very different descriptions. For example, in a problem regarding sales of computers, students may be led to the conclusion that 2 months' sales of IBM PCs correspond to 5 months' sales of MacIntosh computers. Or 2 months of rain in Manaus, Brazil, corresponds to 5 months of rain in Boston.

There are advantages in directing discussion toward issues that crop up along the way to the solution of the problem. Once students have found a solution by means of common multiples, one can ask, for example, whether there will be other common multiples. What about near misses? How can one generally express the relationship between Maria's taxes and her income? Are there other means of solving the problem (e.g., through weighing)?

With a straightedge and compass it is possible to break up the line segments into equal units. This corresponds to the common factor method. Students can test hypotheses about the ratio of the quantities by repeatedly testing hypotheses on instances of the segments. What degree of precision is there in such cases? On a computerized version of the common factor task, there are no limits to precision because algebraic feedback is never ambiguous. This is a topic worthy of discussion.

The multiplication—division method can also be used. Results are likely to be more accurate if multiplication precedes division. Even so, results should be close regardless of the order shown. Do the three methods discussed in this chapter (common product, common factor, multiplication--division) produce similar results? Are they based on the same ratio? If there are differences, which are more likely to be accurate? Do the algebraic statements that correspond to each method mean the same thing? For example, does "5 × Taxes = 2 × 1.

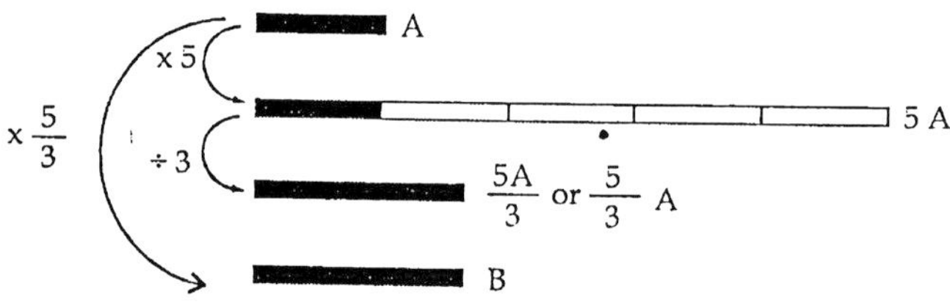

Fig. 9.8. Relation to typical school tasks.

Income" mean the same as "Taxes = Income × E"? Are there in principle, or in practical reality, pairs of line segments for which there are no clear-cut solutions—for example, for which there are no common multiples, no common factors, no pair of integers that makes one magnitude become equal to the other? What are the implications of the conclusions students will draw? What are the relations to the concept of irrational number?

Once students are satisfied that they know the ratio of the line segments, it is possible to determine the unknown value, in this case, of the segment referring to the taxes Maria paid. Hopefully, when students have looked at the relationships from many perspectives, as we have suggested here, they will find the computational side of fractions easier to understand. Another way to approach the problem is to measure the lengths with a ruler and to engage students in discussions once they have obtained their measurements. It may be interesting to suggest using different types of rulers (e.g., in inches and centimeters) and then have students reflect about how the choice of standard may or may not affect the answer to the problem.

Some Questionable Premises Regarding Fractions: The problem just given entails a part-whole relationship, because taxes are part of one's gross income. As we saw, this type of relationship can be captured in a two-line-segment model. It can also be represented in the classic pie format.

But we cannot represent common multiples, common products, or multiplication-division in a pie representation. Imagine that the ratio of taxes to gross income is 2:5. If we take five instances of the taxes (5 gray slices) and two instances of the gross income (2 whole pies), there is no way to know through visual inspection that these quantities are equal. So we must be told the relation between taxes and income. The problem then reduces to a computational exercise. This is one disadvantage of pie models for fractions.

But there is an even more serious limitation to the pie model, namely, that it cannot depict ratios that are not conceptually part-whole. Consider, for example, the problem of comparing the populations of two countries, for example, Brazil and the United States. A comparison of appropriate line segments permits us to see that Brazil's population is about % that of the United States. Once we have a notion of the ratio between the two quantities, we can attempt to use it for answering further questions. By what fraction (or percent) would Brazil's population have to increase to equal that of the United States (presuming that the population in the United States remains fixed)? If the population in Brazil doubles in 30 years, by what fraction would the population of the United States have to increase in order to then equal that of Brazil? But this information cannot sensibly be shown in a pie chart. All ratio and proportion problems can be sensibly represented through fractions, but not all ratio and proportions problems can be adequately depicted in pie-chart models of fractions.

The model discussed in the present chapter begins by drawing the students' attention to a relation between two segments, A and B. The quantities could be identified as 1A and 1B, so in the beginning one does work with "units" in the sense of measures assigned the value 1. Fractions first appear as operators that act upon unit segments. These operations produce other measures such as 3B, ¾A, 2*C. These fractional results can become the operands for subsequent operations. When this occurs students can begin to reflect about what it means to multiply a fractional measure by a fraction. Hopefully such ideas will some day make sense to the majority of students. I believe that this understanding depends in the beginning on students' success in associating mathematical operations with actions on quantities. With time, the mathematical operations may become fairly autonomous of such translations and references to quantity. But I suspect that mental representations of quantities will continue to play an important role in advanced mathematical thinking.

Concluding Remarks

In order to understand what fractions are, as psychological concepts, we must try to understand how they relate to what students already know. Here we looked at two sources of knowledge that students can draw on in learning about fractions: (a) understanding of ratio and proportion, and (b) knowledge of integer arithmetic.

Investigations of ratio and proportion paint an apparently contradictory picture of students' abilities. Studies in the area of mathematics education seem to suggest that the greater part of students in the 11 to 15 years age range have difficulty with ratio and proportion. Yet psychological studies show that children develop rudimentary skills in ratio and proportion as early as 6 years old. It is likely that ratio and proportion understanding begin very early but take many years to fully develop. But, more importantly, children seem to grasp ideas about ratios of quantity long before they work with numerical ratios. A fully developed understanding of ratio and proportion, on which the concept of fraction must rest, entails being able to work with both sorts of ratios and their interrelationships. Traditional notation used in instruction about fractions is incomplete and unsatisfactory for bringing out these interrelationships. A fractional numeral such as p embodies a ratio of numbers but says nothing about a ratio of quantities. Fractional numerals can be understood as shorthand for more general descriptions regarding relations between two quantities. Equations are better suited than fractional numerals for describing the interpenetration of ratios of numbers and ratios of quantity. Equations are special forms of notation that probably do not map directly onto students' natural language descriptions of relations.

One could in principle introduce equations into standard classroom fractions through tasks involving pizzas and cakes, but there are reasons for looking for inspiration elsewhere. To aid students in moving away from analyses based on cardinal number, continuous quantities have advantages over sets of units. Furthermore, comparisons based on length offer advantages over those based on area, because in the former case the students can judge for themselves whether one quantity is equal to the other. This characteristic is important if we want students to use their perceptual judgmental skills in fractions tasks.

An ancient Greek definition of proportion provides a useful context for learning about fractions. Eudoxus' definition of proportion is based on equivalence between ratios of quantities and ratios of numbers. It constitutes an operational definition, a test, about how one can determine whether two ratios of quantities are equal. The test consists in acting on the quantities and observing the outcomes of one's actions.

A modification was proposed in Eudoxus' definition. The modified version provides a means of determining what numerical ratio corresponds to the ratio of two line segments. Three tasks were suggested for discovering ratios. The "common multiples" task is based on the search for a common product segment of the original two segments. The task is solved when the learner chooses integer multipliers that produce equal product segments. This occurs only if the multipliers chosen correspond to the reciprocal of the original ratio of quantities.

The "common measure" or "common factor" task approaches the proportion through division. One solves the task when the integer divisors chosen produce quotient segments of equal length. This occurs only when the divisors stand in direct proportion to the ratio of quantities. Because division by an integer is equivalent to multiplying by a unit fraction, the task provides an opportunity for introducing unit fractions. Mathematically, the "common factor" task is equivalent to the "common multiple" task, although they are conceptually quite different.

A third task was described in which the learner attempts to make one quantity equal to the second through multiplication and division by integers. This multiplication-division task corresponds directly to the case of multiplying by a fraction. The numerator acts as an integer multiplier, and the denominator acts as an integer divisor. Although it is often argued that integer knowledge interferes with students' understanding of fractions as operators, the present task makes clear that a fraction can be defined through integer multiplication and division. In this way, previous knowledge can be used as a resource rather than a stumbling block for the development of new concepts. Seen in this light, fractions are much closer to the topics of multiplication and division than one might expect based on an examination of current textbooks.

A software environment based on the present approach, called Lines of Thought, is now under development. The software comprises a dozen tasks and representational tools that students can use to discuss the relations discussed here, as well as many others. The guiding concern has been to create contexts in which students are challenged to think about how one problem can be analyzed and represented in diverse ways. Accordingly, none of the problems can be solved through computational routines, because computational routines rarely encourage reflection, but rather require thinking about the interrelations among numbers and quantities as well as their embodiment in algebraic statements. Further, in Lines of Thought, problems continue even after a student has found a correct answer. The tasks call for multiple solutions, including those that require integrating knowledge regarding diverse representations. There are several advantages to embodying the tasks in software, the most important being that students can produce data that may give rise to new ideas as well as to provide evidence for testing their evolving conjectures about relations among diverse objects.

The present tasks are suggested as learning contexts rather than demonstrations. Concepts as rich as fractions are not acquired immediately, because they require reorganization of prior knowledge. In order to improve instruction regarding fractions and related concepts, the field of mathematics education needs empirical research regarding how students make sense of the situations described in this chapter. By analyzing protocols of students as they attempt to solve problems, we can gain fresh insights into what is involved in teaching and learning about fractions.

10

Learning Mathematics in Classroom Practice

Introduction

Educational reformers in the United States are calling for sweeping changes in instructional practices, such as the new standards for mathematics instruction from the National Council of Teachers of Mathematics. They argue that students need to be actively involved in practicing mathematics by working in small groups, negotiating ways to define and organize the data in open-ended problems, arriving at multiple solutions, and explaining their ideas to each other. These practices are in contrast to what is seen in more traditional North American mathematics classrooms in which whole-class, teacher-dominated didactic instruction and individual seatwork are the norm. In addition to changes in the processes of instruction, the reform movement is also calling for new instructional goals: from the memorization of number facts and the accurate use of computational algorithms to greater understanding of mathematical concepts and more effective use of problem-solving strategies. Enhancing students' abilities to communicate and to collaborate with others is also emphasized. In addition, the reform movement is interested in changing students' attitudes toward learning mathematics: from anxiety and passive obedience to authority to enthusiasm, confidence, and active involvement in problem solving. Although the reformers call for change in practice as well as content, the new standards for mathematics instruction, for example, contain more information about the latter than the former. More seriously, there is very little justification provided for the connections between changes in practice and desired instructional outcomes.

A number of North American educational reformers have based their proposals on a family of psychological and anthropological theories referred to as socio-cultural theory. Socio-cultural theory traces its roots to the work of the Soviet psychologists Vygotsky, Luria, and Leont'ev, who began writing in the early part of the 20th century. As this work became more widely available to a North American audience in the 1980s, important expansions, modifications, and applications of the theory were made.

The purpose of this chapter is to show how socio-cultural theory can provide a basis for the hypothetical connection between the proposed changes in instructional processes and the desired goals of the reform movement. A secondary purpose is to explicate three crucial constructs: legitimate peripheral participation, activity setting, and instructional conversation, which play a central role in understanding and evaluating educational reform from a socio-cultural perspective.

In order to accomplish these purposes, I show how the three constructs relate to the broader theoretical framework provided by van Oers and outline some of the extensions and applications of socio-cultural theory that have occurred in North America in the past 15 years. Then I use the theory to discuss some observations that were made in two middle school mathematics classrooms taught by Ms. Hanes. The observations were collected during the first 2 years of an educational reform project aimed at fostering high-level reasoning and problem-solving skills for students from economically disadvantaged backgrounds. The goal of this analysis is to illustrate the value of a socio-cultural approach for understanding how changes in social practices in the classroom can affect the learning of mathematics. In the final section of the chapter, I discuss the practical significance of socio-cultural theory for guiding our analysis of the processes and outcomes of educational reform.

Sociocultural Theory

A complete presentation of socio-cultural theory is beyond the scope of this chapter. Interested readers are encouraged to look at other sources for a fuller treatment of this perspective.

The discussion of the Vygotskian approach in van Oers' work provides a useful introduction to the constructs to be presented here. There are four key ideas in van Oers' work that are central to the socio-cultural approach to learning mathematics. First, social, cultural, and institutional contexts do more than merely facilitate or impede learning. Social organizational processes are an inherent characteristic of learning-whether or not it occurs in an overtly social context. Second, learning needs to be viewed as a form of apprenticeship or a means by which novices become experts through participation in activities within a community of practice. Third, learning mathematics is a discursive activity. Fourth, learning involves the negotiation of meaning within the context of situated activity.

Van Oers traces the source of his action-psychological approach to Russian scholars and educators such as Vygotsky, Leont'ev, Luria, Galperin, Davydov, and Bakhtin. In addition to these sources, North American theorists have been influenced by cross-cultural research conducted by Cole, Lave, Rogoff, Saxe, Scribner, B. Whiting, J. Whiting, and others and by studies of the social context of instruction by Bruner, Wood, and Wertsch . Three constructs discussed by North American theorists provide a framework for examining mathematics learning that is compatible with van Oers' action-psychological approach. They are legitimate peripheral participation, activity setting, and instructional conversation. Each concept and its relevance for understanding learning in reform mathematics classrooms is discussed in this section.

Lave and Wenger described learning as a process by which a newcomer is integrated into a community of practice. They called this process legitimate peripheral participation. Legitimate peripheral participation is used instead of apprenticeship to avoid the restrictive connotations of craft apprenticeship.

Unlike many psychologists and educators, Lave and Wenger did not depict learning as internalization, transmission, absorption, or assimilation of information from the "external world" to create some form of "internal" representations. Relying upon Marxist theory, they denied the dichotomy between the internal and the external. They also argued that learning is not an individual accomplishment and therefore the unit of analysis should not be the individual. Instead of learning as intemalization, they proposed "learning as increasing participation in communities of practice". Thus, what matters for learning is not the availability of instructional resources such as computers, small class size, content-rich textbooks, and so on, but access to meaningful practice in a community. Goodnow agreed with this position when she claimed, "it is the nature of one's positions, of one's participation in the social life of the group, that influences the extent to which one picks up, and appropriates as one's own, the skills and ways of thinking valued by the group".

All participants in a community of practice are legitimate, but some (such as newcomers) are more peripheral than others (such as old-timers). Old-timers differ from newcomers in having more power in the community as well as more knowledge of its valued skills. Newcomers can become old-timers, at least in Principle, by increasing their range of practice in the community over time. As their range of practice increases, their knowledge increases.

In summary, Lave and Wenger presented an alternative way of conceptualizing learning. Instead of learning as internalization, learning is seen as participation in the activities of a community. Thus, the ideal conditions for learning mathematics would involve access to meaningful activity within a community of mathematical practice. This community could occur outside or inside the institution of school (Saxe, 1991; Saxe & Bermudez, chapter 3, this volume; Schliemann & Carraher, chapter 5, this volume). If learning is to occur inside school, then the classroom teacher has an important role to play as the old-timer in the classroom community. Some of the responsibilities of the old-timer involve the communication of the norms, values, and discourse practices of the community to the newcomers and the design of meaningful mathematical activity settings.

Both Vygotsky and Leont'ev also attempted to redefine learning using some basic constructs from Marx. They argued, like Lave and Wenger, that one needed to identify a unit of analysis in psychological research which integrated the thoughts and actions of individuals with their goal-directed, culturally specific activities (Cole, 1985; Leont'ev, 1981). Activity setting, as defined and used by Tharp and Gallimore (1988), is one approach to comparing and contrasting learning activity in context. Gallimore and Goldenberg (1993) defined five variables that determine an activity setting: "1) personnel present during an activity, 2) salient cultural values, 3) the operations and task demands of the activity itself, 4) the scripts for conduct that govern the participants' actions, and 5) the purposes or motives of the participants". By focusing on activity settings, one is forced to recognize the connections between what a person does, feels, thinks, and believes; the constraints and supports provided by other people and artifacts in that particular setting; and cultural rules, norms, and values.

Activity setting and legitimate peripheral participation provide complementary and necessary tools for the study of learning in sociocultural context. The concept of activity supplies a unit of analysis for the study of educational reform, and the concept of legitimate peripheral participation permits one to infer something about learning from differences in participation patterns. These two constructs emphasize that learning is synonymous with socially situated activity. What they do not include is the notion of learning as a discursive practice, which is also central to sociocultural theory. That is why the third construct, instructional conversation, is also needed.

If, as van Oers and others have argued, learning involves the negotiation of both cultural and personal meaning, then classroom discourse must allow this kind of negotiation process to occur. Tharp and Gallimore (1988) used the term instructional conversation to refer to classroom discourse that permits the coconstruction of meaning between teachers and students. They contrasted instructional conversations with the more typical kind of classroom talk known as the recitation script. The recitation script consists of three parts: an initiation or Query by the teacher, a student response, and an evaluation by the teacher. The recitation script assumes that learning is a process of internalization, not one of negotiation of meaning. It restricts students' activity to accepting (or rejecting) the interpretation implicit in the teacher's query. There is no opportunity within this script for students to redefine the problem being presented or to offer alternative explanations, unless specifically requested to do so. It also privileges the teacher's evaluation of an answer. In contrast, instructional conversations are modeled after everyday conversations in which the more experienced members of a culture instruct the less experienced via talk. An example of this kind of conversation is the young child learning a first language through interacting with family members, neighbors, and friends.

Instructional conversations involve the integration of concepts from school (i.e., Vygotsky's scientific concepts) and everyday concepts (Tharp & Gallimore , 1988). They serve a similar function in Tharp and Gallimore's theory of learning as does the notion of discursive learning activity in van Oers' approach. Instructional conversations go beyond concept learning to involve the mastery of specialized speech genres such as the mathematics register (Forman, 1992; Halliday , 1975, 1978; Pimm, 1987; van Oers, chapter 7, this volume). In the mathematics register, words may be given new meanings (e.g., "similarity", "identity"), syntax reflects the timeless and impersonal nature of propositions (e.g., there may be no subject in a sentence or the subject may be an impersonal "you"), and particular modes of argument are valued (e.g., precision, brevity, logical coherence).

The three constructs, legitimate peripheral participation, activity setting, and instructional conversation, allow us to ask a number of questions about reform classrooms. For example, how do reform classrooms and traditional classrooms differ in the opportunities each offers for social participation? Within any particular classroom community or activity setting, do individuals differ in their participation? What do these participation patterns tell us about learning mathematics?

Application of Sociocultural Theory

I the analyses described next, three different comparisons of participation in activity settings are made with reference to two of Ms. Hanes' middle school mathematics classes. First, the range of activity settings available in traditional and reform classrooms [2] is contrasted. Second, student participation across activity settings within a single classroom is described. Third, student participation within a single activity setting is illustrated by focusing on differential use of the mathematics register. The aim of this analysis is to use data from these classes to query by the teacher, a student response, and an evaluation by the teacher. The recitation script assumes that learning is a process of internalization, not one of negotiation of meaning. It restricts students' activity to accepting (or rejecting) the interpretation implicit in the teacher's query. There is no opportunity within this script for students to redefine the problem being presented or to offer alternative explanations, unless specifically requested to do so. It also privileges the teacher's evaluation of an answer. In contrast, instructional conversations are modeled after everyday conversations in which the more experienced members of a culture instruct the less experienced via talk. An example of this kind of conversation is the young child learning a first language through interacting with family members, neighbors, and friends.

Instructional conversations involve the integration of concepts from school and everyday concepts. They serve a similar function in Tharp and Gallimore's theory of learning as does the notion of discursive learning activity in van Oers' approach. Instructional conversations go beyond concept learning to involve the mastery of specialized speech genres such as the mathematics register. In the mathematics register, words may be given new meanings (e.g., "similarity", "identity"), syntax reflects the timeless and impersonal nature of propositions (e.g., there may be no subject in a sentence or the subject may be an impersonal "you"), and particular modes of argument are valued (e.g., precision, brevity, logical coherence).

The three constructs, legitimate peripheral participation, activity setting, and instructional conversation, allow us to ask a number of questions about reform classrooms. For example, how do reform classrooms and traditional classrooms differ in the opportunities each offers for social participation? Within any particular classroom community or activity setting, do individuals differ in their participation? What do these participation patterns tell us about learning mathematics?

Application of Sociocultural Theory

In the analyses described next, three different comparisons of participation in activity settings are made with reference to two of Ms. Hanes' middle school mathematics classes. First, the range of activity settings available in traditional and reform classrooms is contrasted. Second, student participation across activity settings within a single classroom is described. Third, student participation within a single activity setting is illustrated by focusing on differential use of the mathematics register. The aim of this analysis is to use data from these classes to illustrate how socio-cultural theory could be employed to describe instructional processes in particular classroom settings and to make predictions about instructional outcomes in those settings. No attempt is made to generalize the results of this analysis to other reform classrooms or even to the entire corpus of data on Ms. Hanes' classes.

A Comparison of Activity Settings in Traditional Versus Reform Classrooms

In traditional middle school mathematics classrooms, students are participants in a limited range of activity settings. For example, Stodolsky found that fifth-grade mathematics classrooms devoted 40% of the instructional time to independent seatwork and 29% to whole-class recitations lead by the teacher. In contrast, she found that fifth-grade social studies classes devoted only 28% of the time to seatwork and 18% to recitations. Work in small groups comprised less than 1% of the observed time in the mathematics classrooms in her study but 34% of the time in the social studies classrooms. Thus, fifth graders in Stodolsky's sample participated in a broader range of activity settings in their social studies classes than in their mathematics classes.

In reform classrooms, students may participate in a wider range of activity settings than in traditional classrooms. In addition, students may be asked to follow a different script for conduct in these activity settings. Traditional classrooms are more likely to use the recitation script than are reform classrooms. Thus, in traditional mathematics classrooms, students have limited opportunity to initiate topics, redirect discussion, provide elaborate explanations of their own, or debate issues. Students who deviate from the official recitation scripts or independent seatwork scripts by talking to their peers can be sanctioned for failing to accept their rights and obligations as students in a traditional classroom.

In contrast to this picture of a relatively restricted range of activity settings and official scripts in traditional classrooms, reform classrooms can provide opportunities for students to assume a variety of participatory roles. In Ms. Hanes' classroom, the following types of activity settings and interactional scripts were observed: whole-class recitation led by the teacher, whole-class presentations led by one or more students, small group work led by one or more students with the teacher's intermittent assistance, individual seat work, and unofficial peer group activities. By providing a greater range of activity settings, reform classrooms also present a wider diversity of task demands and scripts. For example, students presenting their work in front of the class have to learn to communicate their ideas effectively to others through multiple representational formats. They also need to listen to the ideas of other students, even when they do not agree with them, to support their own positions with evidence, and to reconcile the differences between positions. Students can no longer rely on their understanding of the recitation script.

One script employed in mathematics classrooms follows the rules for the specialized speech genre specific to mathematical talk, the mathematics register. Although the mathematics register can be found in traditional classrooms as well as in reform classrooms, students have less opportunity to become fluent in its use in traditional classrooms because their participation is more restricted. That is, in traditional classrooms, students are asked to absorb this register by reading the text and listening to the teacher. In reform classrooms, students are asked to employ the register in more active and creative ways: to explain and contrast different solutions to a problem or to compare multiple representations of a problem. Therefore, students in reform classrooms have more opportunities to use the mathematics register as both a tool for their own thinking and an object for reflection.

These new task demands and new scripts also bring new purposes and values. Instead of just rewarding accurate and automatic use of algorithms, reform classes may also reward effective problem-solving strategies and communication practices. Students need to view themselves and each other as intellectual resources instead of relying solely upon the authority of the teacher and the text. The aim of this more collaborative approach to learning is to establish a community of learners—with all members having differential but important roles to play in assisting each other's learning.

Table 10.1 gives an outline of the values, task demands, scripts, and purposes associated with the different activity settings in traditional versus reform mathematics classrooms. In this figure, the contrasts between the different activity

Table 10.1. Characteristics of Official Activity Settings in Classrooms

Activity Settings and Personnel	*Values*	*Task Demands*	*Scripts*	*Purposes*
	Traditional Mathematics Classrooms			
Teacher-led recitations	Teacher or text are sources of learning	Internalize mathematics facts and algorithms	Recitation script	Introduce basic skills
	Automaticity and accuracy			
Individual seatwork	Teacher or text are sources of learning	Practice mathematics facts and algorithms	Work independently	Individual mastery of basic skills
	Automaticity and accuracy			
	Reform Mathematics Classrooms			
Student-led presentations	Multiple sources of learning	Pedagogical and communication skills	Instructional conversation	Establish community of learners

In reality, any one activity setting may have several, sometimes contradictory, purposes. This is especially true for classrooms in the process of change from traditional to reform.

Interviews with small samples of students from Ms. Hanes' class revealed their awareness of the results of changing instructional practices on their learning opportunities. One theme that emerged from the interviews was that students did view themselves and each other as intellectual resources. They cited the advantages of working in small groups for allowing you to offer and receive help, to share frustrations, and to expose yourself to a variety of ideas. They also seemed to view the small group as a supportive community: a place where you can count on people to listen to you. Another theme was the importance of explaining your ideas. The students understood how difficult it is to communicate ideas in oral or written form. Nevertheless, they recognized that it was crucial to get the members of their group to explain their work, not just to share answers. Finally, contrasts between traditional and reform classrooms (and the contradictions within a classroom in the process of change) formed another theme in the student interviews. Many students seemed to feel that Ms. Hanes' class involved too much work, too much homework, too much writing and explaining. One student complained that the work took longer to do than last year because Ms. Hanes did not show them the shortcuts.

Changing classroom practice from traditional to reform activity settings can involve contradictions and confusions between the old system and the new one. One of the contradictions mentioned by the students involved grading. They saw a contradiction between offering open-ended problems, accepting multiple solutions, and assigning grades. Another contradiction they discussed had to do with their confusion about allowable small group behavior. Sometimes helping another student was encouraged, but sometimes it was viewed as off-task behavior.

Comparison of Student Participation Across Activity Settings in Ms. Hanes' Classes

Reform classrooms, like those taught by Ms. Hanes, provide both opportunities and challenges to students. Some students seem to benefit from having a greater chance to learn in collaboration with their peers whereas others seem confused by the demands of learning alternative scripts. For example, students who are much more comfortable negotiating with their peers than with the teacher are given an opportunity to use their peer networks to participate in the officially sanctioned small group activities of the reform classroom. One student in Ms. Hanes' seventh grade class, Dan, was observed to repeatedly turn away from the overhead projector in the front of the room. Ms. Hanes at one point asked Dan to turn his chair around so he could watch the student presenting at the overhead. When Dan ignored her request, she moved his chair herself. However, he continued to face other students in his group and to avoid looking at the person in authority (who happened to be a student). In a traditional classroom, Dan's active resistance to authority would have resulted in his being excluded from much of the instructional activities. In Ms. Hanes' classroom, however, several other students in Dan's group studiously followed the teacher's instructions and helped him participate in the group's problem-solving work. Thus, Dan's resistance to authority may have been less of an impediment to his learning mathematics in this classroom than in a traditional one.

An example of the challenges of these new activity settings could be seen when other students in Ms. Hanes' class tried to apply the rules for the recitation script to their small group or student-lead activity settings. Some students spent much of their time during small group activity waiting for Ms. Hanes to initiate group activities or to evaluate their work. They were frequently frustrated and confused when Ms. Hanes encouraged them to ask questions of each other and to evaluate each other's work.

These new classroom activity settings with their unfamiliar scripts also result in new task demands, values, and purposes. In Ms. Hanes' classroom, where there was no official textbook and where the teacher shared the responsibility for explaining complex mathematical concepts and procedures with her students, students were required to be effective communicators and collaborators. Any one idea could be presented using a variety of representational formats. No one format was privileged, as it would be in a classroom where seatwork from a textbook and the recitation script predominate. Solutions to problems were achieved through a process of negotiation between the teacher and students or among the students as in an instructional conversation.

In summary, observations of students in Ms. Hanes' seventh-grade class illustrate what a comparison of individual student's participation patterns across activity settings can show. Dan was most active and task-focused when he was able to participate as a member of a small work group. When he was asked to participate as a member of the whole class, either during teacher-led recitations or student-led presentations, he acted in ways that demonstrated his opposition to the person he viewed as an authority.

Other students, such as Betsy and Diana, were more comfortable than Dan when they were given an opportunity to interact directly with Ms. Hanes. However, they found it difficult to sustain task-focused small group activity without frequent assistance from the teacher. Betsy and Diana showed that they relied upon the recitation script, even when Ms. Hanes was not using it, to organize their work. These students tended to be confused by Ms. Hanes' open-ended problems with multiple solutions and frustrated by her unwillingness to evaluate their work. They showed a pattern opposite to that of Dan: resistance to small group work and compliance with teacher-led recitations. All of these students were partial participants in the classroom community of practice. Their participation patterns indicated what skills and ways of thinking valued by the community they were able to appropriate.

Comparison of Several Students Within a Single Activity Setting

Within any single activity setting, each student may participate in a different way. In the example to be discussed here, three students, at different times, presented their work on the problem at the overhead. Only the presentations of two students, Allen and Ulysses, are discussed here. The problem that all three students were asked to explain is as follows: "During the month of April (30 days), there were eight more rainy days than dry days. How many rainy days were there?" Allen's solution to this problem was 23 rainy days and 7 dry days and Ulysses' solution was 19 rainy days and 11 dry days. Ms. Hanes read the problem to the class and called on Allen to explain his solution.

Allen: [Makes slashes on the overhead to represent 30 days—as two groups of 15 slashes.] Then, first I took thirty and split it in half and got two—fifteen and fifteen. And, um, so you said there was eight more so I put one side was rainy and one side was dry. So, wait, rainy, wait, yeah, rainy, dry [labels transparency]. And there was eight more rainy days than dry days, so I took eight off of the 15 [crosses out eight slashes on dry side] and put over here [adds eight slashes to rainy side] and said how many more rainy days were here? So, then, so I had first I added the eight that were here. And, um, that equalled . . . 20, 20, 3, 23. And I said how many more so and there was [counts aloud one, two, three] seven. So, and then take away from the 23 is 16.

At this point, Allen stopped. Instead of evaluating his answer, as the recitation script would require, Ms. Hanes asked Allen to reread the problem (perhaps hoping that he would notice that his answer was wrong).

Allen: During the month of April (30 days), there were about eight more rainy days—there were eight more rainy days than dry days. How many more rainy days were there?

Following this exchange, Ms. Hanes tried to get Allen to reflect on what he had done so that he could identify where his strategy of transferring days from the dry to the rainy group got him into trouble. Unfortunately, Allen did not seem to understand what Ms. Hanes was asking him to do. First, he appeared to think that her lack of explicit evaluation of his solution implied that he was correct. Then, when he realized that she did not think he was correct, he seemed to lose confidence in his ability to provide a correct strategy or answer. Ms. Hanes asked other students to help make Allen's system work. Two other students volunteered but only one of them, Ulysses, actually began with the same system as Allen.

Ulysses: The only thing that made, well Allen's ide—, well Allen's idea was right. It's just that there's two so you

3. divide the eight by two so you only add four instead of adding
4. eight because when you take away four from the dry days, then
5. it makes it four lower and makes the other one four higher.
6. So that would make it, still make it a difference of eight
7. instead of . . .

There are several differences between the explanations of Ulysses and Allen, other than the difference in their solutions. Some of these differences have to do with each student's mastery of the mathematics register. First, Ulysses' explanation is more concise than Allen's. Ulysses assumed that the class understood how Allen had laid out the problem: as two groups of days, rainy and dry (lines 4-5).

He briefly reminded them of these groups in line 18 and then proceeded to work on the problem from there. Second, the syntactic subjects of Ulysses' statements were in the form of the second-person impersonal pronoun or it. In contrast, the subjects of Allen's statements were personal pronouns. Also, Ulysses' verbs were in the present, timeless tense except where he referred to Allen's previous work, whereas Allen's verbs were in the past tense. Third, Allen tended not to use mathematical terms. Instead, he was as likely to use everyday language to represent mathematical operations, such as "split it in half," as he was to use words that have specific mathematical meanings. Ulysses' explanation is full of mathematical terms with precise meanings. One could easily rewrite Ulysses' verbal explanation into mathematical notation.

Finally, Allen's misreading of the problem (lines 14-16) further indicates his difficulty distinguishing mathematical and everyday story problems. That is, in everyday language, it would be considered appropriate to reply to the question, "Did it rain a great deal in April?" by saying, "Yea, there were about eight more rainy days than dry ones." However, this is a mathematical story problem that requires a precise mathematical answer—not an approximate one. Thus, it would be important to know whether the problem states that there were exactly or approximately eight more rainy days than dry ones. In addition, Allen's misreading fundamentally altered the problem when he changed the final question posed from "How many rainy days were there?" to "How many more rainy days were there?" because the latter question was answered in the original problem, which stated that there were eight more rainy days than dry days.

There is another interesting issue that can be raised about the different explanations provided by Allen and Ulysses. Allen's explanation was a direct report of his personal experience with a homework problem. Ulysses' explanation was very academic; he described a procedure that should work no matter when, where, or who did it.

Together, these two forms of explanation (the everyday and the academic) need to be interwoven in an instructional conversation, according to Tharp and Gallimore. The ability to integrate the mathematics register and the everyday register is not just a linguistic skill; it is also a cognitive skill. When one is capable of integrating the two speech genres, one demonstrates an understanding of the relationship between multiple representations of a problem. This example illustrates the notion of learning mathematics as a discursive activity. Full participation in student-led presentations requires the mastery of two speech genres. Students who participate in these presentations are assisted by each other and Ms. Hanes in the use of the genres.

Conclusion

This chapter has focused on describing the range of activity settings, participation patterns, and speech genres of students. I have argued that reform classrooms provide a greater diversity of activity settings for students than do traditional classrooms. In addition, I have proposed that this diversity brings with it new task demands, scripts, values, and purposes. Finally, I have shown that the diversity of activity settings is matched by a diversity of participation patterns within and across them.

What can an analysis of activity settings and participation patterns tell us about learning mathematics? For sociocultural theory, learning is inherently related to social activity and discourse; learning is a process by which newcomers are integrated into a community of practice. Before newcomers understand the valued skills of this community, their participation must be peripheral. As the important skills, norms, and ideas of the community are appropriated, the former newcomers move toward greater participation, thus demonstrating their learning.

Ms. Hanes' classrooms can also be seen as communities of practice that are embedded in and create other communities of practice. These communities would include other educational reform projects in the United States and around the world. As a teacher in a school that is part of an educational reform project, Ms. Hanes is trying to foster the skills being promoted by the NCTM standards. Because teaching in accordance with these standards represents a change in instructional practice for Ms. Hanes, she is a legitimate peripheral participant in the community of mathematics reformers. Increased participation would mean that she can help create and sustain the types of activity settings in her classroom and school that are capable of fostering the skills valued by this community. In principle, the student presentations and small group work activity settings that were observed in her classroom should promote the communication, collaboration, reasoning, and problem-solving skills consistent with those standards. However, ensuring that those new activity settings function as they need to do is no easy matter. Ms. Hanes is only one participant in the activity settings observed in her classroom. Her students bring their own values, feelings, and expectations to those settings. In addition, other participants in the reform project, parents, and school district personnel influence what occurs in her school.

In contrast, the sociocultural perspective would not make the same distinctions between "outward" behavior and "internal" representations. Instead, the continuities, not the discontinuities between intermental and intramental activity, would be emphasized. Thus, indices of learning are as much present in classroom discourse as they are in individual problem-solving protocols. The establishment of a community of practice—with a common communication system, norms, and values—would also be evidence of learning.

In conclusion, socio-cultural theory takes as two of its guiding premises the notions that learning is a form of participation in the activities of a community of practice and that learning is a discursive activity. Thus, it suggests that educational programs that change social practices, activity settings, and classroom discourse in ways designed to support students' active engagement in solving meaningful mathematical problems in collaboration with others should foster learning. The theoretical justification for the reform movement in mathematics in the United States requires further elaboration, however, if it is to be used to evaluate the success of that movement. I have tried to argue that notions such as activity setting, legitimate peripheral participation, and instructional conversation can be used to conduct the studies of classroom practice that would be needed to provide the necessary empirical evidence. Models for this work are available in a small but growing body of educational research being conducted from a socio-cultural perspective. The collective result of this activity should provide the educational research community with an alternative framework for conceptualizing and assessing the processes and outcomes of reform.

BIBLIOGRAPHY

Barnes D. *"Language and learning in the classroom". Journal of Curriculum Studies 3,* 27 - 38 , 1971.

Barnes D. "Language in the secondary classroom". In D. Barnes, J. Britton, & H. Rosen, *Language, the learner and the school.* Middlesex, England: Penguin Books, 1969.

Barnes D., & Todd F. *Communication and learning in small groups.* London: Roudedge and Kegan Paul, 1977.

Cohen E. G. *Status equalization project: Changing expectations in the integrated classroom.* Unpublished final report, Stanford University, 1980.

Cole M., & Means B. *Comparative studies of how people think: An introduction.* Cambridge, MA: Harvard University Press, 1981.

Dewey J. *How we think.* Chicago: Henry Regnery, 1933.

Easley J., & Easley E. *Math can be natural: Kitamaeno priorities introduced to American teachers.* Urbana-Champaign: University of Illinois, Bureau of Educational Research, 1982.

Ericsson K. A., & Simon H. A. *Verbal reports as data. Psychological Review 87(3),* 215-51, 1980.

Erlwanger S. H. "Benny's conception of rules and answers in IPI mathematics". *Journal of Children's Mathematical Behavior* 1, 7-26, 1973.

Garofalo (Eds.), *Mathematical problem solving: Issues in research.* Philadelphia: The Franklin Institute Press, 1982.

Gay J., & Cole M. *The new mathematics and an old culture.* New York: Holt, Rinehart & Winston, 1967.

Hayes J. R., & Simon H. A. "Psychological differences among problem isomorphs". In N. J. Castellan, D. B. Pisoni, & G.R. Potts (Eds.), *Cognitive theory* (Vol. 2). Hillsdale, NJ: Lawrence Erlbaum Associates, 1977.

Johnson D., & Johnson R. *Learning together and alone.* Englewood Cliffs, NJ: Prentice-Hall, 1975.

Johnson D., & Johnson R. *The internal dynamics of cooperative learning groups.* Paper presented at the annual meeting of the American Educational Research Association, New York, March 1982.

Kantowski E. L. *Processes involved in mathematical problem solving.* Unpublished doctoral dissertation, University of Georgia, 1974.

Kilpatrick J. *Analyzing the solution of word problems in mathematics: An exploratory study.* Unpublished doctoral dissertation, Stanford University, 1967.

Lancy D. F. *Cross-cultural studies in cognition and mathematics.* New York: Academic Press, 1983.

Lesh R. "Applied mathematical problem solving". *Educational Studies in Mathematics 12(2),* 235-64, 1981.

Lester F. K. "Building bridges between psychological and mathematics education research on problem solving". In F. K. Lester & J. Garofalo (Eds.), *Mathematical problem solving: Issues in research.* Philadelphia: The Franklin Institute Press, 1982.

Lucas J. F. *An exploratory study in the diagnostic teaching of elementary calculus.* Unpublished doctoral dissertation, University of Wisconsin, 1972.

Lucas J. F., Branca N., Goldberg D., Kantowski M. G., Kellogg H., & Smith J. P. "A processsequence coding system for behavioral analysis of mathematical problem solving". In G. A. Goldin and C. E. McClintock (Eds.), *Task variables in mathematical problem solving.* Columbus, OH: ERIC Clearinghouse for Science, Mathematics, and Environmental Education, 1979.

Mayer R. *The psychology of mathematical problem solving.* In F. K. Lester & J. Garofalo (Eds.), *Mathematical problem solving: Issues in research.* Philadelphia: The Franklin Institute Press, 1982.

Mehan H. *Learning lessons: Social organization in the classroom.* Cambridge, MA: Harvard University Press, 1979.

Nesher P. "The stereotyped nature of school word problems". *For the Learning of Mathematics 1 (1)*, 41-48, 1980.

Nisbett R. E., & Wilson T. D. "Telling more than we can know: Verbal reports on mental processes". *Psychological Review 84(3)*, 231-59, 1977.

Noddings N. *The use of small group protocols in analysis of children's arithmetical problem solving.* Paper presented at the annual meeting of the American Educational Research Association, New York, March 1982.

Olson D. R. "Culture, technology and intellect". In L. B. Resnick (Ed.), *The nature of intelligence.* Hillsdale, NJ: Lawrence Erlbaum Associates, 1976.

Paige N. M., & Simon H. A. "Cognitive processes in solving algebra word problems". In B. Kleinmuntz (Ed.), *Problem solving.* New York: John Wiley & Sons, 1966.

Paivio A., & Csapo K. "Picture superiority in free recall: Imagery or dual coding?" *Cognitive Psychology 5*, 176-206, 1973.

Rohwer W. D. "Images and pictures in children's learning". *Psychological Bulletin 73*, 393-403, 1970.

Rudnitsky A.N. *The graphic representation of structure in similarity/ dissimilarity matrices: Alternative matrices.* Paper presented at the meeting of the American Educational Research Association, New York, 1977.

Schmuck R., & Schmuck P. *Group processes in the classroom.* Dubuque, IA: Wm. C. Brown Group, 1979.

Scribner S., & Cole M. *The psychology of literacy.* Cambridge, MA: Harvard University Press, 1981.

Sharan S., Hertz-Lazarowitz R., & Ackerman F. "Academic achievement of elementary school children in small group versus whole-class instruction". *Journal of Experimental Education 48(2)*, 125-29, 1980.

Shavelson R. J. "Learning from physics instruction". *Journal of Research in Science Teaching 10*, 101-11, 1973.

Shavelson R. J. "Methods for examining representations of a subject-matter structure in a student's memory". *Journal of Research in Science Teaching 11(3)*, 231-49, 1974(a).

Shavelson R. J. "Some aspects of the correspondence between content structure and cognitive structure in physics instruction". *Journal of Educational Psychology 63(3)*, 225-34, 1972.

Trivett J. "The clinical interview: A comment". *For the Learning of Mathematics 2 (1)*, 51, 1981.

Vygotsky L. *Mind in society*. Cambridge, MA: Harvard University Press, 1978.

Webb N. "Student interaction and learning in small groups". *Review of Educational Research* 52, 421-45, 1982.

White P. "Limitations of verbal reports of internal events: A refutation of Nisbett and Wilson and of Bern". *Psychological Review 87(1)*, 105-12, 1980.

Wood B. S., Brown K., Chiosk S. N., Ecroyd D., Hopper R., Rowland-Morris P., & Wrather N. *Development of functional communication competencies pre-K-Grade 6*. Urbana, IL: ERIC Clearinghouse on Reading and Communication Skills, 1977.

Index